To J.J.

Vegas ain't for everybody.
From one southern gentleman
to another.

Best Always,

aka

"Hank"

To J.J.

Vegas ain't for everybody.
From one southern gentleman
to another.

Best Always

"Hank"

House
OF
Cards

*Five Full Contact Years as a
Las Vegas Nightclub Bouncer*

HANK CARVER

The Drunk, High and Reckless Edition

abbott press

Abbott Press books may be ordered through booksellers or by contacting:

Abbott Press
1663 Liberty Drive
Bloomington, IN 47403
www.abbottpress.com
Phone: 1 (866) 697-5310

ISBN: 978-1-4582-1955-8 (sc)
ISBN: 978-1-4582-1956-5 (hc)
ISBN: 978-1-4582-1957-2 (e)

Library of Congress Control Number: 2015916826

Print information available on the last page.

Abbott Press rev. date: 11/5/2015

To K, C, and most of all E.
I'm sorry I couldn't be a better man.

CONTENTS

The names in this book have been changed to protect the innocent as well as the not-so-innocent. The sequence of events is as close to chronological as possible. However some events that happened on different nights are presented together for economy. You don't really want to hear about all the standing around we did anyway. Do you?

VEGAS

Las Vegas is a land of milk and honey for some. For others it is a city that brings only heartache and despair. Nowhere else does there exist a place where fortunes are so rapidly won and lost. Sometimes there's more than just money riding on that roll of the dice, the turn of a card, or that last carom of a ball.

People come here in droves and most of them want the same thing—action. They want authenticity, a Las Vegas trip to remember, a radical departure from their normal existence. Some get much more than they bargained for. For the souls who choose to live here? Their stories are as unique as the people themselves. Vegas is and always will be the place people come to get hitched, get drunk, and get fleeced. The industry here is service. The inhabitants of this city are here to serve the people who come here for those very reasons. The entire city and its economy are based around what occurs on a seven-mile-long patch of asphalt, the Las Vegas Strip.

The Strip is where milk meets honey. It is a playground for the rich and famous as well as the not so rich or famous. It is a place where anything can happen. A place where dreams come true and nightmares are realized. It is a place where the only color seen is green. It's the birthplace of the New American Dream.

The New American Dream lives here because nowhere else can you make the kind of money that is made for doing what would be a menial job anywhere else. Dealers with no skill other than gaming make livings

1

that the failing middle class would envy. In the nightclub industry, obscene amounts of money are made. At the right club, the bartenders and waitresses make a six-figure income working just a three- or four-night week. Their bussers drive BMWs. Even the bouncers can flirt with an executive salary if they're on top of their game.

The life is glamorous, complete with all the trappings. It provides money, power, and a certain cache that can only be had by working a rope in the world's adult playground. In a city where cool is king and hot on Monday is lukewarm by Wednesday, the landscape changes constantly, just like the Las Vegas skyline. It is an environment where anything goes, where anything can be had, and the only limit is how far you want to take things. It is both beautiful and toxic. For all the glitter provided by the club life, there is an equal measure of pain it can exact. This is that story.

Before we get started, you should know a few things. First off, this is written by a bouncer. I'm telling you these stories because, otherwise, you'd never get to hear them. Bouncers don't write books. Fewer still take it to the level I have. That being said, some stories are presented very well, some maybe not so much. I'm not that fucking funny guy who writes those witty books you pass around during the holidays and ask your friends if they read the passage about the time he worked as an elf and shit. I don't have his contacts, and Vegas isn't exactly a hotbed of literary talent, so this book is largely unedited.

These are my words, my experiences. I wrote the original draft from a journal I kept while I was living the stories. As you can tell from the cover, I was drunk, high, and reckless through that time, and this edition will embrace those ideas. If you were in my life at the time and didn't make the book, please accept my apologies. After reading it, you'll probably be glad you didn't. That being said, I have a lot of material that didn't make the book due to size considerations and some of the shit my guys flat-out vetoed—it was that bad. Maybe someone will pick this up and turn it into a fully finished masterpiece, and then I can bring out everything in a new and improved edition. But it's probably not that kind of work.

If you did make the book, we were likely in the trenches together and our lives rubbed up against each other in a meaningful way. Or you could have been included through collateral damage. If I hurt your feelings in here, well, I probably already did anyway. At least now you'll get the whole story.

Second, I'm writing this book under an assumed name. The rest of the names have been changed to protect the terminally stupid and the innocent folks we involved in our crass, wild, and often dangerous behavior. If you know me and you don't want to look at me in a different way, put the book down now. If you don't want to hear about adultery, drugs, violence, prostitution, extortion, suicide, and how I was involved in these activities, put the book down now. If you don't want the intimate and sometimes misogynistic details on my sex life, put the book down now. If you don't want to hear about all the base ways people act in Las Vegas, put the book down now. You have been warned. If you want to hear about all that shit, then by all means, read on.

The stories that follow have been culled from five years of living and working as a security guard in one of the most exclusive clubs in Vegas. During that time, my crew and I handled some of the biggest players, stars, and egos in the world. In the business of security, it's your job to clean up the poop. Most bouncers are untrained, uncouth meatheads, and the wages they are paid ensure they'll stay that way. No one on my squad was like that. They all had personality quirks that made them unique, but no one was stupid. This is a workaday account of what happened when a group of hard-drinking, loose-living alpha males took control of securing a multi-million-dollar operation. It's been said that what happens in Vegas stays in Vegas. It did, until now.

CLUBS

I always wanted to live in Las Vegas. For me, it seemed like a place where anything could happen, a place where a young man looking for his fortune might be able to find one. It also seemed like the last wild place left. In 2001, my girlfriend Shannon and I made the decision to move there together. I was finishing film school in Florida and Shannon was up for the adventure. Las Vegas was to be a steppingstone on our way to California. Shannon had always wanted to live in Hermosa Beach, and Hollywood is the destination for anyone who wants to work in the film business. When it came down that Shannon's job in the private financial group of a local bank was being downsized and she would be given a sizeable severance package, the decision was made easy. Add to that fact that a friend of Shannon's was looking for a little adventure herself and wanted to room with us, thereby lessening the financial burden for all. The stars seemed to align.

Shannon was a great girl—loving, supportive, and beautiful. Our stories were the same in many ways, starting with both of us being the only children of single parents who struggled. She was left with her mother, who was by all accounts a bona fide crazy person. Her mother once tried to commit suicide by jumping off the roof of her single-story house. She ended up with only a sprained ankle. I grew up with my father, a hardworking and honest man who had once been a police officer. When I was born, my father gave up the job and moved to Florida with my mother, only to watch her split soon afterward.

Shannon and I were great together. So much could go unspoken and we understood each other. My peregrine ways provided a challenge for her and helped to open up her rigid world view. In turn, she kept me focused and provided a stable home environment. But she wasn't without her quirks. Behind her ice-blue eyes and blond hair there sat a stubborn streak and a serious self-esteem shortage. Shannon needed constant attention, and her stubbornness would allow for nothing less. I could appreciate this in her, as this proved to be beneficial in keeping me away from the roguish and generally negative avenues that people with a lack of direction usually fall into, a lane with which I was all too familiar. I kept her company; she kept me straight. We were in love and were ready to make a go of it. Shannon was pretty much the only reason I made it through film school.

I graduated in the fall of 2001 and we made the decision to move after the New Year. Shannon's job duties would require her to work through the holidays in order to streamline and coordinate the transfer of all her clients' accounts. This left me a few months with nothing to do until the move. The prior two years spent with me not working had left us with some credit card debt and I decided I'd better get a job, at least in the interim. I had a friend, Stan, who worked security at a local nightclub in Orlando. Stan and I had known each other since elementary school. We'd grown to be good friends after our high school years. We'd partied together quite a bit during those years and our friendship was cemented by shared experience. I called Stan and he put in a word for me. Based on Stan's recommendation, I was hired immediately.

As one would imagine, nightclub security isn't science. As such, being a "bouncer" doesn't put you in a position to command high wages; in fact, you can count on being the lowest paid guy or gal in the club. Make no mistake—your employer views you as a liability and a possible source of litigation. Working in a room full of drunk and/or high people, you cannot avoid problems, and that is why you are there. If you're lucky, you'll ascend to the rank of security supervisor and make a few dollars more per hour. For most nightclubs, all you need is a pulse. To be considered gifted at the job, it means you have some brains, a big heart, and an equal measure of balls. If this is you, you'll be head and shoulders above the norm. Luckily, I fell into this category.

Security is a sort of pack-mentality brotherhood. You don't just sign up for the job, get hired, and get accepted—you're on the fringes until you prove yourself worthy of inclusion. While I'll stop short of calling it combat, it can certainly take on some elements associated with this experience. You work in a noisy, sometimes dirty environment where your job is to come into contact with people who can be agitated, hostile, and otherwise uncooperative. Your job is also to make sure these people are acting in accordance with the policies set in place by the club to govern the safety of the patrons.

Sometimes people are great and they're just having too much of a good time. These folks usually respond to a verbal command and a firm pat on the back. Other times you have to "bounce." This is all that the name implies. Handling yourself correctly in a physical altercation is the quickest way to prove you belong in the brotherhood. The biggest, most important thing in security is getting someone's back. Don't get me wrong—defusing situations should be the number one goal of every bouncer. But any security guard worth his or her salt knows you cannot and will not be able to defuse every single situation. Sooner or later, you're going to have to get down. Unlike combat, though, nobody dies. Usually nobody dies.

I was able to start off near the inner circle. I was fortunate enough to have the benefit of knowing Stan, who was one of the supervisors at the nightclub. Stan vouched for me. They trusted Stan. This smoothed my acceptance into the security hierarchy, because the more experienced bouncers helped me out and gave me their tricks of the trade. It always helps when those in the know believe that they can trust you. That was all I needed, and as a result, I learned the ropes quickly. I was only on the main floor a short time when I was approached by Shawn, the nightclub manager who oversaw the security department.

Shawn had years of experience in clubs and had opened venues all over the world; as a result, he carried heavy clout in the business. Shawn asked me if I knew anything about IDs. I didn't, really, except for a number of attempts at making or procuring fake identification while I was still underage. Shawn gave me the situation straight: our main door guy was moving, and he needed a new face to ID the line. Most of the guys worthy of that spot didn't want it, as it required them to stand out front, tethered to the line. Likewise, the supervisors valued their freedom to roam and get in on the action.

While it wasn't a move to a supervisor position, and it didn't necessarily get me any more money, it meant an opportunity to learn a valuable skill in the nightclub world, something that might be of use down the road. The ability to identify a fake ID and keep minors from gaining admittance was the first line of defense for a nightclub's liquor license. I told Shawn I was a quick study and was willing to do whatever he wanted on that front. Shawn had faith that I'd assimilate this task and he made the move. I was the main man on the door in just under three months of getting the job.

I worked the door and familiarized myself with the different IDs, as well as the varying tactics used by degenerates in training to subvert the system. These varied widely, from using the older brother/sister's expired ID to the downright fake made on a printer at home. One of my favorites was the stolen imposter, when an underager would take an ID from someone who was clearly a decade or two over legal drinking age and try to pass it off as their own. All you could do was laugh and ask them the questions.

Me: "What's your birthday?"

Underager: "Ten-seventeen, seventy-two."

Me: "Really?"

Underager: "Yes. Ten-seventeen, seventy-two."

Me: "So you're forty-two?"

[Never mind that the crow's-feet on the ID picture have miraculously disappeared.]

Underager: Blank stare.

Me: "What's your sign?"

Underager: "I'm a Pisces."

[Most underagers don't bother to learn their fake sign and will give you their real one.]

Me: "You sure? You want to try again?"

Underager: "Virgo?"

(The game's usually up right here, as the truth seldom needs a second chance, but once in awhile, they get it right or say they don't follow astrology.)

Me: "Okay, last question—you don't mind if I show this to those guys over there in uniform, do you? Just so we can both feel better about tonight."

Underager: Blank stare, fidgeting, and a nervous look in the direction of the cops, followed by a timid shake of the head or sometimes a meek "no" squeaking out.

(A lot of nightclubs have cops on property.)

Our club policy was to confiscate the fake. We'd log it in, and after an appropriate amount of time, we'd turn them in to local law enforcement. In the case of the imposters, it was always much worse. Imagine having to tell your mom or dad they had to go down to the nightclub you'd tried to get into, so you could get shitfaced, and claim their ID. Needless to say, we didn't get many parents down at the club. Their ID simply vanished in a haze of bullshit and shame.

The months rolled by until the time came to leave for Las Vegas. As the move and my last day at the club neared, Shawn made it known that he had friends in Las Vegas and that he'd be more than happy to put a word in for me. In fact, he'd spent time working at a property on the Strip, where, given my experience, I'd be a natural fit. This was great news, of course. A cross-country move was daunting enough, but moving without jobs or even prospects added a level of trepidation that Shannon and I did our best to push to the back of our minds. Now, with a single phone call, Shawn would be able to get me set up with a spot at a Strip property. Even if this was starting off at the bottom of the bouncer pecking order, I was certain I'd be able to distinguish myself in fairly short order, just as I'd done in Orlando. I was confident I could do this, even without the benefit of knowing any of the supervisors.

When the day finally came for our cross-country adventure, we packed our belongings and set off in a giant U-Haul with my father behind the wheel. Being a homegrown Southern boy, it was to be the only time I'd been west of Louisiana. Shannon and I were ready to make our way, with only each other to rely on. It was the scariest and most exciting time of my life. Little did I know I'd be saying that for the next five years.

We arrived in Las Vegas after a little less than a week on the road. I rode with my dad in the moving truck while Shannon and her friend followed behind in Jennifer's car. This no doubt kept the proximity effect of traveling from being an issue, and everyone was in a great mood when the valley unfolded in front of as we came in on the 95. In typical fashion, Shannon had done a great deal of preparation for the trip—she'd studied maps, read everything she could on Las Vegas, and even went so far as to join a Vegas chat group. Through her group, she'd learned what parts of town were generally desirable and which were less so. The Summerlin area on the west side of Las Vegas was widely considered the crown jewel of the city, while the east side was decidedly less desirable, as it was populated by a lower income demographic.

The east side was our destination. Shannon had a found an apartment that was in line with our meager budget. This bothered Shannon more than me. I grew up in a blue-collar household. My father swung a hammer for a living and my stepmother repaired appliances, so in essence, we could be classified as a lower income demographic. Couple that with the fact that, throughout my educational years, the letters in my last name and the fact that the alphabet ruled the seating chart gave me friends of a different skin color. I was comfortable with people regardless of income or race. For Shannon, it was a different story altogether. Her mother was a bank executive and she grew up with a Southern exposure much different than mine. We had worked on expanding her horizons in terms of acceptance, but she was still a work in progress.

As the girls settled our stuff into the apartment, I set out to secure my employment. Shawn had made good on his promise to make the call—I had a destination and a name to ask for once I got there. Excitement tinged with a case of sickening nerves crept into my gut. I needed this job. Despite her best efforts, Shannon still hadn't made any headway in the job area. She quickly learned that banking and financial services spots were relegated to tellers and not much else, not without a hookup. Luckily, that's what I had. I soon realized that no one in Las Vegas is quick to help a new face.

The first two times I went to the club, I called to make sure Carl was there. He was in, but by the time I got there, he was too busy to sit with me. I chalked it up to the business and the fact he was running big club in a giant casino. Still, it struck me as unprofessional and a rather callous treatment of a potential employee. But remember what I said about the way security is viewed? We are low paid, easily replaceable, and in general considered not that complex. So I was a footnote in his day. On my third try, I finally got in—Carl met me in a windowless office in the bowels of the club. The conversation was short.

Carl: "So Shawn tells me you ran the door in Orlando?"

Me: "Yeah. He trusted me enough to hand it over pretty quickly. I was fortunate there."

Carl: "That's good. Shawn was my supervisor when I was bartending. Love that guy."

Me: "Shawn's a good guy for sure. He's really helped me out along the way."

Carl: "All right, man—he vouches for you, so we're going to bring you on. It's not a lot of money. We pay twelve bucks an hour and you're not starting on the door. Not out here."

Me: "That's fine by me. I'm just grateful for the opportunity."

Carl: "You have your cards?"

Me: "My what?"

Carl: "Sheriff's card, TAM card."

Me: "No. I didn't know I needed anything. We didn't have any of that in Orlando."

Carl: "It's no problem. I have the info right here. Get your cards, come back, and we'll put you to work."

Carl handed over the paperwork and shook my hand. I tried to contain my elation at this. Twelve bucks an hour was by no means a windfall, but it was a foothold. It meant groceries, electricity, and the ability to make our way. It provided the opportunity for Shannon and I to get headed in the right direction. I rushed to the front door of the casino and out into the warm night air. My head was full with the idea that anything was possible, that anything could be had in this new place. I looked down the Strip. The city was alive with neon.

The next day, I showed up downtown to get my sheriff's card. It looked like a jail processing unit, complete with fingerprinting stations and places to get your mug shot taken, or in this case, the photo for your sheriff's card. This idea was solidified when I saw a woman of questionable taste being taken into custody. The sheriff's card program in Las Vegas is designed to keep criminals out of certain industries. This no doubt springs from the fact that Las Vegas was established and built by organized crime and the Mafia. However, the days of Bugsy Siegel are over, and the issuing of a sheriff's card is basically the defining criteria of whether or not you're going to be able to find work in a bar, as security, or as a stripper—in other words, all the clean professions. I filled out the information card and took it to the window. One look at the woman's face as she scanned my card and I knew there was trouble.

Sheriff's card lady: "It says here you have two misdemeanor convictions."

Me: "Yes, ma'am. They were five years ago."

Sheriff's card lady: "I can't issue you a card unless you get a letter from your employer stating they know about your convictions."

Suddenly, the volume got turned way up. I couldn't even hear the rest of what she said. The droning thump of my skyrocketing blood pressure filled my ears. The elation of the night before gave way to an equal low, a valley of ever deepening and overwhelming sadness. The amazing possibilities were now in jeopardy over a mistake I'd made five years ago. I trudged out of the office, hardly noticing that the woman of questionable taste had begun struggling with the officers and shouting protests against her arrest. I climbed into the car and just stared out the windshield, shell-shocked. I couldn't believe this was happening. All the things you're warned about when you're a kid, that you shouldn't get in trouble because it will come back to haunt you—yeah, that bullshit—it was all true.

I know I'd done all the things to get me there, the misdemeanor pickup for petit theft and possession of marijuana. I did those things and that wasn't lost on me. I'd done a great deal more than that as a youth. Growing up in a single-parent household with little money and even less supervision meant you found your way into things. It had been that way since the second grade, since I ran my first confidence scam.

I didn't know what that was at the time. I just knew that if I offered to stay after class and put the chairs up for the teacher, I could get a few moments alone in the room and help myself to the items my classmates had left in their desks—items my father couldn't afford.

By the time the fifth grade rolled around, my father had married my stepmother and we had finally stopped moving around. Up until then, I'd been in a different school for nearly every grade, including a very short stint in a religious private school. Staying in one place allowed me to finally make some regular friends.

I fell in with a group of rough-and-tumble boys—boys of similar background, with single parents and stepparents—working-class kids. We did what kids with a lot of free time and little supervision end up doing. By the time we got into our later years in high school, we'd moved into burglary and credit card fraud. After high school, I graduated into recreational drug use and petty dealing to go along with a string of retail jobs that I stole from mercilessly. My pockets were lined with ill-gotten gain, and I had plenty of free time by virtue of not being able to hold a job for very long. I never got caught, mind you. I usually just got bored and left. It seemed I had a knack for finding trouble.

The arrest that had me in jeopardy came on a weekend that I'd been partying for a number of days—ecstasy, acid, weed, partying. My friends and I decided we'd go downtown and try our shoplifting game as a means of entertainment. We picked a local shop that sold blown-glass art and the haul was hefty. One of my friends had stolen so much, he couldn't carry it all comfortably, and I offered to stash some of the loot in my pockets. Afterward, we climbed up the stairs of a parking garage and out onto the roof of an adjacent building to smoke weed and look at the Gulf of Mexico.

When we returned to the parking garage, the cops were waiting. Seven of us were arrested that night on a range of felony possession and misdemeanor charges. The cop searching me got so excited about finding my weed that he failed to complete the search and missed the quarter sheet of acid I had in a smaller bag in that same pocket. I stuffed it down the back seat of the cruiser and narrowly missed a felony charge.

So there I sat in my car, keenly aware of how lucky I had been up until this point. Even still, the one slip-up I'd had was coming back to haunt me—the debt that must be paid. It was an unbelievable development. Since I'd met Shannon, my life had done a complete and abrupt about-face. I'd held the same job and hadn't pilfered, and I'd stopped using drugs altogether. Hell, I didn't even drink, because soon after we'd gotten together, Shannon had been diagnosed with epilepsy. That meant no drinking for her, so I just quit, too. Even after straightening out, full stop, here I was, unable to complete the last task that would ensure I'd be able to break free of my old life. I went home to write a letter detailing that night, throwing myself upon the mercy of the higher-ups. When I told Carl the situation, he pointed me in the direction of human resources and the director of the nightclub.

"Good luck," he told me, but his face did not give me hope.

For all my trepidation, the meeting was positive. The director of the nightclub and the head of HR were very understanding of the situation. The arrest had occurred far enough in the past and I'd had it together enough to finish school and stay out of trouble. It didn't hurt that I'd come to the job with Shawn's blessing. They gave me a letter stating that they had full disclosure of my charges and I took that to get my card.

I was issued two cards by the Las Vegas Metropolitan Police Department that day. The first was my sheriff's card, which meant I'd be able to work. The second was a nifty pink card that had *Convicted Person Registration* plastered on the front in bold black letters; on the back, instructions that I was to notify the LVMPD of any new address or residence change within 48 hours. That didn't matter to me. I was in business and determined to make the best of this new life.

I started training in the nightclub on a busy Friday. There was a great deal of manual labor involved, which was to be expected—after all, we were the muscle. We had to set up barricades and ropes and all the usual people-moving, people-herding apparatus. When we moved into the club itself, there was still a great deal of moving to be done— couches, tables, etc. I was being trained by Kani, a barrel-chested islander. He stood about five-nine, and he was that wide, too. Kani was a consummate professional as far as security could be concerned. His suit was too short in the sleeves, but I was convinced he meant business.

13

Kani was also considered a veteran in the hierarchy of the club, and as such, he had the private rooms.

These rooms were considered a "money" spot in the club. The official stand of the nightclub was that security was a non-tipped position and therefore we were not to accept tips. The punishment for taking tips was immediate dismissal. This, of course, was a ridiculous notion, since this was Las Vegas, and the city is driven off tips. Tipping is both the official and the unofficial economy of this city of three million people. There was one caveat to the club's policy: if we were given a tip, we were to notify the manager and they alone had the power to let us keep the money. That was good to know but it was largely a nonissue for me as I had just started training and wasn't in any position to be given a tip anyway. Kani took me to the front door shortly before we opened and there was already a mass of people clamoring for entry.

Both the VIP line and the general admission line snaked deep into the casino and throngs more people mobbed the front trying to get past the rope without waiting in line. It was unlike anything I'd ever seen. It dwarfed anything I'd experienced in Florida, save for the biggest of raves that were popular throughout the mid-nineties. While those were one-night spectacles, what I was experiencing now was a nightly occurrence. Anyone who was anyone and a whole bunch of people who weren't anybody wanted inside those ropes. Anyone who has ever been to a Las Vegas nightclub knows what this scene is about—it's a special phenomenon.

But to truly understand the scale of what I was witnessing, you have to understand the landscape of the time. There was no Hyde. There was no Tao. No Pure. No Jet or 1OAK. There was no Hakkasan. The scene hadn't yet been watered down by the establishment of a nightclub in every casino on the Strip. We didn't know it then, but what we were living and experiencing was the rise of the Las Vegas nightclub.

Kani and I returned to the club and took up our spot at the private rooms. Kani worked a small velvet rope that allowed very select parties access to their room. Kani was introduced to the each of the parties by Andy, the VIP host, as he brought them into the room. The parties had paid top dollar for bottle service as well as a hefty tip to Andy for the privilege of a few hours in the rooms. For the next five hours, Kani would duck into the rooms periodically to check on his guests and he was always there to open the rope as they went back and forth to the dance floor. Since I was there, Kani would escort ladies to the restroom, a special bit of service that would allow them to skip the inevitable line that was waiting.

When the end of my first night was near, I was returning from a bathroom break. Kani had his head sticking out of the curtain and was waiting for me.

"Get in here, man. Help me out," he said.

I ducked through the curtain and saw trouble.

I saw what he needed help with—a sweaty Greek kid was passed out on the floor. He was pale and twitching periodically. I say *kid,* but he was older than me, probably mid-thirties. Kani hoisted his legs and motioned to the back hallway. I grabbed the Greek kid under the armpits and we pulled him into the back hall. Kani made a couple of attempts to rouse the guy, but nobody was home. The Greek kid's twitching got more and more erratic and his breathing was raspy and labored. Kani took off to call an EMT.

"What's he on, fellas? I asked.

"Nothing. We're club promoters from Florida. We know what we're doing. He always does this," they answered, but their furtive glances told me better.

"I've got a little bit of experience here. This isn't normal for anyone."

I hoped the appeal would help get me the information that was going to save their friend's life. The kid started convulsing and I rolled him onto his side so he wouldn't choke on his own puke.

"He always does this?" I asked.

Now they looked worried. So I leveled with them.

"I'm from Florida, too, fellas, and I know how it goes down out there. You're not going to get in any trouble," I told them.

More stressed glances as they had a conversation without talking until finally one of them opened his mouth. "He took Ecstasy, GHB, he's done some coke, and he's been drinking vodka all night."

No sooner did they get it out when Kani rounded the corner with the EMTs in tow. The EMTs took one look at the sweaty Greek's condition and immediately got him ready for transport to the hospital.

I filled the EMTs in on the mixture he'd been playing with that night, and the EMTs rolled the kid out with oxygen strapped to his face. His friends milled around for a few moments before they realized all this has occurred while the club was closing and the party was over for the night. They squared their bill, but the episode had noticeably put a damper on their night's festivities, and the remaining club promoters quietly made their exit.

There was just as much moving to be done at the end of the night as there was at the beginning, and after a long night, most security take stock, trade stories, and move furniture fueled by energy drinks and a very strong desire to get the hell out of there and get some breakfast. Kani and I finished a little after 6:00 a.m. and we headed across the mostly deserted casino floor on our way to clock out for the night. Kani told me that what had happened tonight was just the tip of the iceberg when it came to working the job in Las Vegas. He told me the partying that took place here reached levels that would leave you shaking your head.

No stranger to danger-level partying myself, I just nodded in agreement. A nearly primal scream from across the casino drew our attention towards the table games. A security guard almost involuntarily reacts to sounds like this with a head whip, as his job is made of these. What I saw next was what left me shaking my head. All the Greek kid's friends were huddled around a craps table shooting dice, very loudly, and obviously winning. They were gambling, drinks in hand, without a care as to what was happened to their friend. They just kept the party going. Kani smiled at me. "Welcome to Las Vegas."

The following evening, I reported for work at the usual start time of 9:00 p.m. for my second night of training. The customary furniture moving and setup for the evening took place and the club was soon packed with people. Kani let me roam a bit on my own to get a feel for the energy of the club. I was watching the floor when a call came over the radio: "There are pieces of shit on the balcony."

I thought at first that this was just security guard humor coming through. Through prolonged dealings with guests, some bouncers have become a little jaded towards the folks who help pay their bills. The caller was immediately hit with a barrage of hilarious comebacks and one-liners.

Our humor turned when the caller recognized the comedy and then went on to confirm that, despite the jokes, there was in fact shit, meaning actual human feces, on the balcony, and he was going to need a porter to clean up. I hustled outside to see this for myself. The gathering crowd displayed equal parts disgust and disbelief. As I pushed through the crowd, I saw them—a dark-brown turd was sitting on the rail of the balcony. Another had obviously tumbled off the rail and left a skid mark down the wall on its way to the floor. I asked if anyone had seen who left them. A number of guests stepped up, as they had watched this event take place.

A young woman in a yellow miniskirt had hiked one ass cheek onto the edge of the rail, pulled aside her thong, and taken a dump. She did so without shame and in front of fifty or so people. I made the call over the radio with her description so that we could find her and eject her from the club. I told them to check the ladies' room because unless she used cocktail napkins to wipe her ass, she was most likely going to require a bit of cleanup. I couldn't imagine why someone would get dressed up, go to an exclusive nightclub, and then take a shit in public. The consistency of the turds meant it couldn't have snuck up on her. If it had been like gravy, I might even have been able to understand, as then it would have been an unfortunately timed accident and somewhat forgivable. But this defied logic.

Our porter, Tony, hit the balcony and saw what lay in front of him. Tony's job meant he got to clean up the worst of the worst of the messes in the nightclub. In terms of job description, being a porter is a huge step down from being a busser. Bussers worked sections, keeping them clean and assisting the cocktail waitresses by bringing everything but the booze. A busser was paid handsomely for this, even though they were glorified garbage men. Porters were actual garbage men—they swept the floors, dumped trash cans, and emptied ashtrays. Now Tony had the unenviable task of finding a way to clean this mess up without creating an even bigger mess. Tony was a good-natured kid who was always smiling. This time was no different, and I soon found out why.

His idea to clean up the shit showed he had a devious mind and a mean streak to boot.

Tony ducked into the lounge and returned with pair of glasses, glasses that a busser or a bartender was going to have to wash. He scooped the shit to and fro using the glasses and being careful not to get any on the outside. He scraped the edges clean using the glasses against themselves and soon he had compacted the shit neatly inside with just the faintest of smears near the lip of the glass. He then sprayed the wall with disinfectant, wiped it down with a rag, stuffed the rag into the glasses and then took the glasses inside where he no doubt deposited them in the dish area for an unsuspecting busser to handle. No one on security was going to snitch on Tony for passing the shit on to the bussers—the humor it provided was just too good. I was too new to do anything but relay the information to Kani so he could laugh and then keep my mouth closed. Plus it's always nice when the little guy got an opportunity to tip the scale.

As the days turned into weeks, I was trying to get in as much work as possible. Shannon still hadn't found work and my club wages didn't stretch very far. I started splitting my time between the private area of the club and our larger sister club, where performances took place. They were two distinctly different worlds, but I was suited to both and was making friends quickly.

The hierarchy and your time on the job dictated where your supervisor stationed you. Most newbs started out front and moved their way inside the club, though they'd train in a number of different spots so they'd be able to work any spot in a pinch.

I fell in with a guy who started around the same time I did; his name was Stu. This was by virtue of being stationed in the same spots most of the time. Stu and I spent some time out front together and found that our interests ran along the same lines. He was a pit bull of a man—short, broad-shouldered, and muscled. He was a fan of ancient times and wore the tattoos to show it. If I needed help disposing of a body, Stu was the guy I would call.

I was rotated in to work the GA, the general admission line. I was working the line one night when a couple came upstairs from the nightclub. The man said that he had dropped his wife's ID sometime after they entered the club, and he wanted to know if I or anyone else had found her ID. I made a call on the radio to see if one had been turned in to lost and found. No response. The wife started going all blubbery. She explained that they were leaving in the morning, and she wouldn't be able to get on the plane without her identification. She paced the floor and kept wringing her hands, as though without her ID, she would never get home.

It seemed obvious to me that this wouldn't be the first time someone had lost an ID in Las Vegas and had to get on a plane to go home. From there, it was a short jump to realizing that the airlines certainly had some sort of protocol for just such an occasion. At any rate, it wasn't my problem, further than making the effort to see whether or not someone had turned in the lady's identification. Her husband calmed her down and told her to wait against the wall. He was going to handle everything.

The man approached me and stood the way someone does when he doesn't want his wife to hear what he is about to say.

"Okay, here it is—this black chick stole my money when her hand was in my pocket. See, she was giving me a hand job at the bar, and she pulled out my money, and my wife's ID was wrapped up in the cash," he told me.

He said all this in a matter-of-fact tone, and I was surprised by his economy of words. Most average people, when confronted with a problem of this magnitude, at least stuttered, and some lost all composure, but not this guy.

"Listen, I don't care about the cash—she can keep it. I just need my wife's ID," he continued.

"I appreciate your situation, but I can't go through the club accusing random black chicks of stealing," I explained. "Check the garbage cans—pickpockets discard anything that can link them to the crime pretty quickly afterwards. That's the best I can give you right now. You can always call casino security in the morning. That's where anything found goes after we close," I told him.

19

He headed over to where his wife was standing and she kind of shrank down the wall and started a whole new round of hysterics when he told her the bad news. He was shameless, really. But I admired the grace with which he handled a rather sticky situation.

It didn't take me very long to move out of the positions reserved for newbs and into positions that saw more action. I had a skill that separated me from the rest of the rank and file. I quickly became a mainstay on the GA line out front due to my ability with ID. Las Vegas is a tourist Mecca, and you'll see identification from every state and country. I was very good at spotting fake ID. Don't know why. Something clicked. I could spot a fake as soon as they handed it to me. It was also a psychological game—it's the mannerisms, the body language. They know they have a fake ID, so they usually start giving it away the minute they present themselves. A lot of times, it's these nuances in behavior that make the difference in a situation. A great deal of what makes the difference between someone being "good" at the job of security and just being another warm body are these types of instincts. From the jump, I was very good at the psychological part. I had developed the skill as a kid.

The woman I grew up with was a Class A tyrant. Yelling was her preferred method of communication. I remember leaving church and getting screamed at on the way home more often than not. Needless to say, I spent as much time as possible away from home, usually staying at my friend's house and spending the night to avoid confrontation. I'd rather sleep on his floor than be at home.

When I had to be home, I was always vigilant, always watching for signs of her mood. Picking up on little things could make all the difference between a peaceful night and one marked by screaming and crying. When you spend the bulk of your grade school and high school years perfecting this as a means of emotional survival, it becomes second nature, automatic, instinctual. Picking up on people's behavioral nuances served me well on the job.

While I was on the door, Las Vegas made the jump from a laminated ID to the hard card that's in play everywhere, but they were getting knocked off a week after they were introduced. The technology and ingenuity that go into making a fake ID can be staggering. A week after they made the change, I caught my first fake. It was hands down the best fake I'd ever seen. It probably passed in every club in town. I caught it completely by chance and instinct. I was ID'ing and handing out wristbands to those old enough to drink. I looked at the kid's ID and did a double take—he just looked too young. But the line was huge, economy was necessary, and the ID was one of the new hard cards, so I banded the kid and moved on.

Still, as I went through the line, something wasn't sitting right. He just didn't look old enough—not even close to twenty-one, the age on his brand-new ID. I doubled back and asked to see his ID again. He held up his wristband and said I'd already gotten him. "Sorry. man. I don't remember. Just let me take a peek again and put my mind at ease," I told him. He produced his ID and then I jumped him with a quick question. "How old are you?" I asked him.

"Sixt ... twenty-one," he stammered. The little fucker blew it on the first question.

"Thanks, kid. I'm going to need that wristband back," I told him.

He weakly held up his arm so I could strip him of his band. He meekly asked for his ID back, and I told him no. There was no way I was handing over a new knockoff. Just the ability to study this new-look ID made it worth its weight in gold. I still let him go to the show, mind you—no use adding insult to injury, and he wasn't going to be able to drink.

When the line died down, I pulled the fake and studied it against a real ID. It was a masterful knockoff. The difference was something with the font—it was just a little off. It was like one of those designs you have to relax your eyes to see. But once you did, you could tell as soon as you looked at one. I was snagging those things left and right over the next few months. Someone in town was making a mint selling near-perfect knockoffs.

The following week, I pulled two at one time off a young couple. The guy decided he wanted to play hard, probably to impress his

21

girlfriend. He insisted they were real and he demanded that I give them back. Even after I told him outright that I knew they were fakes, he still demanded they be returned, even going so far as to say that I had no legal right to keep their IDs. So I dropped the hammer on him: I told him that I was going to hand them over to the detail of Las Vegas Metro that we had stationed outside the club.

"I'm just going to let them run these for you and your girlfriend. If they come back clean, I'll apologize and buy you a drink," I told him. I wasn't able to get any drinks comped for anyone, but I was so sure they were fake, I knew I wouldn't need to.

"Fine. Run them," he replied. His girl doesn't look so sure.

"Last chance, man—take the easy way out." I was practically begging him to take the out here, but the kid just couldn't get there.

"Run them. I want you to."

His smug tone changed my mind. I walked them over to Metro. The cops took a look and told me they were good. The kids were good to go.

"Look, guys, I know they're fake. I've been seeing them the last few weeks, and some of the kids have admitted they're fake. The font's off, anyway," I told them, trying to get them to do their job.

The cops couldn't see it, but I wasn't surprised at this. You had to relax your eyes to see, and cops just can't relax. They finally relented, however, and called them in, no doubt more out of their own curiosity than to help me out. Both IDs came back garbage.

Mr. Smug and his girlfriend were now officially in deep shit. They didn't get arrested, but Metro wrote them each a citation, kept their IDs, and then threw them out of the casino. After all that, the kids didn't even get to go to the show.

Metro returned and study the IDs for what seemed like forever. They still couldn't believe they were fakes. "I don't know how, but they must have made a mistake. These things haven't been out very long," They were telling me.

Yeah, me and the DMV are both wrong on this—happens all the time, I thought. They didn't realize I played the game every night at work—recognition through repetition. I was very good at the game and I seldom lost. The GA line was where I made my bones, being a reliable and trustworthy authority on the door. It helped me gain respect among the more experienced members of the team and moved me up a rank on the food chain.

Since I was gaining recognition as a good-standing member of the team, our security supervisor, Scoop, put me on a VIP section on the floor one day a week. It was our night for hip-hop in the main club, and one particularly raucous evening, we had a rap show set to go on. I was working the section behind the soundboard and arguably had the best view of the stage. It was a packed house when the star took the stage. About fifteen minutes into the show, my section was approached by about a dozen black men. Their leader was a slight, fresh-faced black kid, definitely in shape and displaying a lot of ice. He approached the rope with a bottle of champagne in hand. As he reached the rope, he extended his hand to unhook it and enter. As he grabbed the rope, I grabbed the rope. This was not the professional thing for a doorman to do, nor should you challenge someone unless absolutely necessary.

The kid just smiled as his entourage surrounded me. "Man, I got a table upstairs," he said.

"I'd be happy to accommodate you. Just give me a moment to check it out," I replied. His goons were breathing down my neck. I was pretty sure I'd get my ass handed to me without being able to mount much resistance, as all these guys were my height or taller and considerably heavier. I raised my hand to make a call on the mic and his goons closed in.

The kid straightened his diamond bracelet. "Make that call," he ordered.

I started to call just as Scoop walked up carrying an ice bucket. "Yo, Hank. You know who this is?"

I didn't. Scoop filled me in on the iced-out pugilist that I failed to recognize. "He's got a table upstairs. We going to sit him down here for the show," Scoop told me.

I opened the rope and let them in. The members of the entourage spent the show continually mugging me, obviously still angry about the earlier slight to their gravy train. They sat in my section for the entire show, high-signing and acting tough. The iced-out pugilist wasn't bothered by me in the least. He just sat there and enjoyed the show. It was that way with most celebrities—the help is like the furniture.

The show ended and the iced–out–pugilist party made its exit. As people were making their way out, a call came over the radio. A harried female voice was screaming, "FIGHT, FIGHT, FIGHT!" But she wasn't giving a location.

People tended to get tunnel vision when a fight occurred, and just because it was your job didn't mean you'd be any less susceptible when the adrenaline climbed. I looked around for the commotion and noticed people scattering near the front exit. I rushed over and rounded the corner to see two security guards holding a frail white kid.

One of the guards was Cal, a jovial good old boy. He had the kid in a full nelson and under control. The other was a fat-ass Italian kid, Luigi. He was holding one of the kid's arms in one hand and pointing with the other. He was screaming, "GET HIM … GET HIM!"

You could hear the fear in his voice. I looked at who he was pointing at. I saw a huge black guy at least twice as wide as I was closing in on them. He was wearing a blue and gray ostrich shirt and he was definitely pissed off. I did the only thing I could do. Just as he reached back to swing, I hooked his elbow with mine.

This motherfucker was strong as shit and his swing carried me so that when he was done, my back was at his chest. "It's not worth it, sir," I tried to assure him.

He shucked me off his arm and started up the steps after the kid. I grabbed his belt and leaned back. I swear, if I hadn't started moving my feet up the steps after him, he would have drug me the entire length of the stairs. By the time we reached the top, he had slowed down. I think I wore him out.

"Sir, what's the problem? What did he do?" I asked.

"Man, he said, 'Fuck hip-hop.' Fuck that nigga."

Yes, saying "Fuck hip-hop" in the wrong company is enough to get your ass kicked. Luckily, the kid was gone when we got to the front of the club.

As I settled into the routine, I discovered that work was going to be erratic—still better and more frequent than my time in Florida, but in Las Vegas, the stakes were higher. My household was relying on me for support, and I couldn't let Shannon down. She had supported me through more than just school, and this was my opportunity to repay her. The trust she and I had established was on a level I'd never experienced in a relationship. This was really the first time I'd thrown in with a woman on the idea of a future together. My first love in high school was doomed, as most first loves are, and my second was based on codependency due to experimenting with recreational drugs. If you coupled those relationships with my mother's absence and my experiences with my stepmother, it left a big hole where trust for the female gender should have resided.

Shannon had broken that down and helped me change my life for the better. I took this idea of our future together and held it inside me— it drove me. In looking for opportunities to make some cash, it came through Stu that a guy on security ran a tiling business during the day and he was looking for guys to crew. He had a bunch of jobs laying tile in big-money homes out in Henderson. Since I'd been around blue-collar work all my life and basically grown up on construction sites, it was a natural fit.

The schedule was brutal, though. I reported for work at the club at 9:00 p.m., sometimes earlier if there was a special event. Work usually lasted until 4:00 a.m., then it was home for a couple of hours of sleep, only to wake and report to the job site at 9:00 a.m. I'd tile all day, until 4:00 p.m., and then back to the club at 9:00 p.m. If you're doing the math, that equation works out to no real sleep. Hell, there was hardly time to get enough calories in between naps and work. I stand six-foot-four, but the long hours with little chance to grab a meal had me weighing in at about one hundred sixty-five pounds. Still, the ten bucks an hour in cash was needed and I was fully dedicated to that grind.

All in all, things were moving along. The club was good to me, and my daytime work was helping pay the bills. I'd cycled onto the door on a full-time basis except for the occasional time that Scoop would send me inside for a change of pace. As supervisors went, Scoop was one of the good guys. Sure, he only oversaw security, but the future would see him moving into the management ranks.

There are few good managers I have worked for. Those few were exceptional at their jobs. The best ones usually had their own malaise, be it infidelity, drinking, drugs, etc. They knew their business and accepted that other people might have their own. The good ones could identify this in people but still trusted and enabled them to do their jobs.

This was the exception, however. A great many of the managers I have worked for were ineffectual douche bags. These jackasses chose to ignore the fact that when you take a shit on the people you work for, they will fuck you behind your back at every turn. Even if you get some middle-of-the-road employee who won't necessarily fuck you, he or she certainly won't give you their best.

The guy running the show for us in Vegas was some slick club asshole. His claim to fame was that he had opened the first rock-and-roll club in an Eastern bloc country, and he made sure everyone knew this.

Our Monday-night party was the only game in town, and it brought out a who's who of Vegas locals as well as celebrity guests. Working the door of this event carried a certain prestige that I hadn't fully realized yet. My skill set put me there to weed out the undesirables and frauds. But I was a blue-collar guy who was still not entirely up to speed on the selective policy exercised at the doors throughout Vegas. This was to be my first real lesson.

One night, two Latinas came up to the door. They lingered for a moment in front of the sundries shop. Mr. Eastern Bloc leaned into my ear and said, "We don't want them in here ... charge them thirty dollars."

We were charging locals ten and tourists thirty at the time. The brusqueness of his comment and the fact that I loathe elitist pricks elicited an immediate cerebral *Fuck you*. What I failed to realize then was that the entire club experience is based on elitism. The idea that people would voluntarily line up outside a building and submit to the establishment of a pecking order, determined by the basest of criteria, to be decided by people whose main motivation is money, all so they can buy overpriced drinks and be "seen" doing so, is still foreign to me, even now.

I checked the women's identification; both were local. I charged them the local price and let them in. Eastern Bloc went behind me and checked with the doorman.

"What did I tell you?" he seethed. I tried to respond, but his voice grew stern, like a father's would be. "What did I tell you?"—pause for effect—"Huh?"

I remained quiet, knowing I could not win this battle. I did, however, go home at 6:00 a.m. and pen a scathing letter about how I thought his comment had been racially motivated and also how he had so unprofessionally berated me in front of other guests, a huge corporate no-no.

I arrived at the door to our human resources manager's office promptly at 9:00 a.m. She was a sweet-as-pie, rotund, extremely understanding and businesslike woman. She thanked me for maintaining a good moral compass and doing the right thing, even if it meant defying the man in charge. The end result came swiftly—Mr. Eastern Bloc lost his job and I never had to deal with him again. For me it was a lesson learned. He was the first douche bag, but he certainly wouldn't be the last.

I may have won a fan in the front office, but the other result was my being moved off the door. The new man in charge, Ken, moved me upstairs to replace Kani on the private rooms. Kani had parlayed his experience into a lucrative private-security gig that would provide enough reason to quit. I never knew if Ken moving me off the front door was punishment or a privilege, but I think Ken could do without a moral compass off his right shoulder—scruples have no place on the front door in Las Vegas. He was a good manager once you established whether or not you were dealing with drunk Ken or high Ken. Then you could adjust how you dealt with him.

The move proved to be a good thing for me. I met people at a much higher rate and really got the experience of what a Las Vegas club was all about. The one thing that astonished me was the amount of money I was being offered on a nightly basis. Twenty-dollar, fifty-dollar, hundred-dollar handshakes were coming my way just for opening and closing a two-foot-long velvet rope that separated the private rooms from the rest of the club. Needless to say, I wasn't taking anything. I was turning down more money on a single night than I made in a week of working two jobs. This was due in part to my naiveté to the game and mostly because I was afraid of losing my job.

The management's no-tip-taking policy was in full effect, so I wasn't taking anything. I had been successful in turning down money for a while. The reactions were mixed, ranging from utter disbelief to looking as though I'd called them an asshole and then insulted their girlfriend, all because I wouldn't take their money. One night, as the evening was winding down and the last of my guests were leaving, the drunkest guy and the last one out of the room stopped and lingered in the doorway as I held the rope open for him.

"Have a good night, sir," I bid him farewell as he continued onto whatever after-hours party was on the itinerary, most likely the late-night spot at Barbary Coast.

"Did anyone take care of you?" he asked. "Me? I'm good, sir. I appreciate it, though." A number of his party had offered me money throughout the night, all of which I had turned down.

"No. No. Absolutely not. This is the business we're in," he said as he pulled out a ten-dollar bill and forced it into my hand.

"Sir, I can't take this," I told the guy as we uncomfortably held hands outside the private room.

"Take it. Take it. Just take my money."

No doubt this phrase had been uttered many times in Las Vegas. As the discomfort of holding a sweaty drunk's hand grew, I finally took his money.

"Thank you," he told me, the smell of vodka heavy on his breath.

The close-talking that's made necessary by the volume in a nightclub gives you a familiarity with the scents of other people—a familiarity you'd rather not have. Despite my offer to return his money, he wouldn't take it back.

He walked down the steps and disappeared into the people flooding out in the direction of the front door. Now I was stuck with ten dollars I didn't want.

I actually did want the money. I needed the money. I just didn't want the hassles it represented. I thought about just pocketing the money and moving on to my closing duties. But if someone saw me and decided to snitch, I could be in real trouble. Just as Shannon and I were getting our footing, I could be at risk of losing my job, and that would be a huge setback. So I decided to do the right thing. I called the floor manager, Napoleon.

Napoleon was a five-foot-four-inch weasel's asshole. Stu always said he looked like a James Bond villain, sans cat. Now as a manager, he had the power to let me keep the tip—that's why I called him. In one fell swoop, Napoleon plucked the ten dollars out of my hand and said, "Thank you for your honesty."

He deposited the money in the pocket of the crisp designer shirt he was wearing, and I know that's where it stayed. In that moment, he bought all the respect I had for him for ten dollars. That also marked the last time I turned down money.

Now that the money situation was wide open, I was looking for an angle. I say it was wide open now because all a policy like that really does is make sure there is no line drawn between a tip and a bribe. Whereas you might take a tip for opening the rope or escorting a lady to the restroom, you would not take money to look the other way while someone snorted coke or fucked. But when you can be fired for both, you take both. The first place I started was with IDs. While Ken had taken me off the line for the high-profile Monday-night party, he left me on the door for the rest of the week, when the ability to handle volume with accuracy was necessary. He needed bodies in the club fast so they could buy drinks. That meant me on the door.

By now, I could tell a fake as soon as I got it in my hand. If they presented me a fake, the result was the same—confiscation. If I hit you on a Friday, it was at least a hundred bucks to get it back. Saturday or Sunday, we could negotiate a deal. I made a good bit of cash doing this. This is where Greasy and I fell in.

Greasy was a jovial cat of close to three hundred pounds. He'd worked clubs in Las Vegas before and had a knack for establishing a rapport with everyone he met. He was also a cat who'd attempted suicide when he exited a moving vehicle traveling fifty miles an hour on I-15. Still, he was genuine person. He was one of those people who gave you a good feeling whenever you were around him.

I ran the regular line and he ran the VIP line. I would confiscate the ID and Greasy would take the payoff. When I was sure he had the cash, I would give one of the people in their group the ID. This system kept the cash separate from the ID and ensured survivability for both of us. It would be difficult to spot unless you watched it over and over again on casino surveillance, and we all knew casino surveillance was focused on the games or was only called up if there was an incident elsewhere. We quickly learned that no one from the nightclub cared to look for this sort of exchange and in the end, I was essentially doing my job barring minors entry to the club. The minors didn't care because they most likely went through hell to obtain a fake ID in the first place, so a payoff was part of the game and added a level to their Vegas story. I was happy to split the cash with Greasy for the added security.

So through this part business transaction/part game/part job, Greasy and I made a nice bit of side cash. Not paying was always foolish to me. A fake ID was usually not obtained for free, and if you got it confiscated on Friday, your weekend was ruined—no clubs, bars, or gambling for you. Basically, your whole reason for coming to Vegas for the weekend was off the table. A few that didn't want to pay resorted to threats, weak protests of calling my boss, the casino, and the cops to tell them I was using extortion to squeeze money out of them. This, of course, never materialized, because my boss paid me to confiscate fakes, their parents would love to hear about how they were trying to get into a nightclub, and telling the cops you were committing a crime to tell them I was committing a crime might be the dumbest move ever.

I seldom lost the ID game. But once there were two boys from Georgia. They gave me two obviously bogus IDs. I used a common bluff I'd used many times and threatened to call Metro to run their fakes. Metro wasn't at my disposal on that particular night, and these two rednecks called my bluff. I even went so far as to make a fake radio call for detail. They didn't budge. They waited and waited for the cops to show. I made them wait twenty minutes and they did so patiently, which was the surest sign of my doing something wrong. Holding an honest person's ID for any length of time would make that person go apeshit. I finally had to give them back. That's the only time I remember losing.

I was learning the ropes and beginning to make some money, but the stress was definitely real. I felt like every time I took a handshake, it could be my last. After Napoleon's bullshit move, I felt vindicated in taking money. Still, I had to be on my toes. Working the private rooms on Monday was proving to be my best night. When the VIP hosts sat tables for bottle service, you could count on them dropping thousands of dollars, and that usually meant an extra duke for the guy holding the rope.

For every VIP host I ever worked with, maybe one in twenty was actually cool. VIP hosts are the used-car salesmen of the nightclub industry. You'll see them out front with their faux-hawks primped like peacock feathers while working their phones like a video game. Out there with fat-knotted ties threatening to choke them, if they unbutton their jacket, it reached to mid-chest. The Rat Pack rolls in their graves as these clowns disgrace Vegas.

They do have value for the club, and the best of them make exorbitant amounts of money for "working." Even the best had to scrape their way up to make it, and this made them especially grimy. Most VIP hosts are nothing more than pimps and drug dealers, but it's dressed up in the lights of whatever nightclub they work for. Most hosts grovel for money. You can watch as their guest sits down and they begin to salivate like a hopeful mongrel. At least used-car salesmen sell a useful product. VIP hosts peddle hangovers and regret.

But every once in awhile, you'd run into a cool host that knew their business and wasn't smarmy. A host that's so good at what they do, they make sure everyone gets taken care of, including security. Jensen, our lead host at this time, was one of those guys. He was a genuine guy who always said hello. He was sure to let you know who you were getting and what their story was. It made sense that he would brief security, as we would have a lot of hands-on with their guest and helped to shape that guest's experience. But you'd be surprised at how many hosts treated security like useless jackasses.

On one Monday night, a couple came up to look at the rooms. They had yet to be sat, and I was awaiting my guests, so I gave them a polite, but firm, no. I didn't need the rooms occupied by non-paying squatters when my parties arrived. That would get the night off on the wrong foot and could potentially put a dent in my ability to make some cash. The gentleman produced a crisp one-hundred-dollar bill and offered it up. "We just want to sit in there for ten minutes with the curtains closed. What do you think?"

I took a quick look around to see if anyone could see us. I snatched the bill with quickness, opened the rope, and closed the curtains behind them. I was all nerves, as I knew they were in there and up to no good. Cocktail waitresses, bussers, and porters were using the hallway I was working as a pass-through to execute their jobs. The cocktail waitress working the rooms stopped in front of the curtain.

"Are we sat?" she asked.

"Nah, we're good," I told her.

She could tell I had a case of nerves, and this piqued her curiosity. She reached for the curtain.

"I said we're good," I told her.

She was bent by the way I was talking to her. She shot me a nasty look and pushed the door to the back hallway open.

Now I had a problem. All I needed was an uppity, pissed off cocktail waitress telling Napoleon I was pulling some shit in the rooms. I pulled back the curtain to see the woman on her knees and the gentleman in the throes of finishing.

"I need you guys to wrap it up," I told them.

The woman tidied herself. She was more than a little embarrassed by the fact that I had interrupted them. The gentleman, though, was all smiles as he waved me off. "Yeah, buddy, sure, no problem. We're good here," he said.

"Nah, bro, we're not good. I need you to zip up and make it out of here. I'm not tossing you, but I need the room," I told him.

I was waiting for Napoleon to come through the curtain at any moment. If this dude had his dick out when he did, I was the one who was going to get fucked.

"Zip it up, chief. You and the lady got to go," I told them again.

They finished composing themselves and headed out into the lounge area. I was just relaxing from what I considered a close call when Jensen walked up to the rope. "Did you let a couple in these rooms?" he asked.

Oh, shit. The uppity broad told Jensen. She was really going for the jugular. One word from Jensen, and I'd never get another party again. I'd be relegated to some bullshit duty like watching the patio.

"Yeah, man. I did. Sorry. They just wanted some privacy for a minute," I told him. I figured I had to at least cop to that. No one saw the dude getting head but me, and I hoped I could get by with Jensen reprimanding me on how to handle the rooms.

"Did they give you money?" he asked.

Damn, I thought, *now I'm screwed.* With that question, Jensen left me only one way to go. I couldn't tell him the truth because of the official no-tip-taking policy. That put my job on the line. But lying to him was the second worst way to go, because if he didn't like or trust me, he could send me to the equivalent of security Siberia.

"No, Jensen. They didn't give me anything," I told him.

Jensen's shoulders dropped and I immediately knew that was the wrong answer.

Did he see me? Did the cocktail waitress or someone else see me take the cash? I couldn't be sure. But Jensen's body language told me everything I needed to know. I hung on his posture, waiting for him to speak.

"Hank, don't you fucking lie to me. They gave you cash because I told them to," Jensen said. His voice was like your dad's when he's disappointed in you.

"I'm sorry, Jensen," I hardly started before he cut me off.

"Shut up, Hank. I like you, and that's why you're on these rooms. I trust you to take care of my people. But I have to be able to trust you. Do you understand?" he asked me.

Now I felt terrible, like liars do. "Yeah, man. I get it. My fuck up. Won't happen again," I told him. I was hoping I hadn't screwed myself all the way here, but I was in a no-win.

"I sent them up here so you could make some cash and you handled things just fine. You're going to do well in this business." And with that, Jensen shook my hand and headed back into the lounge.

I was left to ponder this lesson on how the business worked, and it helped shape the thinking that, if everyone's dirty, then everyone's clean.

Jensen was a great guy and an awesome host. He had connections all over the place and he was no doubt heading for great things. He helped school me in the way Las Vegas worked and his lessons were well received. The guy taught me a great deal about taking care of people and about the nightclub business in general. It's too bad he was killed in a drunk-driving accident.

Celebrities and pseudo-celebrities permeate the atmosphere in Las Vegas. The latest reality-show star will commonly get to "host" a night at a local club. There is no end to the D-list names that host these parties. They run the gamut from pop stars' deadbeat boyfriends to a stupid rich girl from Orange County and our own Vegas cocktail waitress turned celeb, whose sole achievement was getting banged by a megastar actor. It says something troubling about society when these people are considered celebrities. But in a town that makes winners and losers on a roll of the dice, anyone can be king or queen for a day. But I also got to deal with actual stars throughout my tenure. Movie stars, rock stars, boxing heavyweight champs, superstars from football, basketball, and baseball—even the former director of the Agency— these are the real folks people want to see, and they all came to the club because it insulated them from the masses.

Our Monday-night party was gaining steam. It brought out the best in nightlife society and was beginning to attract celebrities. I learned at our pre-shift meeting that a certain Sultry Pop Princess was to be a guest in the club that night. Ken saw fit to put me on her detail as an escort throughout her visit. She had three separate areas in our club dedicated to her. She had a couch in our main room, one in our hip-hop room, and a separate private room, my normal spot.

She arrived with two local casino moguls and a friend of hers she called Julie. She also had a very large black man with her, a personal bodyguard named Desmond. Desmond was a wall of flesh and he was constantly working two cell phones coordinating her itinerary for the evening. I said hello to the moguls, who I'd seen on a number of occasions before. They were generous, as they always were, with both of them leafing off a few hundred each. The two of them stayed for a brief time and made an early exit, leaving the party to our Pop Princess and Julie.

It was then that Desmond came out of the private room and produced a large wad of cash. He turned over hundred after hundred as I watched. By the end, the stack was three grand. He held the stack in one hand and returned the rest of the wad to his pocket. He offered up the money and as I reached out his giant paw took a vice-like grip on my hand with the money still in between us. "You know what this is for, right?" he asked me. Silence was the first thing that jumped to my head, though I didn't speak this. I couldn't be sure. So I just nodded. I had three grand in my hand and didn't really care what it was for. The level this young lady was on was stratospheric at the time, so I was certain I was being paid for discretion.

I escorted Princess, Julie, and the bodyguard on several trips to each of their sections throughout the club. She wanted to be highly visible. During one of these trips to the hip-hop room, Princess had her back turned to the crowd and was talking to Julie. The room was packed and jumping, as it always was, and the rope was the only barrier between Princess and a few hundred people. I was making space at the rope the best I could but the room was wall-to-wall. People stood at the rope and gawked. I guess this kid got it in his mind that he was going to touch her while her back was turned. As he reached out, Desmond grabbed this kid's arm and turned it down. The kid resisted but I watched as Desmond slowly twisted the kid by the forearm until the he was standing on his tiptoes to relieve the pressure. "Keep your hands to yourself," he told the kid as he let his arm go. I think the kid was just happy to have his arm still attached to his body.

Each rotation through the club included a stop at the private employee bathroom. We did it the first time, which wasn't surprising, but when we did it again, and again—well, I can just say that now I was certain why Desmond had given me the three grand. Each time, Princess and Julie went in together, and each time, Desmond looked extremely annoyed. Given my experience with Princess, the later revelations of her drug use came as no surprise. I will say that she was polite, gracious, and respectful, even considering the drugs. She said thank you every time I opened the rope for her. Again, celebrities seldom acknowledge your existence, much less speak to you, and save for Julie's cartwheel and stripper-pole mounting of the pillar in their private room, they were well-behaved.

The main reason security exists is to dissuade an altercation or, in the event a full-blown fight breaks out, to gain control of the combatants and stop the fight before serious injury occurs. For those reasons, security runs nightclubs. Sure, they do so by mandate of the owners and the managers they've appointed, but make no mistakes—security is the law in the club. They make the rules. Whatever the management has put in place, you can be sure there is a second set of unwritten rules that security uses.

I was working one night when a fight broke out in the middle of a sea of people, so in I waded. Making your way through a crowd of people who have no idea why you're moving them against their will can be a monumental undertaking. First and foremost, people are oblivious to their surroundings. They're there to have fun with their friends and most likely have a good buzz going. The music is loud and bodies are moving frenetically around them. They're having a great time, so they don't even see, much less understand, that ten feet away, someone isn't having a great time. Second, they almost always feel as though my moving them out of the way with a firm hand is rude and unnecessary, so sometimes they resist or, even worse, confront the bouncer. They also don't understand that your typical fight has one side that doesn't really want to fight and is awaiting rescue while trying to avoid being hurt. I've seen grave injury occur with a single blow, so the seconds it takes me to move them matter. Luckily, this usually subsides quickly when the person realizes what's going on and gets the hell out of the way.

When I got to the fight, I grabbed the first combatant I saw. The kid struggled a bit but he didn't weigh near enough. I grabbed him around the waist and I pulled him out of the fray. As we neared the steps, he took a death grip on the handrail. He was trying to get back to the fight. I pulled, but the kid wouldn't budge. I suddenly felt his entire body shudder, and less than a second later, he shuddered again. Someone was blasting this kid in the ribs. I released the kid so I could stop his attacker. You can imagine my surprise when it was Stu. He blasted the kid's ribs again with a two-piece that made the kid go slack.

Stu snatched him up in a chokehold and I followed close behind. The kid was out cold by the time we hit the top of the stairs, and there were only three of them. Stu hustled the kid's limp body toward the front door. I rushed to catch up so I could try to open it before they got there. I missed. The kid's head slammed into the door a split second before I pushed the bar to open it. "Oops," said Stu through a shit-eating grin.

It was a good thing the kid was unconscious. Stu sat him down and gave him a chest rub. The kid sprang back to life. "What happened?" he asked.

"Bro, I think you fell," I told him. I changed the subject to the egg that had formed on his forehead. "That's going to need some ice, man," I said with a grimace.

I watched as the egg grew before my eyes. He reached to touch the horn growing out of his forehead.

"Don't touch it. I'll get the ice," I told him, then retrieved the poor kid some ice. "Why you fighting security, man?" I asked. "I was trying to get my shoe. It came off in the fight," he answered.

Normally, one would feel bad that this kid had gotten beaten, choked unconscious, and then had his head used as a battering ram to open a door. I didn't, and Stu certainly didn't. The rules between security and patrons are simple. Rule 1: Follow instructions. Rule 2: Do not resist. That's it. Failure to follow these rules comes at one's own peril.

If this kid had made anything of the way he was treated, Stu and I would have closed ranks and told the story the way it happened—the kid started a fight in the crowd, then resisted when we intervened. We made him compliant using force equal to what we were experiencing and the kid was injured in the process. Trust and believe that our sober version would be much more credible than your drunk version. I said that security is the law in the nightclub, and it's true. We're like the cops, only with less oversight. At least the cops have internal affairs. The only thing close to IA is my boss, and he doesn't want to deal with security issues. He's way more concerned about the numbers than how you "fell down" in the club.

After six months on security and spending a great deal of time together on tiling jobs, Stu and I were tight. He was upstairs in our sister club most of the week, and when the second spot opened after an old-timer moved on, Stu offered me the spot. I jumped at the chance to get into a suit full-time and make furniture moving and line duties a thing of the past. This was huge. I was looking at four solid days a week in the rare air of a private, members-only club. Better than that, Stu and I were the only security in the room. That meant only two pairs hands awash in what was certain to be a pool of money.

Plus the added benefit of not having to absorb the nightly payoff for Scoop. Yes, that was a concern. While never spoken, it took me exactly one shift to realize that Scoop made the final decisions on who worked the money spots and that this was contingent on him getting a share. Things were still tight at the house, so I made the decision to keep all my money and failed to make the payoff one Monday night. The next Monday, I was tethered to door duty, keeping an exit door clear. I was back at the private rooms the following Monday and was sure to hand Scoop his share at the end of the night with an apology for forgetting a few weeks prior. While the amount handed over was variable, Scoop had been in the game long enough to know who made what, where, and how that depended on business. This was an unspoken deal, and since no one would talk about it, it was better to err on the side of keeping Scoop happy and fed. After the first instance, I always made sure this was the case. Now you can see why supervisors are an easy call to make management. They know the numbers, too.

The first thing I noticed after making the jump was that hotel executives were always coming and going. From the VP down to the assistant banquet manager, if you had a business card, it was your ticket into the club. In the microcosm of the casino, you never knew where someone sat in the pecking order. Just because their card said assistant banquet manager didn't mean that person didn't bus tables years ago with the executive assistant to the VP. A title didn't necessarily say it all. So you had to watch your step. Attitudes varied from humble and gracious to downright arrogant, and the title didn't always parallel the attitude.

I was on duty one Friday night, a regular members-only affair, when I saw a commotion in the middle of the room near our most popular table. I hurried over to see a younger gentleman shying away from a young woman who was attempting to smack him. She was being restrained by another young woman, who was apparently amused by the entire situation. I could tell by the wide grin plastered across her face. I separated the parties and told the aggressive girl to relax. She didn't.

"Tell me what happened," I said.

"That fucking asshole bit my friend," she replied, still agitated.

This was new. Never had anyone bitten before.

"Well, did she like it?" I asked.

Her agitation ceased as she searched for an answer. I relieved her of the trouble. "I mean, it seems like you're the only one mad here. She's not trying to fight this guy."

"He's an asshole," she ranted. "You don't treat women that way."

I turned toward the younger gentleman, not entirely sure she wouldn't climb over my back to get at him. The young gent looked sufficiently flustered. He was still straightening his suit and smoothed his hair repeatedly. He handed me his card and, of course, he worked for the hotel, casino marketing.

"Did you bite her," I asked.

He smiled nervously and wondered how to answer the question of whether or not he was a bit of a sexual deviant. He denied the biting, though I could tell he was lying. His nervous hair-straightening bit gave it away.

"Look, do me a favor—just call it a night so the girl's friend will calm down. Any more of an incident and someone downstairs might find out. You don't want that problem, do you?" I said to him in an appeal to the job-first mentality that was prevalent in most casino suits.

He agreed to leave. I turned to the girl, who had now turned her wrath upon her friend.

"I can't believe you'd do that. He's not even good-looking." She was ripping her friend like she was her mother.

I interrupted to tell her I'd had him removed from the club and that they were free to resume having a good time.

Much later in the evening, I saw Miss Agitated feverishly making out with a young man she'd just met. He wasn't good looking either.

On Mondays, our security was fully staffed. We had a detail of around twenty guys or so working. Throughout the week and on Friday and

Saturday, we ran two guys. Stu and I were working a busy Friday night—we had in excess of 1200 on the list. I was standing on the perch, a short set of stairs that led to our smoking room. The perch provided a view of the entire crowd in the lounge except for one spot, which was obstructed by a large column. One of the bartenders signaled me from the bar. As soon as I stepped down, I saw the problem.

A pretty raucous fight was taking place at the end of the bar. As I cut through the crowd to get there, I radioed Stu. As I came closer, I saw that he was right in the middle. I touched his shoulder as I entered the fray to let him know where I was. He looked at me and then turned toward the combatants he wanted. It was three on three, with two older gentleman and a lady taking on three mid-to-late-twenties yuppie types who were faring miserably in the fight. Stu took the yuppies, leaving me with the old men. When two guys are breaking up a fight between multiple combatants, you have to enter with ferocity.

I shoved the old men as hard as I could. I alternated pushing them until they had no choice but to exit the door out onto the patio. One split off as soon as we got outside. Apparently, he was done with the fight. But the other squared up on me and raised his fists.

"I'm security," I shouted, trying to penetrate the rage haze that covered his face.

He knew exactly who I was already. Ten minutes earlier, I had told his wife to put her shirt back on. She was wearing only her bra in a crowded lounge. For a lady of fifty, she had a tight body, though.

I identified myself again. "I'm security."

He swung and I closed the distance. His bicep glanced off my arm as I grabbed his shirt and swept him off his feet. I landed on top off him and pushed my knee into his face. I looked behind me to see if his partner was coming. His wife was standing over me with a rocks glass over her head.

"Don't even think about hitting me with that. Put it down," I yelled.

I pushed off her husband and grabbed her by the arms. I am generally opposed to putting my hands on women, but I shook the shit out of her until she dropped the glass. I let go of her and her husband was back on his feet.

"Don't touch my wife," he said, acting as though that were the mitigating circumstance.

My general manager rushed onto the patio and the wife burst into tears. He ushered them back into the lounge and offered to buy them a drink. It seems the yuppies were invited guests of the casino, but they weren't members, like our older couple. This immediately made the older couple right and the yuppies wrong, regardless of who started the fight. Lucky for me, the wife's theatrics went away in a wash of gin and vermouth. One of the bystanders on the patio told me the only thing that kept me from getting hit with that glass was slamming her husband to the ground. It seems she had narrowly missed.

After the confusion, Stu and I reconvened on the perch. The light shone off his forehead, nicely accentuating the swollen outline of a rocks glass. I guess the wife hadn't missed after all. I suppose you could call it karma for the shoe kid.

The following night was Saturday. "Hank, come to the private rooms," Stu called over the radio.

I could hear the smirk through the radio. I made my way from the perch to the private rooms, where Stu was lining the doorframe with just an edge so he could see into the room through the side of the curtain. I moved to the other side and did the same. Sitting on the ground with her back to us was the fattest lady I had ever seen naked.

"She doesn't have a stitch of clothing on." Stu chuckled.

The woman was gyrating violently on the floor between the couch and the table. "What the hell is she doing?" I asked him. I was half-afraid to disturb her to find out. "I guess we should tell her to get dressed," I said. Neither of us really wanted to see this woman any closer than we had too. She looked like she had gotten spanked with a waffle iron. "You found them, so it's your deal, brother."

Stu didn't look pleased, but he went in first and I followed.

"Miss, I'll have to ask you to get dressed," Stu said.

She leaned back further than a woman of her girth could be expected to manage. It was then that we saw what she was doing. She was fucking the skinniest guy I had ever seen. This kid was all of about twenty-two or twenty-three and couldn't have been one hundred twenty pounds soaking wet. I put her around thirty-five and over three bills, easy. She stood up and her body relaxed. Her gut covered her snatch. The kid stood up. He was smiling like he had just won something, but she was no prize. The two of them got dressed and we escorted them from the club. They left together, no doubt headed to finish what they started.

That same night, I was in the midst of closing down the room for the evening when I was approached by a couple wanting to take a look at the view. He was an older man with jet-black hair graying at the edges. She was a bottle blond in her mid-forties with huge fake tits. She wore a skin-tight black dress with a sequined playboy bunny on the front. They wanted to look at the view. I told them we were closing and the balcony was closed for the night.

"Don't you know so and so, the casino host? He was the one that got us up here," he told me.

"We just want to look for a second." She smiled. She did have a nice smile and was definitely hot for her age, so I let them go.

I opened the door to the patio and let them know I'd be returning in a few minutes. I made my rounds through the club and all was clear. I went back to the lounge side of the balcony, as that was the side with the view. The couple was nowhere in sight. I stepped out on the balcony and walked the length. As I rounded the corner, I saw them. The woman's dress was in a band around her stomach. The man was furiously pounding her doggy style. He had a handful of titty and was going at her like it was the last piece he was ever going to have. I watched them screw for a few moments, really relishing what I was about to do.

"AHEM," I cleared my throat.

The startled old man stumbled backward, exiting her, and there he stood, bathed in the lights of the Strip, glistening and erect. "We were looking at the view," he said.

"Yeah, I know. Me, too," I told him.

The woman smiled again as she pulled her dress down and struggled to wedge her giant tits back into the elastic fabric. The man pulled up his pants and put his equipment away. The couple was grinning. I gathered that getting caught was the exciting part for them.

"You two got to go. I have to get this place shut down," I told them.

They were arm in arm now, like two schoolkids who just got caught making out. Not a retiree and his trophy wife, who just got caught humping dog style on the balcony of a multimillion-dollar club. The two of them made their way toward me. The man produced his hand and wanted to shake.

Now I was smiling. The thought of shaking this guy's hand, covered in twat slime, amused the shit out of me. "Forgive me if I don't shake," I said, a wide smile across my face.

He nodded in agreement.

As 2002 came to a close and the holidays were upon us, I made plans to go home and visit my father in Florida. Shannon wouldn't be able to make the trip with me, as she had found a job as a bank manager and hadn't yet worked long enough to accrue any vacation time. I was disappointed that Shannon wouldn't be able to make the visit home, but I was happy that things were finally looking up. We'd both finally managed to find good jobs, though I was still working the tiling gig during the day with the club ruling my nights. I was optimistic that I'd be able to go down to one job after the first of the year, and I was looking forward to spending more time with Shannon. Money was becoming less and less of an issue with each passing week. Our Monday-night party was becoming THE ticket. We had the prime space and the best view of the Strip, hands down. Add the celebrity factor, and all of Vegas wanted to be there.

Bottle service is a Las Vegas institution. The money spent on these tables reached the obscene. People plunked down thousands of dollars just to own a small piece of real estate in your club for a few hours. These people with so much disposable income were the security guards' bread and butter—as well as the cocktail waitresses, the bartenders, and the VIP hosts. Everyone was looking to get paid. There was so much money floating around that you could literally pick it up off the floor. I was working the private rooms one evening when I spied the unmistakable smoky-green hue of dollar bills lying on the floor at the base of the steps.

I was beginning to make some money, and I wanted to get a sense of the environment I was experiencing. Plus standing outside two rooms for hours on end with little or no human contact beyond cursory greetings and the occasional request for a bathroom escort can get supremely boring. So I decided to see how long it would take for someone to pick up the cash. It sat between two sections of VIP tables and was in plain sight in the middle of the walkway. People kicked it. People stepped on and over it. Somebody had to have seen it. Everybody had to have seen the cash sitting on the floor. Yet no one picked it up. It sat there for forty-five minutes.

One of our security supervisors, Big Sal, who stood around six-eight, came to fill up the doorway. I said, "Sal, pick up that dough right there."

Sal picked up the cash and stripped apart two crumpled fifty-dollar bills. He smiled and handed me one. That's how it was in the club—people couldn't be troubled to pick up one hundred dollars off the floor. Even if you saw the money, the potential harm wrought on your carefully contrived image by the fact that you would actually stoop to pick up cash from the floor would certainly dissuade all but the poorest soul. But that soul wasn't allowed in our club.

It was New Year's Eve and I was excited because I'd heard Las Vegas puts on a tremendous show. Every year, they shut down the Strip and people flood the street. Most of the hotel/casinos lining the Strip take part in a coordinated fireworks show. The club was also flooded with people. We had the best view of the Strip from our balcony, and the members were paying a premium for dinner and an open bar.

I was working the rope for a private party in the media room. The guests were older, well dressed, and generous. A few younger gentlemen, obviously sons and nephews, were with the party and were less enamored with the room and more intent on taking full advantage of the open bar. The lounge was wall-to-wall and the mood was festive. As the midnight hour approached, the balcony filled with people.

One young gentleman had swayed a young lady to keep him company in the now-empty media room. The kid worked his game and the young woman gradually warmed to him, no doubt succumbing to the effects of the open bar. What started as conversation soon moved into heavy petting, and soon after they were feverishly making out. I checked in on them from time to time from my spot at the rope. There wasn't much need for me at the rope, as everyone had rushed the balcony. I had to turn one elderly man away because he wasn't with the party. After I sent him away, I checked in on the couple. The kid was good. He had her top down and her very expensive boob job was on display. Always one to appreciate good work, I stood in the doorway for awhile and watched. The kid was sucking her nipples like booze was coming out of them. The young lady glanced up and saw me watching but made no effort to cover herself. She just clasped the kid's head and pulled it to her chest. I just smiled and she smiled back. *No shame,* I thought to myself as I returned to the rope.

The countdown had passed and we were in the year 2003. Arguably, the two young lovers were having the best time. But partygoers began returning from the balcony and I went in to let the couple know that they had to make themselves presentable. The woman fixed her top and bid the young man farewell. He said his nonplussed goodbye and smiled a wry smile. He looked like the frat guy who had just gotten off a sorority girl.

My party wrapped and I was cleaning up the room and moving the furniture back to its original position when the young lady returned. She was frantic. She kept wringing her hands and pacing back and forth looking for something.

"Can I help you?" I asked.

"You have to help me find my fur coat," she told me.

A missing coat is a minor problem. She must have seen that I wasn't giving it the proper weight.

"It cost twelve thousand dollars," she clarified.

Fucking twelve thousand dollars for a coat? I thought. A missing coat is a minor problem. A missing coat that cost twelve grand is a giant felony-theft problem. I had to help her find this or my boss was going to be pissed.

"I know it's not in here. I didn't see you come in with it, and the same party was here all night," I told her, going into immediate high-alert status.

45

"We were in the other room having dinner."

I took her down the back hallway to the private rooms and we looked in the room where she claimed she'd eaten dinner earlier in the evening—no coat. She nervously clasped her hands together. "I know I left it in the other room."

I was sure she hadn't. "Why don't you go look again and I'll check the lounge," I told her.

I surveyed the lounge and spotted an older man in a tuxedo with a fur coat under his arm. I approached him and noticed it was the elderly man I had turned away from the media room while the rich broad and frat boy were ensconced therein.

"Sir, there is a young woman looking for her fur coat," I told him.

"Well, that's good, because I'm looking for her—she's my wife," he replied.

It was a sad, nearly cinematic moment: old rich man looks for trophy wife while she sullies their marriage with a zit-faced frat boy partying on his daddy's dime on New Year's Eve. The woman walked up while I was explaining to her husband where she was.

"I was looking for you, darling. I couldn't find my coat." She took her coat from him and replaced it with her arm. "Thank you," she said to me with so much syrup dripping off that you'd think I'd done something. Her husband stood silently by as she looked me up and down. She winked at me, thereby cementing the fact that I was privy to her transgressions.

I knew her boob job was expensive.

I'd been in Las Vegas for less than a year and things were going well. After I had hurdled the initial stumbling block of getting my sheriff's card, I'd found myself in a job at which I excelled and quickly moved into a position that anyone who puts on a suit and throws people around for a living would kill for. The club was growing into a destination. Scratch that—the club WAS a destination, and I was growing into the idea of what I could accomplish there. I'd distinguished myself in rather short order and as such, I'd just been given the tiniest glimpse of what I could attain economically, not to mention the people I would have access to as a result of working in one of the premier nightclubs in Las Vegas.

Like I said, things were going well and I was looking forward to the New Year and all that it held. I felt like I was making my way and all the positive strides I'd made in my life were paying off. It was just like everyone said—work hard, fly straight, and things will go your way. I'd never really believed that bullshit before. But here I was living that very thing. Little did I know, that feeling wasn't going to last.

You know, it's a funny thing making your living off reading the nuances in people's behavior. Everyone possesses this skill on some level. It's coded in our DNA after thousands of years of perfecting communication. Hell, people used it before they could talk, when grunts and motions were the language of the day. I think that in the growing technological age, people are using it less and less and therefore it's underdeveloped in a lot of people. Do you wonder why people seem to be more oblivious than ever? I think mine is hyper-developed as a result of my childhood, and it's proven useful throughout my life. It's kept me out of a whole bunch of scrapes and really smoothes out the process when I'm dealing with people. The only bad thing is, you can't turn it off.

I'd returned from spending Christmas at home with my father and had to go right back to work for New Year's. Shannon couldn't go on the trip because she hadn't accrued any vacation time at the new job. I was looking forward to spending some time with her. We had agreed to have our Christmas together after the New Year's craziness died down. I thought nothing of it when she told me that she still had some shopping to do and needed to go out. I offered to go with her and promised I wouldn't peek. I wanted to hang out with her and spend at least a little time before I had to go back to the nightclub-and-tiling grind. We hadn't been seeing much of each other at all. But she told me she could get it done quicker on her own, so I let her go off alone.

The next day, I came home from tiling and walked in as she was on the computer checking her e-mail. She quickly closed the window she was looking at. In an instant, I knew something was wrong. That small action coupled with her reaction sent a message that was loud and clear: something was going on. It ate at me while we had dinner and watched television. I was so sure, I almost confronted her then and there. But I couldn't play my hand, only to have her deny it and go back to cover any possible tracks.

When in love, you have to be willing to play the fool; it's part of trusting someone. Now, I'm down to play the fool, but only if you're really good. The thing about proximity is, you let your guard down, but as I stated, it can't be turned it off. I also have a knack for memorization that allowed me to recall her e-mail password as soon as she clicked that button to close the window. I waited for her to go to bed, and when I was sure she was asleep, I went into the office, logged in, and checked her e-mail. There it was, in black and white.

The nervous panic hit my stomach. She was cheating on me. How could this happen? I paced the room, stunned, dismayed. I read the e-mail again. The words threatened to sear my eyes. I read it again: *I can't wait to get back inside your hot pussy.* This one sentence proved the most stinging. Partially because it proved that another man was familiar with my girlfriend, but even harder to reconcile was that her sex was so very vanilla. Rage would be the salve for my wounded pride. I pushed the door to the bedroom open.

"Wake the fuck up, bitch." I turned on the light. I said, "WAKE UP. How long you and Terrell been fucking?"

Terrell was one of her coworkers, a man who had been in my house and shaken my hand. Now that's ballsy, to look another man in the eye while fucking his girl behind his back, and this showed that Terrell was a special kind of asshole.

"HOW LONG?" I yelled.

Shannon's feeble attempts at denial began through her grogginess. "What are you talking about? We're not ... I'm not," she stammered.

"Drop the bullshit—I read the e-mails."

She was awake now. Her face ashen and pale, she dropped her head and wisps of blond hair covered her eyes, shielding her from my rants.

"How could you? I'm breaking my ass and you're out fucking another guy. You're a fucking whore."

It was pretty standard fare for this sort of exchange. I knew well she was capable of such a thing when we began our relationship. Shannon had let me know that she'd cheated on every single one of her boyfriends before me. She was very matter-of-fact about it. When she was younger, she'd screw every guy that showed her a little affection. All the things I thought brought us together—being the product of a broken marriage, raised by a single parent, yearning for attention, approval—all those things in her that I identified with were all the same things that made it so easy for her to cheat. It was all very clinical if you think about it. I imagine a psychologist would think it cliché, even.

Her primary excuse for cheating was that I didn't spend enough time with her. This cut deepest of all. I was killing myself working day and night from tiling to security back to tiling. For the first time, I felt like I valued hard work and that I was repaying a kindness to someone who'd believed in me. To be able to do this for her after she'd done it for me meant everything to me. It was a chance to back her up and allow her to lean on me for a while, to put forth my best effort and set a foundation for our future. I was finally doing the right things for the right reasons. Her betrayal of that idea stripped it out of me in one shot. I was mad at myself for investing in the naïve belief that hard work and doing the right thing would work out. I felt like a fool for ignoring my gut and going against what I knew to be true—what I watched growing up—that working hard and doing the right thing meant fuck all.

Even afterwards she was the victim. She felt like she couldn't handle what she'd done. She threatened to hurt herself. We took her to a crisis counselor and I found myself trying to be strong for her. We tried to carry on like nothing had happened, going out to dinner, sleeping together, and acting like a couple. I was trying to delude myself, even though I knew it was over. I just didn't know yet what I was going to do without her. One thing I did know was that I fully intended on paying Terrell back in some fashion. You couldn't just run roughshod over a man's life and home and expect to walk away whole.

Shannon gave me all the information I asked for concerning Terrell and his situation. He had a girlfriend that he also lived with. She even gave me his work schedule. But the last morsel was the best—Terrell was an ex-cop. I decided against heading over to the bank, where there were only a thousand cameras, which would only provide evidence in the event of a confrontation and escalation. I finally settled on paying Terrell's girlfriend a visit while she was at home and he was at work. I wrote a long letter detailing the situation, including dates, times, and locations. I walked up to the door of their shared apartment, rang the doorbell, and handed her the letter. "You don't know me. But Terrell and my girlfriend, Shannon, have been a busy pair. I'm sorry you have to hear it from me, but I'd want to know," I told her.

She stood there, mouth agape, as the realization of what was happening came over her. As I turned to leave, I heard a kid in the background. I guess I thought this would make me feel better—it didn't.

Since Terrell was who he was and I'd certainly not made the situation any friendlier by taking a huge dump on his home life, I thought I might need protection should Terrell want to come back on me. Stu took me to a gun shop he knew and they gave me a deal on a used .40 caliber. I wasn't sure that having a gun at hand when I was an emotional wreck was the best idea. But neither was being exposed to a piece-of-shit ex-cop with character problems, so I armed myself. I also began drinking.

The situation at home was far from ideal. I was living with Shannon while we "worked on" things. In reality, there was nothing to work on. Shannon's infidelity hurt me deeply. It sapped every bit of strength from me. My insecurity was immense, a leviathan that crawled inside of me and wrested my confidence from me. I sat on the balcony one night by myself. This balcony was only big enough for one chair, and I sat with my feet propped up on the wall. There wasn't a view, just a tree and the housing development we lived next to. I drank slowly from a bottle of bourbon. I wondered what I was going to do. Shannon had helped me turn around a life that was headed for the worst kind of disaster. I couldn't see what was going to become of me. I drank until the bottle held just a shot. I sat there with the pistol in my lap, and for the first time in my entire life, I thought about suicide.

I pulled the slide back until it locked. The clean copperhead winked at me. I looked at the way the barrel sat slightly askew when the slide was back, knowing that it would straighten out when I chambered the round. Then I'd put the gun in my mouth and squeeze. The forty-caliber report would be followed by freedom from pain, from regret, from a cloudy future, freedom from a life devoid of love. Shortly thereafter, shattered glass would rain down from the sliding glass door covered in viscera. And finally, the mushroomed bullet would lodge somewhere in the apartment ceiling with a bit of my gray matter still attached. All the pain would go away in the simplest of actions. Literally one second would fix the pain I felt in my heart and in my head. I looked at the gun. I looked at the bottle. I decided I would take a shot or a shot.

I pointed the gun at my head and really got to the root. I could feel the powder burn on my face. I gritted my teeth and looked right into the barrel. In one simple action, I could have relief. But then my father's face crept into my head. I realized the thought of his only son blowing his brains out would destroy his heart and make all the sacrifices he'd made for me just a fruitless waste. I asked myself what that would make his life worth. That's the only reason I didn't shoot myself. If he had been gone, so would I.

I took the last shot from the bottle, stood up, and fired the gun into the air. I had to get that bullet out of the chamber. It carried the worst of intentions. I was drunk and off balance, so I struggled to get the sliding glass door open. When I entered the living room, the light was on and Shannon was standing there. It's a scene I will never forget. Her face, her body language—everything read the same. She was disappointed that I was alive. You see, if I'd committed suicide, she could have been the victim, and that was a role she relished.

My despair was all-enveloping; it invaded my mind constantly, following me everywhere I went. I threw myself into work so I could forget for a while. I was looking for comfort and there were high levels of comfort to be had in the nightclub. One of these comforts came in the form of female attention. If you're going through a breakup, nothing makes you feel better faster than attention from the opposite sex. As base and shallow as this seems, it's an important component in the healing process. It makes you feel good for the obvious reasons, and especially in a case of infidelity, it helps to soothe that bruised ego. I was free in this sense, and there was no shortage of female attention to be had in the club. As Greasy would say, *It's time to shake out your lion's mane.*

Bouncers, in particular, receive a great deal of this attention for one simple reason: we're safe, or, rather, we're perceived as safe. Now, don't get me wrong—it doesn't hurt that most of us are among the larger and taller individuals in the club at any given time, and I don't need to go into the female attraction to tall men, as this is well documented and has a basis in mate selection throughout recorded history. But why we really receive an inordinate amount of attention is due to the fact that we project an image of safety. After all, that's our job. We're a captive audience and we have to at least maintain a professional level of respect due to the fact that we are working. Also, we're not drunk assholes who are going to be creepy or too forward. All of these reasons make a woman feel comfortable about sidling up to a bouncer and striking up a conversation. That conversation also gives them a friendly face should they run into that drunk, forward, creepy asshole later in the evening. These reasons are also why a bouncer with any game at all will never find himself with an empty bed if he should choose.

This didn't just extend to patrons of the club. A Las Vegas nightclub also has a fabled phenomenon that is maintained at a level higher than anywhere else on the planet: the cocktail waitress. There are pretty girls everywhere, in every town in the world, and some could even challenge for the crown—New York, L.A., Miami. But Las Vegas has the highest concentration of pretty per capita over any of those cities. The money they make means there is no lack of beautiful women from all over the place lining up to apply for these jobs. Nowadays you can walk into any club on the Strip and find a parade of dimes at the ready to deliver cocktails and sell overpriced bottles to slobs who can't wait to part with their money.

Clubs print ads hiring "Cocktail Waitress/Models." This tells you all you need to know about what that lineup looks like. At the time we were working the club, this concentration was even higher because there were simply fewer nightclubs in Las Vegas. Pretty sells and Las Vegas is all about the sell. The news about my breakup spread quickly through the gossip-driven world of cocktail waitresses, and I immediately received a great deal of extra attention from Angie.

Angie was a spunky blond with a straightforward manner and porcelain-white skin. She asked me to hang out in short order, and after a couple of lunches together, the nature of our relationship was made evident.

The oft-joked-about myth about single mothers and Las Vegas is not really mythology. I suspect this is because there are a plethora of men with poor impulse control and no willpower. But it's not like this fails to apply to the women. Las Vegas doesn't exactly provide a recipe for marital or relationship bliss, a fact I was all too familiar with. There are just way too many pitfalls in a city built on the bones of temptation. Angie was taking care of two kids and our time together was limited, mostly relegated to her coming over to my house and us having sex. It was a rebound for both of us and that was where the relationship thrived. I was definitely shaking out the lion's mane.

Angie had a weird way of making you feel like she was about to suck your balls out through your dick. In the locker-room atmosphere of the security team, where our sexual conquests were a matter of sport, one of the guys asked me if it was weird-good or weird-bad. Crazy thing is, I wasn't really sure.

Angie and I both needed the comfort the other provided; still, I found myself trying to get into the boyfriend zone of dinners at home and movies on the couch. But Angie was too shell-shocked from her marriage and the aftermath of a messy situation with her ex to allow me to get too close. We began dating, and in many ways, it was the perfect relationship. It was because of Angie, I developed an affinity for mommies.

People always ask, what's the worst part of the job? The fights? The egos? While these are definitely hazards of the profession, one group takes the flag: pukers. We've all done it. Drank too much, too fast. Mixed booze we shouldn't have. I'm guilty, and I'd bet you are, too. But can you at least have the decency to throw your guts up somewhere disposable? If you can't make it to the restroom, lose it in a garbage can. Puke in your fucking purse. I've seen a woman fill a wine goblet up with scarlet venom she squeezed through her teeth. Good for her. If you're going to puke, make it your problem. No one wants to clean up the putrid, bile-soaked remains of your last meal.

I worked a long Friday at the beginning of a fight weekend. Fight weekends in Las Vegas are insane. That happens when the population of your city swells by ten to twenty percent in the span of a couple days. I had been sick with the flu for the week leading up to the fight, and when I get sick, I have a tendency to drop a lot of weight. Plus the fact that I probably wasn't eating as much as I should have been due to my state of mind, and that put me about twelve pounds lighter than normal when I took a seat at the poker table one night after work. I played a lot of poker—it served as yet another distraction from my situation. I did this mostly because I was still living with Shannon and didn't want to go home.

I ordered a beer from the cocktail waitress. I was sitting next to an attractive Asian girl. We chatted while we played. She was twenty-six and from L.A. We talked about poker, the weather, and assorted mundane bullshit. I lit her cigarettes as a gentleman would, told her a few lame jokes, and all was going swimmingly. The hours whiled away and I steadily kept drinking, even though it had been years since I'd done any serious imbibing. The alcohol, long shift, and lost weight slowly acted on me until my suave, witty Dr. Jekyll turned into a slobbering, obnoxious Mr. Hyde. When she politely asked for a game change to the No-Limit game, I said I'd go, too. She smiled and changed her story, citing fatigue, and said she was going up to her room. I told her goodnight and let her know I'd put her on the list to come up to the club.

After sabotaging an almost sure thing, I decided I'd get drunk. I didn't even notice the sun rise as I drained one green bottle after another. I felt my stomach turn and I staggered away from the table. I knew where the bathroom was and hustled to get past the sports book. I didn't make it. I sat on the planter just outside the book and puked foam all over the marble. At least I was coherent enough to spread my legs and not get any on my shoes. It was ten in the morning and the casino was full of people coming and going. Cups full of coffee and pastries in hand. Parents and children headed to the pool. And on display, one drunken degenerate in a suit and tie puking his guts out. Casino security came by and did their job. All I could muster to identify myself was the name of the club. Another round of liquid foam escaped my face, and I blacked out.

I have jigsaw pieces of recollection. The security guard summoned a manager. They got a wheelchair and put me in it. They wheeled me up the disabled ramp and down a hall. I was jolted awake by horrible electronic noise. My headache was tremendous, like I'd been hit in the head with a hammer. Another horrible grating electronic noise reverberated off the walls and sung through my aching head. I looked out over the stage of the club. A band was on stage and a sea of people were watching them. A sickening feeling filled my empty guts—I'd slept all day in a skybox at my job.

I looked at my watch. It read *7:30 p.m.* I had to be back to work in an hour and a half. It was fight night and we were going to be slammed. My head pounded. I gathered myself and tried my best to straighten a dress shirt that was wrinkled to all hell. Fuck—where was my jacket? I only had one suit. I straightened my tie and took a deep breath before I stepped into the employee hall. It was empty, thank God. *The poker room—my jacket has to be there,* I thought as I hustled down the hall. I reached the room and the day manager handed me my jacket and asked me to sign for two racks of chips. Apparently, I'd won a few hands the night before. I drove home, showered, and drove back to the casino.

My hangover was tremendous and it was busy as hell. The room was filled with the well-to-do fight crowd. I rallied halfway through the night and made great money hustling a few tables. All night, I was waiting for someone from downstairs to come up and relieve me of my job. I had no idea how I'd gotten into the skybox or who put me there. Big Sal came up later that night and filled me in. Casino security had summoned a manager, Kirby, who put me in the skybox to sleep it off. Kirby didn't know me very well, and I'd only met him a couple of times in the course of work. But still, he kept it to himself. The only reason Sal knew was because Kirby checked in with him to see if I was a good guy. Reputation can carry you a long way in this town, and the good guys get protected while lames get ground up and tossed aside.

This episode should have been a warning—about the drinking, about the gambling, about the dark road I was heading down—but it wasn't.

My love affair with taking chances was born into me. I don't know why, but if there's nothing risked, then there's no juice for me. Las Vegas is built on this concept. The casino business makes billions every year, and not because you win. They have planned this down to the minutest detail. The fact that they regulate and control the atmosphere is a foregone conclusion. Why do you think the drinks are free? I have fallen under a roulette table and struggled to get back into my seat, only to have the waitress bring me another cocktail. The idea that the casino cares how drunk you get and how much you wager exists only if you're winning.

I once went on a run so wild at a blackjack table inside a casino that I was doubling down for people I didn't know. The entire deck was hitting me in the face and I couldn't lose. The people I was doubling down, they were winning. The pit boss received a call and informed me that I was no longer allowed to double down for anyone else. If I was losing, do you think he would have gotten the same call? There is a reason that the casino is playing "Crazy," a seventeen-year-old song, over the P.A. system. It is in the hope that it will speak to you on some level, unconscious or otherwise, and cause you to take a risk to "get a little crazy." Otherwise, you won't survive, right? Couple this with the fact that, subconsciously, every day, we're working against the J.J. Rousseau belief that, but for the benefit of a few ambitious men, the rest of us are forced into a life of servitude. And isn't that what we're working against, the grind?

These are two very powerful forces to be caught between: the grind that most of us hate—oh, my fault, you love selling insurance, electronics, etc.—and the idea that, for just a moment, we get to lash out at the forces that control us every day is very appealing, and if we could just win, then maybe some reprieve might be won as well. The glut of "professional" poker players in Las Vegas proves this. I wish I had a dollar for every douche bag I've listened to at a poker table who claimed they played professionally and then watched as they pulled a two outer and acted as though it were a genius play. They cling to the dream. It's packaged and sold to us slick. The subculture is the mainstream and everybody's the rebel of their own story. Television helps perpetuate the myth, and at the time, people were eating it up heartily. Poker tables swelled with rookies and folks who were going to be just like Chris Moneymaker. Yes, I was one of them.

Now, even though Shannon and I were over, I deluded myself for time with the idea that she and I could reconcile. We attempted through sex to exact some measure of catharsis. This could have possibly resulted in her getting pregnant. She came to me on a cold, gray day and my response was just as cold.

"If you can be sure it's mine, have the baby."

I certainly didn't want the child. I grew up in a less than ideal situation, and bringing a child into a situation where the love and trust had been completely fractured just wasn't going to work. Ultimately, it was up to her, though, as she was the one carrying the child. I guess she couldn't be sure whose child was inside her. She scheduled an abortion. I certainly don't blame her, as there was only one side of the equation that would do the right thing if the child were his. This was the thing that drove me out of the house.

I'd nearly found myself in a life-altering situation simply because I was scared. I had to get out before it was too late. So I moved up the road to Henderson and into Stu's two-bedroom apartment. He had just broken up with his girl and was in need of a roommate. We were both newly single and had a doomsday outlook. I continued working the club and tiling during the day. I spent my nights off drinking and playing video games with Stu, mostly drinking. Any spare time I had was spent at the poker table in the idea that I could maybe one day play professionally, and then I'd truly be free. The fact that when I played, I was usually drunk or hungover and spent a lot more time losing than winning did nothing to dull this idea. The losing seldom bothered me—there was always another handful of cash to be made the next day or the next weekend.

Being drunk or nursing a hangover on a daily basis means, more often than not, you're driving under the influence, or at the very least, without your full capability. In my mind, this vagabond existence was the one I was meant for.

The regulars of the club varied. Most were of the uncool, overworked sort—the kinds of people who have let their bodies go to attain money. Some were just social lepers except in a business setting. They ponied up their hard-earned dollars in hopes it would grant them some exclusivity and an air of cool that they couldn't possess otherwise. I suppose in their minds it meant success just to belong, and to bring guests or meet someone in the confines of the club saved them the embarrassment of having to speak about just how successful they were, though some felt the need to hold court and talk about it anyway.

These regulars generally fell into one of three classic archetypes in their dealings with security. Snobs couldn't be bothered with you, as you were just the help. To them, you were a feeble-minded, low-paid Neanderthal who was only there to keep out the riff-raff. Nut-swingers were always guys who thought it was cool to be down with the bouncers. Nut-swingers loved to sidle up to you and ask shit like this: "So do you live in Vegas?" My answer to this one was always the same: "No, they fly me in from Tahoe. I'm that good." They reminded me of the cartoon in which the little yappy dog was always following around the bulldog trying to be his pal. They liked to be around tough guys because they felt like it made them look tough, and looking tough, whether you are or not, attracts a certain type of female, usually the ones that will sleep with you. What nut-swingers never got is, in a room full of them, we always looked like the tough ones. The last group of regulars was the Joes, the average people who were there and, short of an altercation or issue, were indifferent to you being there and would just as soon acknowledge you as not.

One night, I walked the long corridor that led to a secluded private room. Adjacent to this room was a larger room that we used for private events and our Monday-night party. Also lining the hall were various rooms, including the old managers' office, which was now used for storage. Early in the evening, the private room was used for dining. As I passed the doorway, I saw a young lady standing on the table, which was strewn with plates and surrounded by about a dozen men in pressed khakis and Polos. The men were hooting and catcalling and I saw why. The lady had no top on. Her breasts were small, and the men were snickering as she danced awkwardly. The young lady was doing her best to be seductive, but her drunken state, coupled with the fact that she had no rhythm whatsoever, made it painful to watch, and I didn't have the benefit of a few drinks to ease the pain.

I grabbed the woman's shirt from the side table and helped her off the table. She just smiled as I handed her the shirt. "It's okay," she protested. "I know these guys from college. We all went to Indiana together," she told me.

"Really, so it's kind of a reunion for all of you, then," I replied.

"Yeah, I haven't seen these guys for years. I live in Cincinnati and they're all in town for a convention," she prattled, then hugged one of the guys around the waist.

"That's great. Could you put your shirt on, please?"

"Oh, sure," she replied, then struggled to get it over her head.

The guys were all laughing. I mustered a smile. People who got this drunk amused the shit out me, as I'm sure I did them. I wiped the smile off my face as she finally pulled her shirt down.

"Do me a favor, darling, and go back to the lounge. Let these gentlemen finish their dinner."

She obliged after giving a few rounds of hugs.

"Fellas, come on—I can't have that," I told them.

They loved it. One of them put his arm around me. "Man, we know her from college."

"She was a stupid bitch then," another of the guys said, then almost in unison, they said, "and she's a stupid bitch now."

If it wasn't for stupid bitches, guys like you would never get laid, I think to myself. I fail to understand why men are foolish enough to condemn women for giving them what they want. Men spend their time trying to get laid, and then after the deed is finished, they attempt to trash the woman's virtue in some kiss-and-tell locker-room ritual. Here's a news flash for the morons who do this type of shit: *Guys, women want to sleep with you—don't talk them out of it by being an asshole.* At any rate, the men taking part in the college reunion were exactly those types of guys. I wondered if they thought about how their wives acted in college.

One day, another bouncer approached Stu and I and wanted to know if we were looking for a third roommate, or, more specifically, he was looking for roommates to live in his house. Gil was an older European cat. He was built like a fire hydrant and spent a good deal of time at the gym. Charismatic and witty, he wasn't at all out of place in a club where most of the people were twenty years his junior. He had a slight accent that only showed itself when he said certain things. "You cocksucker" was one of them. Gil was a rough-and-tumble sort of guy who had mellowed some with age, a rolling stone who had spent some time in jail. As Gil would tell it, the guy "threw him a wobbler" in a pub and Gil punched him in the face while still holding a beer mug. The mug slashed the guy's face badly and he was charged for assault with a weapon. He admits he meant to punch him in the face but says he was so drunk, he forgot he was even holding the mug.

Being a bit of a loose cannon, he gave up the drinking but picked up a nice gambling habit, hence the need for two roommates. We moved into Gil's three-bedroom house in a quiet neighborhood on the east side of town. We all came to call it Desperation Court. A favorite pastime of living on Desperation Court was driving home completely loaded and firing my pistol out the window into the air. I had reached a point where I just didn't care anymore. I wasn't yet ready to kill myself, but I wasn't going to shy away from any behavior that might get me killed or set off a chain of events that might just get bad enough to force my hand. I was truly lost, but I was also truly free. It's an intoxicating thing to just let go, to take on a nihilistic approach to your daily life, to carry with you no fear of ruin or death. It's also a very dangerous thing.

Navigating the waters of a high-profile club can be a sticky proposition. You are handling guests with a sense of entitlement, which gives them the idea that they own the club. You think the moneyed people are the worst? Nope. Rest assured that just about every time, it's the hangers-on whose egos have the worst bloat. You're dealing with celebrities and their entourages, who have their own special set of needs and expectations that are almost always out of touch with reality. All of this is why it was so surprising that the demise of Stu came during the course of fulfilling a rather mundane request for a group of guests spending a considerable amount of money in the club. He was asked to provide female accompaniment.

This was a nearly nightly request for our clientele. A party isn't a party without females, and any security guard worth his salt can provide female entertainment. An invitation of this sort must be handled with kid gloves. Because offending a female guest could pose a serious problem. To minimize this, you had to do a bit of profiling. Younger women in a group together were a safe bet, as they most likely came out to party and most were looking for free drinks. Most times, this was an amicable agreement—the men got company and the girls got drinks. This was the way it worked. Girls like this weren't yet being called bottle rats, a name that's become de rigueur since. I don't really get this, because only cheap, broke-dick clowns would worry about how many girls are drinking off their bottles anyway. One thing I never heard while I was working was, *There are too many girls in my section.*

Stu had been given the unenviable task of finding a group of mature women. This is the one and only time I have heard of this being requested. He approached a group of unaccompanied older women and said that the gentlemen occupying one of the private rooms would like to invite them for a drink. The ladies declined and the request went unfulfilled. Stu still got his tip by providing a group of younger ladies to drink with the men. The older women, however, saw this and became offended. We were at work one night when Stu suddenly got a call to head downstairs for a meeting. Being called downstairs on shift was never a good thing.

Stu handed me the .25-caliber pistol he kept in his pocket and I deposited it in my jacket. Of course we had a gun in the house. We had no metal detectors or security of any kind frisking guests at the door. A very large assumption was made that when the guests are moneyed, they aren't dangerous. But when the idea evaporates because you have to tell two members of a very well-known motorcycle gang that they can't come in with their guns anymore, and you only discovered they had them because you put your arm around one of them to talk to him over the music, that's when you quickly realize you might need an added level of protection.

Stu headed downstairs unarmed to find out what awaited him. It seems that on their own time, the ladies contacted the GM of the entire venue and said that Stu had propositioned them as though they were hookers. This was a complete fabrication, because if the men had wanted hookers, we would have gotten them hookers. That would have been a hell of a lot easier than to risk asking a bunch of worn-out hags to have a drink with a few rich men. It's been said that hell hath no fury like a woman scorned. It should be changed to *old woman scorned*. It was clear that these women knew absolutely nothing about hookers.

Stu was relieved of his position and demoted downstairs. He quit a short time later. Stu's replacement was Kelvin, an amiable kid with a good personality and an easy smile. Since Stu was gone, I took over as de facto head of security, even though the staff numbered only two.

I brought Kelvin up to speed and let him know we'd been pooling tips. The nervous look on Kelvin's face was somewhere between not knowing if he should take the bait and talk about money in the open or if I was serious about pooling, since he was the new fish in the room. What Stu and I knew was that competition for spots and money would breed all sorts of problems and mistrust. Plus you would never know if someone was going to try to backdoor you for your spot and get you caught with money in hand. The solution was simple: if everybody was dirty, then everybody was clean. Kelvin caught on quickly.

Now that Kelvin and I were both comfortable, we got off to a fast start and made increasing our opportunities to earn a top priority. Kelvin was definitely an earner and had the chops to maximize his dough. To my eyes, life was starting to look a little less bleak. We were having a lot of fun. We were making good money, I was still seeing Angie on a regular basis, even if it was just for our Tuesday-morning trysts, and I was in charge of security at one of the most exclusive clubs in Las Vegas. The chaos was becoming normal.

One night, I was attending to my appointed rounds on a weeknight when I saw the curtains were drawn on one of the private rooms. This was the universal signal for something shady going on. I crept to the edge of the curtain and peeked inside. I saw blond locks of hair bouncing back and forth. I pulled the curtain back just a little more and saw a woman on her knees sucking dick. The dick was attached to one of the nut-swinger guests, a short Pakistani who had an odd way about him. We tolerated him like most nut-swingers because he was always quick with a tip in hand when he saw us. He mainly broke us off because it gave him a way to show his affluence and look cool with tough guys. It was obvious that this strategy had paid because he was now being sucked off in the club by a pretty blond woman.

She was facing him and he was facing the entrance of the room with his head leaned back and his eyes closed. I radioed Kelvin to the private room and stopped Garby, a barback who was carrying a case of beer. A server from the restaurant was returning from the employee restroom. "Take a look at this," I told them and threw open the curtain.

The rings sliding against the curtain rod got his attention and he saw the four of us looking at him. He smiled at us and then grabbed the sides of her head and started banging this broad in the mouth ... hard. We all looked at each other in disbelief. He looked at us and it was easy to tell he was quite pleased with himself. I told the guys to beat it and made my presence known to the woman by clearing my throat. She was presumably embarrassed, as she tidied up and he zipped up. We escorted them out and he gave us a final smile and a "See you next time."

I have to believe that he finally felt validated in the eyes of tough guys because he banged this broad's mouth in front of us. Whatever gets you off, I guess.

I took over Stu's section after his demotion. His section was the most coveted space in the club. It had a large 4x8 rectangular table that people just couldn't resist dancing on. It was also the most lucrative section in the club. I worked the section like a consummate professional, with skills honed culling tips from guests on the private rooms. Underneath the "consummate professional" was a seething, reckless heathen with a growing mean streak. A suit hides a lot, which is no doubt why politicians wear them.

On a Monday night, the club was just getting started and I'd just received my first party. It was a club owner from Dallas with a number of his employees accompanying him on a junket. *Nice perk,* I thought as I introduced myself to the big man. He pressed a bill into my hand that I knew was a hundred. People in the business know the drill, and it was certainly appreciated by me. I cleared the few people sitting on the back of his couch and the last one was the asshole. A kid of about twenty-one or twenty-two, he listened and chose to ignore me, taking a slug from his glass.

Maybe he didn't hear me? I spoke directly into his ear. "I'm going to need you to get off the couch. My party's here."

No. He heard just fine.

This was something I never got during my tenure as a security guard. Why challenge security? What you have to understand upon issuing a challenge like this is that WE HAVE TO WIN. Security is the law in the club. If you act up and we don't check you, that means you're in charge of the club. That can't happen, nor would it ever on my watch. Another bouncer, Rex, was working the room with me and came over from his spot when he saw the exchange. A hulking kid about my height and weighing in around two-sixty, he was a former wrestler with a baby face.

Now that Rex was involved, the kid's chance of holding his own was razor-thin. But the kid squared up, determined to resist. He started flailing his arms—this was the equivalent of a rooster flapping his wings to prove he's the cock o' the walk. The kid didn't want to fight; he knew he couldn't win. He just wanted to show he was tough. Just in case he was, I grabbed the arm holding his glass to deprive him of a weapon. Rex saw the move and grabbed the other arm and we had the kid off his feet and moving toward the back hall, which was out of sight of the public. We were nearly to the stairs when I felt someone grab my leg. I immediately released the kid, expecting that a friend of his was "getting his back." I spun around, ready to throw blows.

What I saw was Romeo, one of the other security guards we used from downstairs, holding my leg. Romeo was experiencing what folks inexperienced in confrontations go through, the adrenaline spike. Your body responds to confrontation by upping its adrenaline; you know this as *fight or flight*. Since he couldn't run, Romeo was jumping in, but he was having a hard time controlling the side effects of the spike—things like tunnel vision, loss of fine motor control, etc. The adrenaline spike is why fights usually end up with two guys rolling around on the ground like jackasses instead of a nicely choreographed battle, like in the movies. It's also why Romeo was trying to get me off my feet and was having a hard time of it.

I smacked him on the head. "Romeo, it's me, you asshole," I yelled.

Romeo let go of my leg and I turned to see Rex holding the kid in a sort of modified full nelson with the kid's head under his armpit. I grabbed the kid's legs and picked him up. My thought was to get him out of the room and under control. Just as I did, his girlfriend came smashing into all of us.

Rex and I folded the kid in half and we both landed on top of him. I pushed off Rex and he sat up. The kid was out cold. The commotion had drawn the attention of just about everybody in the lounge, and the people in my section were looking right at us.

"Rex, wake that motherfucker up before somebody sees," I said.

Rex slapped the kid across the face and his eyes rolled white before the brown came back. The kid was in no shape to walk, so Rex and I scooped him up and pressed on to the back hall.

We sat the kid on the floor. He was still reeling as it registered with him what had happened. "You ... you choked me out," he stammered.

Rex and I looked at each other half smiling, half freaked out. This was the sort of thing you lost your job over. Lawsuits that cost corporations a lot of money happened over things like this, and there were a shitload of witnesses. Danny, one of our managers, came into the back hall.

The kid pleaded his case. "They choked me ..."

He almost got it out before Danny yelled, "SHUT THE FUCK UP."

Damn, Danny's pissed off, I thought to myself. Not prone to losing his cool, this was a new look for him.

"Did they tell you to leave?" Danny asked.

"But ..." he protested.

"DID THEY TELL YOU TO LEAVE?" Danny went mushroom cloud and seethed in the kid's face, complete with drops of spit.

The kid shrank. "Yes," he answered.

"Well, now's your chance—get the fuck out of my club." Danny stormed out.

The kid collected himself and stood up, revealing a huge piss stain all over the front of his pants. This could happen when someone lost consciousness, and it was funny as hell when it did.

"Damn, man, you pissed yourself," I told him.

He glanced at his pants and the look of defeat on his face was priceless.

"Hey, Rex, tough guy in the club pissed himself. What do you think?"

Rex choked back the laugh and shook me off, wanting me to cut the kid some slack. The kid's girlfriend came into the back hall. I contemplated letting him have it in front of his girl. I thought better of it when I realized that she'd see it anyway, and I could think of few things more emasculating than pissing yourself in front of your girlfriend. Later, when Danny had cooled off, I asked him what had happened.

"Kid's bitch girlfriend slapped me across the face when I was coming over to ask her what was happening. Then she takes off flying into you guys, which served her boyfriend right, didn't it? Fucking kids." Danny finished with a twinge, as even the recollection of the event was enough to get him worked up.

I told you my boss doesn't care what your problem is—he's just there to make sure no one interrupts the cash flow.

Regulars of the club came from all walks of life. Always, you had the requisite attorneys, doctors, investment bankers, quite a few gaming executives, etc., etc. They paid top dollar for access to the club so they could impress friends or clients; some to rub elbows with the celebrity clientele. While I'm touching on the offbeat and problematic dealings I had with them, we also had cool and funny folks up there as well. The common thread I found united a great many of the people who came through was the fact that no matter what they did, where they came from, or how much money they had, at the end of the day, they were out to get drunk, high, or laid—sometimes all three.

One such regular was Greg. Greg was a forty-something white guy. His balding was of the cul-de-sac variety and he had the paunch of a man made comfortable by too much money. On a Friday evening, I was standing at the entrance to the lounge watching Greg sway to and fro in front of the bar. He had a habit of drinking fast until he reached obnoxious, then he'd maintain steadily through the night. The idea that we "cut off" people who were too drunk wasn't generally observed. We were there to police the situation and keep people in line no matter how much they consumed. I approached Greg because it was my job to do so, but members were given plenty of leeway.

Greg had his pockets emptied out on top of the bar—money, credit cards, papers, gum, matches, all of the random things that find their way into the pockets of a drunk.

"Hey, Greg, how's it going?"

"Good."

His breath reeked of booze so bad, my eyes began to water.

"Your stuff is all over the ..."

"Yeah, help me out with my ... with my shit," he cut me off.

I straightened all of his personal effects and handed them back to him. He deposited the bundle in his pocket, then fished back in and came out with a crisp hundred.

"Here," he said, handing me the bill. "But you have to share it with the Negro." He pointed over my shoulder to Kelvin, who had taken up a spot by the lounge door.

"Sure, Greg, whatever you say," I told him.

I headed over to where Kelvin stood and began to tell him what Greg had said. When I reached Kelvin, he was already smiling. I turned around to see why, and Greg ran into me.

"What's up, Greg?" I said.

"Nothing, man ... tell him what I ... go ahead." He gave me a summary wave.

"Kelvin, Greg gave me a hundred and told me to share it with the Negro. That's you," I told him.

Kelvin's smile widened.

"You know, I'm buying you guys a drink. We got to go for a drink," Greg said.

"Sure, Greg, I drink beer and tequila," I replied.

"Yeah, we'll drink beer and ... tequila.." Greg's speech trailed off as he watched a woman's ass enter the lounge.

"What do you want, Kelvin?" I asked.

"And you'll drink that cognac," Greg returned to the conversation with vigor.

"Oh, right, I'll drink that cognac."

"Right, right, isn't that right?" Greg looked for me to affirm his pop-culture summation of Kelvin.

I helped him out. "Sure, black people drink that cognac all the time. I've seen the commercials."

"Well, you guys ... when you get off, we'll get that drink," Greg told us as he steamed off to another part of the club.

We never did go for the drink, though, because later, we had to ask Greg to leave the club for the night for getting into a shoving match with his business partner over who was paying the bill.

That's one thing I can say for sure—if you are black and a security guard, you will be called a nigger. I promise. It's not right, but it's a hazard of the job. The thinly veiled prejudices that people hold near their heart usually come out with just a drink or two.

One late weekend night, we were having a problem with a couple that was having an argument. He was Fat Tony, an Italian guy, about thirty-five. She was an equally rotund blond, probably older. The two of them were sitting on a couch by the fireplace and their body language said it all.

Confrontation is certainly not the vibe you want in your club. Spend enough time standing around in a nightclub, and you will see that energy like that seems to be contagious.

I approached them and asked that they stop arguing or take it out of the club. They smiled graciously and complied ... for awhile.

A short time later, Kelvin called on the radio, "Hank, lounge, now."

I knew it before I got there. The couple was standing and Kelvin was talking to the husband. Kelvin excused himself and came over to explain the situation.

"This guy was basically screaming at his wife and the bitch is crying," he told me. "They got to go. I already warned them once."

We headed over to give Fat Tony the bad news. He complied, but about halfway to the door, he stopped abruptly. "I'm not leaving. I don't have to," he protested.

I stepped in and let him know that he was leaving one way or the other. This statement, with emphasis in the right place, usually achieves the desired effect. But Tony wasn't moving. I gave Kelvin a look and Tony knows what it meant.

"Don't touch me, n—" He checked his mouth when Kelvin's eyebrows rose in anticipation.

One thing that irks me is disrespect. After all, I wouldn't come to his job at the realty office and call him a stupid wop.

"Man, it's time for you to go," I told Fat Tony as I grabbed his chubby wrist. He tried to resist, so I wrapped my arm around his neck and under his arm to get him off his weight. We were chest to chest and I was walking backward, with Kelvin pushing him from the back.

"Don't do this, man," I said.

He tried to punch me in the back anyway. I shot him a knee to the groin and another for good measure. By the time we reached the elevator, Fat Tony was pissed.

"Just relax, man," I told him, but he wasn't buying. As soon as the elevator door opened, Fat Tony used his weight advantage to bull rush me into the wall. I let go, so as not to get my back smashed into the metal handrail. Fat Tony took this reprieve to swing. I got my head down and his shot glanced off the top of my head. Kelvin applied the chokehold from behind. I knew it was a fight or flight response, but even I'm not immune from time to time.

We struggled with Fat Tony during the ride down the elevator, with him trying to get loose and Kelvin and I restraining him without putting his lights out. The door finally opened and we tumbled out of the elevator onto the bench in the lobby. Our doorman Pauly knew Fat Tony and told him to calm down. Pauly's a savvy doorman and he knew he could potentially defuse the whole situation if he stepped in. But he didn't know the background.

Fat Tony tried to get up off the bench and I shoved him down. "Sit the fuck down NOW," I yelled.

"I'm leaving," he said.

"Nah, you had your chance. You think you're going to swing on me and walk?" I yelled again as I shove him back onto the bench.

"You hit me, too," he told me.

Shit, maybe I did hit him after the initial shot? I was about ninety-nine percent sure, because I know how I react in a situation like that, but I truly didn't know for certain.

"Bullshit, you're talking to the police tonight," I informed him.

I pulled Kelvin aside and asked if I did hit him.

"Nah, brother, you didn't," he affirmed.

The wife pulled me aside and pleaded for me to let him go. This was the reason cops got killed dealing with domestic violence—the husband acts a fucking fool and she ends up defending him. I could only speculate that Fat Tony was only a few choice words from slapping her around.

"No, no way—he's talking to a cop tonight. He's obviously out here to hurt someone. What if that's you?" I asked her.

In my eyes, it's better to have a dude who probably beats his wife off the streets rather than cut him loose and let him take out the fact he just got handled by two bouncers on his old lady.

Casino security arrived to cuff Fat Tony up and take him to the holding cell. We went through the formalities—paperwork, pictures—and Metro was called.

This was where I got my first lesson in Las Vegas-style justice. In Las Vegas, a fight is a non-issue, unless someone is maimed or killed.

Metro arrived, wrote Fat Tony a ticket, and cut him loose. I might have been better off letting him hit her, then maybe he would have gotten some matching bracelets and a night to cool off. At least the asshole probably had to attend anger management for assaulting a bouncer.

On Halloween, the room was throwing a party for the members with the requisite costume party. The club was decorated in Halloween style. The cobwebs that were strung all over the ceiling throughout the entire club added to an already-creepy feel, with all the rugs and a long hallway straight out of *The Shining*.

The guests turned out in droves, filling the place with genies and ghouls, doctors and nurses, and of course pimps and hos. There were more than a fair amount of imposter Hugh Hefners, and the women didn't disappoint—most were dressed as scantily as possible. One woman with a tight body showed up in nothing but a white, skintight, see-through mesh body suit. Not so strategically painted black spots completed the outfit and made her a cow, I suppose.

Making my way through the club was fun except for the constant "Where's the president?" question. I was standing in the unoccupied dining room, looking out the window at the less popular side of the balcony. Frankenstein and Bride of Frankenstein were looking at the view when a couple of women dressed as slutty cops made their way past them and to the farthest end of the balcony. There they were, out of sight around a slight corner, and one of them produced something I could not see from a small pocket on her barely there vinyl skirt. I learned what it was quickly when she pulled a spoon from the vial and held it to her nose. She handed it to her friend and I emerged from the dining room.

"Good evening, ladies, what are you up to?" I interrupted.

The woman quickly closed her hand around the vial, dropping it to her side while her friend fidgeted with her shoe. "We came down here so I could fix my shoe. See? It's broken," she told me. She wanted me to look, but I kept my gaze on the other woman.

"What's in your hand?" I asked her friend.

She immediately shot her hand behind her back.

"No. See? My shoe." The other woman wanted my attention. She tapped my arm and lifted her leg up, placing her foot on the rail of the balcony. The vinyl skirt retreated across the back of her ass and was but a strip of vinyl around her waist. This revealed the fact that she wasn't wearing any panties, and her smooth-shaven twat was clearly visible. "See? Look. My shoe." Her hand moved between her legs. "You see?" she asked me again with a coy smile.

"Yeah, I see your shoe. Look, ladies, I'm not going to toss you, but please try and be a little more discreet, if you get me," I said.

"Thank you," the women said in stereo.

"Good luck with your shoe." I bid the ladies farewell and returned to the lounge.

They appeared a short time later and put on a show on the dance floor about ten feet from where I was standing on the perch. They kissed and carried on, at one point attempting to come up to the perch and handcuff me with a pair of cheap plastic handcuffs.

I suspected my being privy to their naughtiness on the balcony as well as having seen one of them in a state of undress made me their confederate in a sick way. This was par for the course in our beautiful city of Las Vegas, and it was right up my alley. It also marked the graying of the lines between right and wrong concerning my job. The ladies had committed an offense that was in the realm of—or, rather, the exact reason—why I was there. Still, it was easier to let them go and look the other way, while taking advantage of a most petty reason for doing so—it felt cool. The cheap seduction of two coked-up tramps pumped up my ego.

Kelvin eventually moved on to become a VIP host. This was better suited to his personable demeanor and a better place for him. It also allowed him a way to network and move forward with his real career. The kid had a talent that made him a short-timer for the world of security, and I was happy to see him move out of a dead-end job. In his place, I got Cal. Cal was a good old boy of the NASCAR and country-music variety, and as such, he had a laid-back approach to bouncing. Cal approached the job so casually that I had to reprimand him once for eating a salad while directing the dinner guests of a major pharmaceutical company.

With Cal came Dolby. Dolby was an ex-boxer who was past his prime but still had the attitude of a one-time tough SOB. If Jim Croce's Leroy Brown had lived to be older, he would have been Dolby. I was getting the problem children from our sister club or, rather, the people less suited to the demands of the job. They were giving me two guys to replace one, and while this potentially meant more opportunities to earn, it also meant an extra hand in the pot. Plus these guys were older and would take quite a bit more work to mold, if that were even possible. While that was fine, I was used to having guys who would listen, and there are very few older people who enjoy taking orders from a guy who was in diapers when they were teenagers.

Early one Friday evening, I was headed out of the lounge to put a guest on the list for a member. Standing off to the side was a rail-skinny, pale, bespectacled asshole. This guy was giving one of our managers hell. He was on and on about how he wasn't too intoxicated and he wasn't going to leave. As if he really had a decision on either of those. I watched as our GM approached and the guy gave him the same bullshit. Except this time, he added that he was a lawyer and he knew his rights. I gave the name to our maître d' to add to the list, and by the time I reached the group, I was tired of hearing this guy talk. I pushed between the manager and the GM and smiled at him.

"Hi, I'm Hank, and I run security for the club. I'm going to ask you to leave now," I said.

He immediately said that I couldn't legally touch him.

"I know," I said as I reached my hand around his back, being careful not to make contact.

His elbow shot out instinctively to knock my hand away. As soon as his elbow hit my hand, I snatched him by the arm and spun him around. I doubled him over himself with his arms behind his back.

"You see, you shouldn't have touched me. I wasn't touching you. You made me afraid," I told him as I shoved him towards the elevator.

Cal hustled alongside me and pressed the elevator button. Specs was now wailing about how he was going to sue for assault. He was so vehement in this that, by the time the doors opened, I partially believed I might get in trouble for this.

The doors closed and Specs kept crying.

"SHUT UP," yelled Cal in an uncharacteristic display of emotion. From the risk-management side of his brain, Cal quoted an NRS statute with the numbers and all. He explains to Specs that if he didn't leave quietly, he could be arrested for violation of said statute. "How do you like that, Mr. Lawyer?"

Specs went speechless and stopped struggling. I, too, was speechless and let go of him. Specs adjusted his rumpled clothing. When the elevator reached the bottom, he quietly disembarked and waited patiently for Pauly to open the rope. He bid us a quiet good night and walked into the casino.

Me: "'How do you like that, Mr. Lawyer?' What the fuck was that, Cal?"

Cal: "He left, didn't he?"

Me: "Yeah, in the gayest way possible. We're bouncers. Dude needed his dome split."

Cal: "You do it your way and I'll do it mine"

Me: "No arguing with that."

Later that same night, a known working girl approached me while I was on the perch. While we couldn't be certain she was a hooker, she was usually seen in the company of various males. She wasn't particularly attractive, but she made the rounds, and my observation of this phenomenon taught me a couple very important things about hookers, at least on that level. First, for men with money, discretion is more important than looks. This woman who was a great deal less attractive than some of her younger counterparts still had plenty of clients. This could have been a matter of taste, but I think it had to more to do with the fact that she wouldn't be calling at inopportune times in the course of trying to lock down a sugar daddy. Secondly, she taught me the damage was real. She always had this forlorn look on her face, a kind of thousand-yard stare that even her creased smile couldn't hide once you saw what it looked like underneath.

Minutes before, she had been trying to get me to dance with her, and she knew I always treated her nicely. Now she was complaining that she had been accosted by a man in the lounge. Apparently, the man had groped her and stuck his finger in an uninvited place. I asked her to show me where she had been touched. But she declined on the grounds that she was Catholic and drunk. I didn't need hooker complaints about invited guests—it created problems for both her and me, occupational hazards neither of us wanted. While I completely believed she had been accosted—or, more to the point, sexually assaulted—I couldn't exactly raise the alarm, as it would be a her-word-against-his situation. I didn't need a crystal ball to figure how that would work out. Also, the resulting involvement from management would most likely get her barred future access and result in a drop-off in her clientele and opportunities to make money.

While this may seem a petty justification, one has to understand that first and foremost, I'm there to protect the club. While I hadn't been asked to aid people in the commission of crimes against others, it went unspoken that I was there to mitigate problems of ALL kinds. I needed to execute this with discretion as well, and it was this that made me great at the job— the ability to see the end game quickly, make the efficient decision, and massage it to the appropriate outcome. I know this was morally wrong, to manipulate a situation where a woman had been assaulted in order to make my life easier. But I knew if we chased down this complaint, everyone would lose. The guest would lose face, the hooker would lose access and clients, and I would lose time to make money. I told her to return to the dance floor and continue enjoying herself, as that would be best for everyone. I made myself scarce to further defuse the situation and to give her time to have another drink to drown her memory of the thing.

It was a weekend night and I was headed toward the private rooms when I ran into Dana. She and her friends were in Las Vegas celebrating a birthday. They wanted the nickel tour, so I obliged. All I could see was her big blue eyes and a wide smile. I hardly even noticed her friends and the dude who was following them like a lost puppy. Dana and I stared at each other like we'd known one another in a past life. Her friends quickly became bored with the closed-off conversation and left. We kept talking until one of her friends returned to retrieve her so they could go get a drink and actually celebrate the birthday.

A short time later, I found myself swinging back to the rooms to see if she had come back. I peeked in and saw the puppy-dog kid had one foot up on the couch, one on the floor and was fucking the birthday girl's face. I watched and waited until just the right moment. I stepped into the room all at once.

"What are you guys doing in here?" I yelled, making my presence known and scaring the shit out of the kid.

He stumbled backward and fell over one of the couches, pants around his knees. "No, just one more minute, please," he begged. I no doubt had preempted his orgasm.

"No way. Zip it up. You're lucky I don't throw your ass out for that."

The birthday girl rose to her feet, her face red partially from embarrassment and partially from the pounding it was taking. "Happy birthday," I told her with a smile.

She straightened her hair, and that's when I saw the wedding ring.

"Thank you. We're just out here celebrating," she replied as she straightened her hair.

Dana found me later to apologize and invite me for a drink after work. I accepted her offer and found that I couldn't wait for the shift to pass. I met her after work in the casino-center bar. She was there with her friend, who was tired but was doing her part by playing wingman.

Dana would come to say that it was the fact that I seemed unengaged by a group of girls trying to flirt with me that caught her attention. In truth, I wear a stoic mask to hide my shyness. For me, it was her smile and the fact that she wore tattoos.

She took me by complete surprise when she stated that she was not going to have sex with me. I thought we were getting along quite well. Plus, add the fact that her friend was of the loose, cheating, get-your-face-banged-in-the-club-by-the-guy-you-just-met variety, and I was sure that's where the night was headed. Dana, being a strong woman, stated it right up front. I loved that.

We had more than a few drinks and talked. She was from Southern California and was extremely funny. She had a bullshitters wit and could dish it out as well as take it. She could also hold her alcohol. When the sun came up, we were very drunk. She said that she had to go back to her room and pack, as they were going home that morning. In a moment, I said I would take her home. That way, we could spend the day together. I failed to mention that Angie was meeting me at my house that morning, as she always did on Tuesdays. I was sure that if I got Dana alone, a marathon session of drunken sex would ensue, and I was willing to blow off Angie for the opportunity to hang out with Dana. She agreed to let me take her home and we went back to her room to grab her luggage. Her friends were a bit startled when we arrived and their very drunk friend announced that she was going home with a strange guy she had met in a Las Vegas club. They took a picture of me in the event that I turned out to be a psycho killer.

I took her to a local spot for breakfast. I had to wait until I was sure Angie had come by the house and left. Angie called me a few times and I just let the phone buzz in my pocket. We reached my house and lay down together. I had nervousness in my stomach—being with Dana felt crazy and reckless and right. She lay next to me and we began to kiss. Even when things became heated, Dana remained true to her word, and she preserved her virtue. We slept away the day and left for California that night. She and I talked all the way. She didn't want me to drive home, so we went for drinks and stayed at a hotel the following night; we didn't have sex then either.

Dana and I called each other nearly every day. Being party girls, it came as no surprise when Dana and her friends returned to visit the very next month. It didn't hurt to have friends in a private Las Vegas nightclub. It was the first they were in town and their buzz had them wanting to continue the party at a local after-hours spot. Personally, I hate after-hours clubs. Everyone is too drunk or too high or out there with a need to prove something. But the girls were ready for action, and after a few shots of tequila chased by a couple beers gave me my sea legs, we were off. A few guys from work went along. There was no shortage of chaperones willing to accompany attractive, boozed-up twenty-something females to the club.

They were Colin, a short bartender with a smart-ass mouth, and Maurice, a busser from back East. We kicked it at the club for awhile, having a few drinks and some laughs. The action is the same no matter what club you're in—dancing, loud music, and drinking. When the fun had been had, we left the club via the stairs that led back up to the casino floor. We were standing at the rope while one of Dana's friends was chatting with one of the club managers. Dana and I were talking to a promoter I knew. He was having a party at another casino and invited us over. We were discussing whether or not we were going to head over when a short dickhead came shoving past and pushed Dana out of his way. I had a nice buzz going and recognized the rudeness of his action. I thought I would show him the error of his ways.

Me: "Hey … HEY. That was rude of you push the lady. How about you do the right thing and apologize to her?"

We are nothing if not polite.

Short dickhead: "Man, fuck you."

The kid launched his protest and tried to posture. Any asshole that was going to push a woman out of the way would not fold to her man.

Me: "How about I just fuck you up right here, then?"

Colin: "Don't do this here, Hank."

Me: "Tell this motherfucker to take a hike, then."

I smiled at the kid, knowing he wasn't going to do anything. I got paid to throw people around. He didn't know this, though. All he saw was the fact that I was a head taller than him.

Colin turned to the kid and told him something that made him walk away. In my mind, justice had been served and the kid had been thoroughly rebuked for his rudeness. Dana's friend finished her conversation and we all started heading for the door. I stopped to shake hands with a few people I knew at the door, and when I turned to catch up with the group, the short dickhead sauntered up with two of his friends.

Short dickhead: "Talk that shit now."

Now, two things had happened in my life, making only one response possible. First, when I was in the ninth grade, I was lifting weights with the seniors on the football team. I was a tall and skinny freshman that weighed one hundred forty-five pounds all day. After training, I heard my name being called outside the weight room and I hurried out and saw a senior approaching me. I was completely surprised by the fact that a senior even knew who I was. This was the youth equivalent of ladder climbing, and I smiled as he approached. My smile faded as he punched me in the mouth. Apparently, sometime during the session, I'd offended him enough that he'd decided to confront me after training. It didn't hurt, and I just sort of stared at him, stunned that he'd hit me when I thought I was making a friend. Either this satisfied his idea of right or he was afraid of me, since he'd just given me his best shot and I'd hardly flinched. He walked away as I dabbed the blood from my split lip.

Lesson 1: Getting punched in the face doesn't really hurt all that much.

The second memorable event took place at that most storied of high school institutions, a Friday-night football game. For most teenagers, cruising the football game on a Friday night was the thing to do. You had to make sure you looked your best while making your way around the track and socializing while the game was being played. I had on my favorite hat, a hat that my Dad had bought me. In my high school, hat snatching was popular, and when I felt my hat being pulled off my head, I spun around to see who had stolen it but the thief had quickly disappeared into the crowd. I was heartbroken. My family never had very much money growing up, and my dad had bought that hat for me as a gift. I cherished that hat. I scanned the crowd looking for the person who had stolen from me. I worked myself up as to what I was going to do when I found that person. I finally spotted the culprit after the game.

It was a tall black kid who was walking with four of his friends. I saw him with my hat and I knew it was mine because my Dad had bought it for me while we were out of town visiting family, and none of the stores in our area carried that style. Now was my chance to get it back, but then something happened—fear crept over me. I was afraid to confront him. I was afraid of what might happen, afraid of getting jumped and beaten up. So I went home without my hat that night. I thought it was the fear that kept me awake, but I soon realized it was anger. I was angry at myself because I didn't even try. Someone had taken something from me that my father had paid for in sweat, something his knuckles had bled for, something he'd worked for to provide for me so that I might take some measure of pride in the way I looked. As I lay awake that night, I promised myself that I would never let anyone take anything from me again without a fight, no matter what the odds.

Lesson 2: Wounds heal quicker than pride.

This is why few experiences in my life have provided me a moment of pure, unadulterated joy like the one I received from the look on that kid's face when I snatched him up by his shirt and snarled, "I am going to kill you." I then smashed his head into a slot machine.

His friend took his best shot and hit me somewhere in the head. I only know this because it hurt to chew for a few days afterward, but at the time, I was unfazed. By now, the bloodlust had set in, and I wanted the kid to know that, even if his friends got me, he was going to be injured badly first.

I closed my hands around his throat in a murderer-style stranglehold. His eyes bulged. One of his friends hit me again in the face, raising a weird, almond-sized lump on my cheek. I continued strangling. His friends tried to pry my hands away from his neck, but to no avail. One of his boys stepped back to hit me again. Maurice came out of nowhere and leveled this kid. Colin stayed in the cut and didn't help at all. I wasn't surprised, as he was an all-talk, no-action sort of character and you see who's made of what when there's something like personal safety at risk. I felt an arm slip around my neck. I released the kid and grabbed the arm, only to have my legs swept out from under me by a female casino security guard. She pressed her knee into my face and identified herself. I stopped struggling and told her I was going to be cool. She stood me up and I explained the situation.

I told her how it had started out as three-on-one, and I couldn't let them get the upper hand, so starting the fight bettered my chances of winning. In the end, it was a case of mutual combatants, and we were led out separate exits. Casinos seldom report fights unless someone is gravely injured, and Metro is usually too busy to deal with minor tussles. Las Vegas is the Wild West big leagues, and conflicts are treated accordingly.

On the following night, I was taking out a drunk on what seemed a routine escort. The gentleman launched into a level of protest normal for anyone being asked to leave while their friends remained. But midway through the elevator ride, his voice began to annoy me. When you ask a bouncer three times why you're being asked to leave and he explains, the fourth time you ask should be an answer in itself.

"Stop talking," I told him. "You're drunk, you're stupid. I've already explained. STOP TALKING," I yelled at him.

"But ..." he started again.

I closed the distance between him and myself. "You are going to stop talking, the elevator's going to stop, and you are going to get off," I told him.

I was uncomfortably close to him. Most people have a basic response when you invade their personal space in an aggressive manner, and nine times out of ten, the response is fear.

He stopped. So did the elevator. He walked out, and I opened the rope so he could leave.

I have to explain something about a nightclub rope—it has magical properties. When a guest who wasn't talking or had been abusive and was made to stop either through intimidation or force reached the other side and the rope closed, that guest's mouth magically opened.

"But—" he started again.

"I told you, stop talking. So stop and walk," I said.

He put a finger up and just had to say one last thing. "Can I ask you a question without talking?" he said.

I was immediately disarmed, as I cracked a huge smile. "Sure, ask me a question without talking," I told him.

A jigsaw look covered his face as he pondered just how he was going to accomplish this. I stood there waiting to see what he had in store. But it never came. The gent just wandered off without saying a word.

I headed back to the floor and was looking to make some money. I had a trip planned to go see Dana in Southern California. The easy-come, easy-go lifestyle I was leading was simple to maintain during the season. But during the inevitable slowdown that occurred over the holidays, it was harder to keep up on my bills and still execute the freewheeling, devil-may-care lifestyle to which I'd grown accustomed. I walked onto the floor in the lounge when I was approached by two blonds who looked nearly identical.

"I want him," said the one with the light curl in her blond tresses.

I was to find out that while they looked like identical twins, they were in fact not, and the one who was interested in me was the younger of the two.

The older sister, whose hair was straight, looked at me with an equally hungry eye while she explained that it was her sister's twenty-first birthday and she had told her she would get her whatever she wanted. She suggested that I meet them downstairs for a drink after I got off work. So I did just that.

I knew that my budding whatever it was with Dana might preclude me from wanting to see anyone else. But attractive women who threw themselves at you proved a workplace perk/hazard that didn't change with your relationship status. I wasn't in anything serious yet, meaning no exclusivity, nor had anything been stated as such, so I was simply exploring the perk aspect of the situation. Plus it was a short leap considering Angie was still coming over, and that was about as far from exclusive as you could get.

I met the girls at the center bar, where the older sister was happy to buy all the drinks. They explained that they were from California, somewhere north of L.A. They were in town for the younger sister's birthday, and she liked clean-cut guys in suits who had it together. That was me to a T, at least on the outside. They shared the information that they lived together and were very close. When I say they were very close, I mean, they used the same vibrator.

I made out with the younger sister while the older sister watched. She told me she'd wanted to join in but didn't want to step on her sister's toes, as she had promised to get her whatever she wanted for her birthday. After awhile, the older sister returned to her room, but not before extending the invite to stay with them in Cali when I was going to be there next month. The younger sister and I continued our conversation for a while longer before I escorted her to her room. She began to invite me in, then thought better.

"My sister's probably sleeping already, and we share everything."

She, too, invited me to stay with them and so the date was set for me to visit the sisters. I headed home in the knowledge that the ever-present, unreasonable, completely ludicrous fantasy of a threesome with sisters was on the horizon.

The next month flew by and it was time to make the trip. The purpose of the trip was twofold. I was going to San Diego to visit Dana and then on to Pasadena to visit the vibrator twins. Their invite to stay with them, coupled with the porn-fueled fantasy I imagined would greet me upon my arrival, had me itching to get there. I arrived in San Diego and checked into my hotel. Then I continued on to see Dana at her parents' house. Dana's family was very warm and accepting. I felt at ease the moment I set foot in the house. We ate dinner together and I got to know her family, including her sibling.

Later that night, Dana took me into downtown San Diego to show me around and so we could go bar hopping. The parade continued until we were blind drunk. We closed the last bar down and it was time to go. I climbed behind the wheel of my truck and threw it in reverse. The passenger side mirror clipped Dana in the shoulder. "You just hit me," she said as she climbed in.

I apologized and went careening down the levels of the parking garage. As we reached the guard gate, I plowed over three cones that had been placed to divide the lanes. I handed the guard my ticket.

Me: "How much do I owe you?"

I watched his partner retrieve the cones from underneath my truck.

Security guard: "You paid when you came in."

Me: "Oh, my bad."

Security guard: "Why don't you let us call you a cab?"

Me: "Nah, I got this. Just raise the gate."

He did and I took off. What followed was probably a harrowing forty-minute drive on the highway at high speed. I can't be sure. I was in the grip of near-blackout mode. I remember very little. Just glimpses, really, like the thought, *I can get the speedometer over one hundred.* Almost missing the exit and checking my mirror after I crossed three lanes of traffic, but only to look for cops. No reason I shouldn't have crashed or been stopped by the police before I made it to the hotel. But we made it without incident.

For me, it was just another instance of dumb luck or divine providence. Dana and I went upstairs and had sex for the first time. We would laugh that neither of us could remember who started it. Nor do I remember if Dana woke me or I woke on my own. But when I came to, Dana was convinced there was someone in the room with us.

"Someone is sitting in the chair," she whispered.

I looked at the chair, and through my haze, I could make out a silhouette of very broad shoulders rising above the back of the chair. I fished on the floor for the bag where I kept my gun. I fished the gun out of the bag and leveled it at the figure in the chair. "Hey motherfucker, stand up" I said.

There was no movement.

"You got one more warning, and then I'm going to shoot your fucking ass," I said again, trying to sound convincing.

There was still no answer.

"Fuck it. This is going to be loud, Dana," I said.

Dana jumped up and turned on the light at the last possible second. There in the chair sat my jacket, perfectly upright and looking like a broad-shouldered dude who nearly got shot.

Dana laughed. "You almost killed that chair."

We went back to bed and drifted off to sleep holding each other. I never made it to Pasadena that week, though I'm sure it would have been fun. I felt good with Dana and her family. I felt safe, cared for, and I didn't need anything else, at least for a while.

It wasn't long before we decided that Dana should move to Las Vegas. I was all for the move. I'd finally found someone to play Bonnie to my Clyde. I'd found someone reckless like me In actuality, I was just feeding off her, warming myself by her glow to forget my own misery.

She came into town so that we could look for a place, and we decided on an apartment on the west side on the outskirts of Summerlin, which is generally considered the "nice" part of Las Vegas. I told her I would take care of the deposits and rent until she could come out and find a job.

I was making good money, but I hadn't anticipated the holiday slowdown—no one really goes to Las Vegas to party over the holidays. But I was also drinking and gambling. So it went out as fast as it came in, sometimes faster.

I was still living with Gil, and I was on the hook for at least a month's rent for my room on Desperation Court. I had no intention of leaving Gil in a bad spot, as he needed the money as badly as I did. He was gambling at a pretty good clip and it threatened to cost him his house. I wasn't going to be a party to that. As the first of the month approached and Dana's move was imminent, I was still woefully short of the needed funds to pay Gil and make the necessary payments to secure the apartment. I paid Gil out of the tips I had made that weekend. All that was left was the deposit on the apartment, so I cashed my check at one of the local casinos and headed to the poker table.

I played a long up and down session that slowly ate away at my bankroll. I bought in for my last three hundred and picked up a few hands, building my stack to just over seven hundred dollars. I was just a double-up away from being where I needed to take care of the apartment and to make it to the following weekend so that I could work and get back into the money stream. I just needed to clear the deposit, get Dana here, and get back to work, then I'd be flush. I vowed to wait until I picked up a hand that I could make a move on and make the number I needed. I was already nearly thirty hours in when I looked down and saw AA-pocket aces, the best starting hand you can have.

This was my chance—the bet came to me and I bet out, thirty-five dollars. The ten seat called and so did the one seat. The pot was a little over a hundred when the flop, the first three cards, hit the table. The flop was A-J-10, which gave me top set. The one seat bet out fifty dollars. I raised the pot, making it one hundred fifty to go. The ten seat called without so much as a blink, and the one seat called even more quickly than that. I felt like I was behind at this point, with three-way action making snap calls and looking at a straight on the board. Still, these players weren't that good, so they could have had a whole bunch of different hands.

The pot had swelled to over five hundred dollars with the turn card coming. The dealer dropped a 10 down and paired the board, giving me the top full house and nearly the lock nuts. The one seat checked and I bet out two hundred fifty dollars. The ten seat raised me all-in and the one seat made a crying call for his last two hundred with what he knew was an inferior hand. I couldn't wait to get my money in the pot since my only fear was that someone hit quad 10's on the turn, but the odds were so astronomically small and the pot was so large that the cards played themselves at this point.

We flipped the cards over with one card to come. The one seat turned over K-Q suited. He just couldn't get away from a made hand in such a huge pot. But still, his hand was counterfeit—he couldn't win. I turned over my aces and waited with bated breath for the ten seat. He frowned when he saw my cards.

"You got it," he told me. He flipped over J-10, which gave him the under-full house.

I sat back in relief and waited for the river card. The cash was mine. I could rack up my chips, cash them in, and straighten out my situation. I watched as the dealer peeled off the river card. It was a 10.

85

My stomach dropped and a groan went up from the table, which also included a host of people who had gathered to watch a nearly 2G pot go down. The case 10, the only card in the deck that beat my hand, hit the board. The dealer pushed my pot, which included the last money I had in the world, over to the kid in the ten seat.

"Oh, man. That was awesome. It's my first time in Vegas," the kid exclaimed.

One of the spectators patted me on the shoulder and said something to me. I couldn't hear what they were saying over the roar of the jet engine in my head—maybe it was just my blood pressure. The fatigue and stress washed over me as I staggered away from the table. What was I going to do? I was supposed to drive to California the very next day to pick up Dana and all of her stuff. I had lost all the money I was supposed to use for rent and I didn't even have a buy-in to get back in the action. I went home and frantically paced my tiny room. What the fuck was I going to do? No bank account, no credit cards, nothing. Desperation came over me like a sickness. This was the place people found themselves in right before they made a life-altering decision.

I looked at the black bag that held my gun. *This is why people kill themselves,* I thought. *To get away from a burden like this.* This option once again whispered to me. One second, and the pain melted away. Its saccharin invitation sat at the base of my skull slightly below where the bullet would exit. I quickly thought of something else: armed robbery. A minute or two of your life and the problem's fixed, maybe. This would no doubt end in disaster, as most crimes of desperation do, and prison time was actually a step down from being dead. The final option presented itself: pawn the gun and get back in the game.

I had no choice, and if that didn't work, I was truly fucked. I drove from one pawn shop to another to find one that loaned on guns. Finally, I found one in North Las Vegas. I went to the night window, which was adorned with a shotgun to deter any would-be robbers. I fed the gun through the window and back out came two hundred twenty-five dollars. I felt the renewed energy a gambler got when they were back in the game. I decided to go home and sleep. Rest would help, and I needed to be sharp the next day. I stopped for a twelve-pack of beer and that alone led me to slumber. I awoke the next evening and was ready to go. I headed to a casino on the east side, not far from Desperation Court. It was a fitting arena.

The casino sat in a less affluent part of town and most likely served as a depository for blue-collar paychecks. The very atmosphere, with its brown and black appointments and the smell of stale cigarettes, made it feel like a last stop for the down and out. I was sure a dingier place existed in Vegas, but I didn't want to see it.

I took a spot at a table with worn felt. Easily the youngest player at the table, I was convinced I was surrounded by rocks, card players who are notoriously tight with their money. After playing awhile, I was convinced. This would benefit my aggressive style but would be like pulling teeth in terms of time. The time was a problem for sure—I had a deadline to pick up Dana. But I had a larger problem than that: I was afraid.

Afraid to pull the trigger on bets I knew I should make, afraid of losing a pot, afraid of losing the last money I had in the world, afraid of losing Dana, afraid of the conversation we would have, afraid of losing my mind. Fear hung over me. It watched over my shoulder and told me not to put the money in. The odds were already long against me and I was frozen. So I did the only thing I could—I ordered a drink, and another, and another. Then it happened.

Two older gentlemen sat down around three in the morning, looking as though they had just woken up. They were avocado farmers from California in town on vacation and had decided to play poker. Lucky for me, they couldn't play a lick. Now the table was turned on fear. The rocks at the table were afraid of these newcomers. My heart, emboldened by liquor, pushed the edges of the game. I forced the rocks out with bet after bet and kept getting heads up with one or the other farmer. They dumped hand after hand with draws and low pairs. I made my share of hands and kept winning. Was it dumb luck or divine providence? I don't know. But before I knew it, I had sixteen hundred dollars in front of me. It was enough to make the deposits and have a little left over.

I walked out of the casino that morning just as the first rosy fingers of dawn crept over Sunrise Mountain. I breathed deep and looked at the beautiful sky. Reds and pinks to the east, purple and blues to the west. *Now I know what purple mountain majesties means,* I thought to myself. Exhausted and drunk, I drove home to take a nap before I left for California to pick up Dana and begin again.

HEARTS

A new year began and I was looking forward to a fresh start. The business at the club was growing exponentially. Fridays and Saturdays were thick with people, both members and a cavalcade of women, along with the young and hip. Our Monday-night party was growing in popularity. There was talk of expanding the night to encompass more of the club. That would most certainly mean an opportunity to make more money.

I was happy. Dana and I were living in a new apartment and I had a great job. It sure felt like a fresh start. Life was a party. I was paid well for hanging out in a nightclub, and after work, Dana and I continued the party through the night, only to get up and do it all again the next day.

MMA in general wasn't yet the juggernaut it was going to become. While it was becoming more and more popular, it still carried the stigma from being called "human cockfighting" by morons trying to get re-elected. But Las Vegas was the epicenter of that world and fighters would come into the club from time to time. It was a fight weekend when a former MMA heavyweight champ and one of the most beloved fighters of all time came into the club with his entourage. They were enjoying themselves and basking in the adoration of a number of MMA-savvy fans the night before the event was to take place. While he wasn't competing, he was still staying sober, pressing the flesh, and acting as the ambassador to the sport he was to become.

One of the members of his entourage had put his hat back on after being asked to take it off at the door. This was a common occurrence because people's hair seldom looks good after wearing a hat. But still, it was club rules, and the lack of baseball caps certainly dressed up the environment. A dress code is never a bad thing. I stepped down and was in the process of asking the gentleman to remove his hat when I looked to see the champ's massive frame bearing down on me.

This is going to suck, I thought. I knew I was no match for a man who mangled some of the biggest and best fighters in the world. I, like many people, carried the small-minded notion that fighters were unsophisticated cavemen. I couldn't have been more wrong.

The champ was extremely polite and gracious. He put his arm around my shoulder and asked me if everything was okay. I put my arm around him as I explained the club's dress code. His lats were like two steel wings protruding from his shirt. For a veteran of the sport, he was the paragon of fitness for any age. He told the hat guy to take it off and follow the rules.

"Help these guys do their job," he said. All of the fighters I had the occasion to meet while working were extremely polite, very nice, and well behaved. While that may have been the case for fighters, it was a different case altogether for the guests.

There was something new in the ether whenever the fights were in the events center. You could feel it enter the club with the patrons after the fights ended. Fueled by testosterone, blood, and booze, even the most unassuming man was transformed into a brawler of renown, if only in his hometown, and even if it was some twenty-five years ago.

But sometimes you ran into a guy so hard or just plain stupid that he wanted to try security. The energy in the club was frenetic. If you work in a club long enough, you can almost feel when something is going to go wrong.

The fights had been over for a couple of hours, and by 11:30, our club was packed. People were crammed together like sardines. Writhing, sweaty, drunk sardines that just finished watching people beat on one another in an attempt to remove their opponent from the realm of consciousness.

Cal's voice came over the radio. "Hank, come to center bar."

I pushed through the crowd and met Cal in the middle. He was standing with a short kid who looked to be in his mid-twenties.

"This guy's pushing people while he's walking through—girls, too. A couple people have complained, and he was an asshole to me," Cal told me.

That's three strikes on his part right there.

"All right, bro, we're going to have to ask you to call it a night," I told him.

Naturally, I expected him to leave quietly since Cal and I outweighed him by about three hundred pounds, but the kid postured up, sticking his chest out. "I'm not fucking leaving."

All right, cool—he wanted to negotiate. I got right in his ear. "Look, one way or another, you're leaving this club. Do you understand?" I asked him.

This single statement was my easy-way/hard-way speech and normally this thinly veiled threat did the trick. But not for this moron—he fired up. He started shaking with a typical adrenaline-climb response. I saw what was coming and grabbed hold of the arm he was holding his glass in. Cal, in his typical laid-back fashion, was a step too slow.

The kid grabbed my tie with his free hand. This was the only drawback to wearing a tie. Fashion over function, I suppose. I immediately swept his legs out from under him, and in the process, we went down in a pile. Stepping in to throw him while he had a death grip on my tie left me in a bad position, and now he had me in a headlock. I grabbed his wrist and tried to pull my head out but the tie gave him control. I tilted my head down so as not to eat the punches that were imminent from his free hand. Cal finally realized I couldn't get my head out and got the kid to let go of my tie.

Since I never let go of his wrist, I stood up and torqued his arm just as high as I could behind his back. The kid was wailing for me not to break his arm by the time we reached the elevator. I let up because people had started to stare at the kid screaming in pain. Plus I'm not a sadist and I didn't really want to hurt the kid. Still, I had to give him a reason not to try and fight security, and hopefully the memory of nearly having his arm broken would do the trick.

While physical altercations took place from time to time, most confrontations ended with the statement, "Sir, you're forty-five years old and out of shape—you're not going to do anything." I guess you could consider it peace through superior testosterone.

I was now firmly in charge of security for the room. As my responsibilities grew and the club became busier, I was given more and more leeway. It became a sort of out-of-sight, out-of-mind mentality from the management with concern to security. This was more out of necessity than design. They had to oversee the smooth workings of a business that made over twenty million dollars a year. This was their primary concern. They couldn't watch the money come over the bar if they had to watch what security was doing and give them direction on how to handle things. They didn't want to have problems in the club, period. They knew there would be problems, but it was my job to make sure that they didn't spill into their line of sight and generate paperwork or meetings. I took this aspect of the job very seriously since if we stayed off their radar, we would have all kinds of opportunities to make cold, hard cash—the kind that comes in crumpled, sweaty wads. This was the bread and butter of my squad. It was the reason it became a ninety-grand-a-year position. We had to hustle for ours and we pulled down that much. I remember a cocktail waitress who was serving a foreign dignitary, a member of a Middle Eastern royal family—she was given an envelope so stuffed with cash that it made her nervous to keep with her.

Business was increasing and it came time to add another member to the squad, and I was given oversight to select whom would be coming up. I had a large pool to choose from as just about everyone who worked downstairs wanted to make the move up. I wanted Greasy to come up full-time, but he was still working the VIP line downstairs and making his money, so he declined the move. My next choice was a smooth brother named Hank. He had showed his mettle in a few confrontations on Monday nights when security from downstairs was needed to come up, and his sense of humor and smooth-talking way made him stand out from the rest. Hank marched to his own drum and was alpha male through and through. He wore a suit well and his first priority was pussy. He had no qualms about this, even though he had a girl at home. He and I fell in immediately as we were closer in age than me and Cal or Dolby. We stood the same height and people soon found the novelty in two security guards named Hank. The only difference was that he's black and I'm white. Black Hank solidified the team at four and we were ready for the increase in business.

For some reason, people found it impossible not to give into the urge to dance on the table in my regular section. I imagine this stemmed from the fact the table was located in the center of the room and everyone could see you. Women and men, too, jumped up and put themselves on display. The management didn't want people on the table, as it posed a considerable risk to allow drunk, high, or otherwise unsteady people to dance on what amounted to an elevated slip and slide.

The women were gently coaxed down from the table while men were told to just get the fuck down. Men should never dance on a table—there is nothing cool or sexy going on there. Even if you can dance, you look like an asshole, and every once in a while, one of these assholes got their comeuppance.

On a busy Friday night, I watched from the perch as a guy who stood about 5'4," wearing the requisite khakis and button-down, cleared a path to the table. I was already off the perch, pissed, and making my through the crowd when he took off. He took three steps and put his foot on the edge of the table. The expensive leather-soled shoes he wore provided no traction. I watched from a distance of five feet as his foot slipped off and his face slammed into the table. Undeterred, he rolled off the opposite side of the table, jumped up on the speaker, and began gyrating. When I reached him, I snagged him by the arm and pulled down. I spun him around to face me. "What the fuck—? Oooh, that's going to need stitches," I said as I saw the two-inch gash that opened up under his eye.

I escorted him to the bathroom so he could clean himself up. Teague, our bathroom attendant, was there as usual. He and I exchanged looks and all I could do was shake my head.

"Pleased to meet you," Teague said to the guy. "That looks like a good one."

Teague had been a boxer in his younger days, and one look at his weathered hands was all the proof you needed. While he was an older cat, he was still in great shape and could rip off more pull-ups than anyone on the security team. He came up the hard way and had more stories about Las Vegas than you could imagine. Everybody in the club loved Teague.

"Yeah … shit, I can't believe this," the dancing asshole replied.

"That's going to need stitches, bro. Get the bleeding stopped, then take it to the hospital," I told him, but the guy didn't want to end his night by going to the hospital for a wound that clearly needed stitches. He'd rather stay out and drink.

Teague proceeded to tell him about a boxing remedy they used to use in the old days. If it meant he could keep drinking, this guy was all ears. It involved making a mixture of sugar and liquid and basically filling the wound.

"So you want to waive actual medical attention and do that?" I asked.

"Yes, all my friends are here and we're going out," he replied.

I had to see this. I retrieved some sugar packets from the bar and watched as he filled the gash in his face with wet sugar. He formed it into the gash and cleaned the excess from around the edges. It immediately took on a pinkish hue as the blood looked for a way through.

"How's it look?" he asked.

It looks like you've got fucking sugar on your face, I thought to myself.

"Looks good, man" I said. "I'm just going to need your ID and for you to sign this saying you refused medical treatment."

In all things, it was important to protect the interests of the club. The potential for liability was huge, and a signature bolstered our case should this guy wake up realize he had sugar in a facial wound and decide to sue.

He gave me ID and it turned out he was from Florida, not too far from where I grew up.

"Hey, I'm from Florida, too. How's the weather in Boca these days?" I asked him, making small talk and keeping his mind off the fact that he had decided against medical help. I just wanted him to sign the paper and leave. Feigning interest in his life was the surest way to get him to do what I need him to and let me get back to working the room.

He signed and we left the bathroom. He joined his friends at the elevator and the first thing I heard was, "What is that on your face?"

We were an exclusive club and we had to preserve this for the people who paid the most. But we also had an obligation to make our numbers and keep cash coming over the bar. Plus the management knew that you had to allow a certain demographic in to keep the crowd mix right and the energy going. Plus our main demographic didn't fall into the young ladies aged 21 to 30, and no one wanted to hang out in a sausage fest. It was necessary to keep the proper balance.

Spring break came and with it came a crowd of youngsters. In the Southwest, the popular spring break destinations are Lake Havasu, Arizona, followed by Anywhere, Mexico. Those that didn't make it to those places came to Las Vegas. College-age kids came for reasonably priced rooms and free booze. They also brought with them a lack of sophistication and self-respect. The exclusivity of our club, as well as the ratio of attractive women to men, proved a magnet for kids. Most of them just wanted to say they had gotten past the rope. Few were savvy enough to pull it off through tipping or charisma. Those who did make it in didn't last very long inside, as they soon revealed themselves by drinking like they were at a frat party or treating the women who were there like a sorority pledge.

It was as though they were wild animals brought into the zoo, albeit a very nice zoo. Our job as zookeepers was to pluck these kids from the crowd, whisk them down the elevator, and return them to the wild on the other side of the rope. We couldn't have them upsetting the other animals, the ones in another tax bracket.

Monday night was another story. The Monday night of spring break was a free-for-all. Kids were showing up in droves, and even though we were as selective as possible, the club swelled with scores of amateurs. Drink till you vomit was the order of the day and stupidity reigned. Most of the offenses were benign and we threw the offender out, so as not to have to deal with them again that night. I was working my section when I received a call from the door. Casino security was on the way up in force.

I hustled to meet them at the door and I knew there was a problem when their supervisor, Dave, was with them. Dave was a gruff old guy who didn't put up with bullshit, but who also understood that to do the job, you sometimes had to get your hands dirty. He and I had a good rapport.

"Somebody threw a chair off the balcony," he told me. He handed me a twisted piece of painted aluminum scrollwork, a remnant from one of our chairs.

"It didn't hit anybody, did it?" I asked.

"No, luckily, it did not."

For someone to throw a heavy metal chair from atop a forty-story building into an area that was heavily traveled by people struck me as pretty brazen. It was also supremely stupid. That person deserved to have it land on their mother or brother. Cal, Dolby, Black Hank, and I all went out on the balcony to look for the culprit. We asked around but the kids closed ranks. Nobody saw anything. Nobody knew who threw the chair. There must have been three hundred people standing on the balcony, and we made enough noise to let every one of them know we were looking for someone, but not one of them stepped forward. I thought, *If this is the future of our nation, it's a bleak future indeed.*

But a nightclub can be an uncaring environment, and as long as you're not spoiling their good time, customers are largely indifferent to a problem. For the most part, the management doesn't care about the customers, just the dollars in their pocket. Security doesn't care about the customers either as long as they're not interfering with the smoothness of the evening or hindering their ability to make money. The waitresses have the hardest job of all because they have to feign interest in the new faces they see every night, plaster a fake smile on, and laugh at the same tired jokes and innuendo that come their way on a nightly basis. That's not to say that people who work in clubs don't like some of the people who come in or don't have relationships with some of those people that are based on mutual respect. But the transient nature of the town and the people who come in to use it as their three-day-party toilet and then head home ensure that most relationships will be based on mutual disposability. People took *What happens in Vegas, stays in Vegas* way too seriously, and they continue to treat the town accordingly.

As soon as Black Hank hit the floor, I could see he was about the hustle. I had figured as much, which is why I wanted to add him to the team. I was going to build a unit that would maximize the opportunity to make money and Black Hank was all about that. He gave me one very sound piece of advice. He said, "You can say anything to these broads," and he meant that. You could say anything you wanted to a woman, whether it was nice, complimentary, forward, sexual, or just plain rude. You could be assured that a woman's reaction to what was said would be as varied as the women themselves.

I can say from experience that the majority of women in Las Vegas aren't operating in the "respect me for who I am" category, anyway. Whether they chose to act stupid, like one woman did when she argued about a city in England with our bathroom attendant, who was raised there. She was right, though, because, as she put it, "I have English money," even going so far as to pull some coins out of her purse. Or whether they chose to act tough, as one woman we were escorting out was, when she chucked a glass onto an elevator loaded with people. The glass hit the wall of the elevator, showering the crowd with pieces of shattered glass. Or whether they chose to suspend their self-respect, as one woman did when she dived onto the floor to retrieve a couple of one-dollar bills that a pimp had showered the crowd with. She looked up at me because I was standing on one of the bills. "Come on, get off," she said as she tried to pry my foot up. No matter how they acted, they were governed by a seemingly predictable set of rules that were in play in Las Vegas.

Black Hank proved his theory one night when we were drinking in the center bar of the casino. "HEY, GIRL," he yelled out to no one in particular. No matter how many times he did this, some looked. He would wave them over and a short chat would follow with Black Hank alternately flattering them and then talking shit. Some would stay awhile, some would walk away, and a couple of them were even coaxed away to drink with us at another bar. I was convinced.

I was fascinated by this "power of suggestion" theory that Black Hank had discovered simply by yelling "HEY, GIRL" into a crowded bar, and that fascination would lead to trouble. Since ass was his motivation, he gravitated toward identifying the prostitutes that worked the room. One night, Black Hank brought me a proposition.

Black Hank: "Hank, you know how we be drinking downstairs at night and these broads coming up to us, some of them be prostitutes, right?"

Me: "Yeah, man. I know."

Black Hank: "And you know how we know all these hoes be infiltrating and coming up in here and making their money, right?"

Me: "Hoes gotta eat, too. But what's that got to do with us?"

Black Hank: "We should start getting some of those hoes' numbers downstairs and getting them to work up here. We kick out the broads who don't break bread to us for working the room."

Me: "So they just kickback to us for working the room?"

Black Hank: "Exactly. We be getting cash for doing nothing, well, except throwing out these other broads. Shit, they can identify the ones we don't know, so we can get rid of them, too. Plus that will help us grow the stable."

Me: "Grow the stable? I'm not going into pimping, man."

Black Hank: "Well, call it whatever you want. But we ain't going to have the headaches of a pimp. It's easy money."

Easy money—now Black Hank was speaking my language. We were simply controlling access to the room. It was a pay-to-play scenario, and throwing out hookers was a zero-exposure risk for us. Hookers don't make noise when you're throwing them out—they don't want to burn themselves with the casino.

It took us a very short amount of time to find girls willing to kickback to us for the privilege of working a room with so many moneyed clients. The fact that we were a bunch of well-built men dressed in suits and sitting together without female company led to us getting approached by any and every prostitute who was working the bar on a given night. In turn, and just as Black Hank thought, those girls were very helpful in identifying the hookers who had infiltrated the room without our knowledge.

It wasn't quite pimping. It was more like branching out into a business that was taking place under our noses every night of the week anyway. Prostitutes ply their trade in every casino up and down the Strip. If you throw a rock at the main bar in a casino after midnight on a weekend, chances are, you'll hit a hooker.

I met my fair share in the course of working the club. Prostitutes came in all shapes and sizes. You had your high-class girl. These were actually call girls, as they worked with an established clientele. Most often, you would not recognize them if they came in on the arm of a wealthy, older man. They resembled trophy wives in dress and manner. These girls are well taken care of by rich clients, and you seldom knew they were prostitutes. Another type was your bar girl, a little ghetto regardless of color, pretty but worn due to the stress arising from their choice of profession. Many had drinking or drug problems, some had pimps. Mainly you would see them trolling the casino bars picking up stray convention-goers and men looking for adventure. The last and lowliest in the hierarchy was the bullet/stab-wound girl or "track" ho. These were the girls who worked the streets and they acted accordingly. I had the occasion to work with all three.

Their stories were as varied as their ethnicity but the damage was almost constant. The demand was there and the supply was readily available. Anything that would up our income suited me fine, and knocking around with prostitutes sounded anything but boring. I knew Angel and Anna, two ghetto-talking white girls from Hawaii with very visible track marks. Sky, a young black girl of about nineteen years—she should have been a model. A beautiful call girl named Mimi, a Korean woman, was very sophisticated. She could have had any man but would rather control the purse strings herself. I proposed marriage the very night I met her. She declined.

Then there was April, aka Wendy, aka Marie. I'm still not sure what her real name was. She was a white-trash girl from Washington, thin and pale with stringy, dirty hair. She reminded me of a young runaway, but I sensed this was her appeal. I also worked with Janet, aka Marie Sweets, a sweet blond with a beautiful smile. She was mildly out of shape but had an innocent face. She was a budding porn star. She was also bipolar, and after sending her boyfriend pictures on her phone of her with a gun pointed at her head, she shot herself in the chest so she could have an open-casket funeral. Instead of dying, though, she had a stroke and now presumably lives in a great measure of pain. Finally, there was Colette.

I met Colette during one of our usual post-work drinking sessions at the center bar. She was a beautiful mixed-race girl, half black, half white. She wore a tiny black skirt and had blue eyes. I know—a black girl with blue eyes. They were contacts. By this time, drinking was a sporting event, one that took place nightly. The general manager of the club condoned a shift drink after a night's work. He, too, was an alpha male, and he understood the importance of building camaraderie. This nightly ritual usually took the form of tequila and beer. After a few rounds, we would leave the club double fisted and head to the center bar located in the casino or to the upstairs VIP area of our sister club. This was how we built our "stable," which was our first foray out of the gray areas of selling IDs and drinking on the job and into the criminal arena. No one had any reservations about making the leap.

The first time we shook someone down, it was completely by accident. When I say by accident, I mean we hadn't gone into the exchange looking for a payoff. It sort of unfolded organically. Security was called into the men's restroom because Teague had heard a man in one of the stalls using cocaine in a very loud fashion. His sniffs could be heard by everyone in the room.

Discretion is key when using drugs in a nightclub. We all know it's a part of the game. But it is ILLEGAL and puts the club at risk. The man in the stall finished powdering and came out. He was dressed in a white suit and was of Latino descent. He reminded me of Bucho from *El Mariachi*. Black Hank and I flanked him.

Me: "Let's have a little talk."

We escorted him into the hallway and he was crazy nervous.

Me: "You know Las Vegas is a zero-tolerance city, and you know what that means?

Bucho: "No. What does that mean?"

Me: "Someone here leaves in handcuffs, and it won't be him or me."

This was intended to scare him and to serve as entertainment for us. It worked. The guy shook to the point that he began to tremble.

Bucho: "Is there anything I can do? You know, so I don't have to talk to the cops."

I was enjoying this, so I felt like I could let him dangle a little longer. I had no intention of turning him in. If this guy wanted to get high, that was his business. My only interest in it was protecting the club. I shook my head.

Me: "No, you see, I have to protect the club. I have to protect this gentleman's job and my own. This is our livelihood. This is how we pay our bills, and business like this could cost us our liquor license. I just don't see any way."

You could feel the stress coming off this guy. He looked like he was about to implode.

Bucho: "There's got to be some way to work this out. I just had a baby. I just got a DUI last week. I can't get in trouble. There's got to be something I can do."

He was so vehement that I was convinced he put the idea in my head. At any rate, it finally dawned on me.

Me: "What's it worth to you?"

Bucho: "I don't know. How much do you want?"

Me: "How about five hundred?"

Bucho pulled out his wallet and discovered he only had about sixty dollars. He dabbed at the sweat that had begun to form on his brow.

Bucho: "I can go to the ATM."

Me: "No, forget it. This is getting to be too much."

Bucho: "No, let me go the ATM. I'll get you the money."

He insisted, nearly begging us to let him go to the ATM. Then Black Hank chimed in.

Black Hank: "Yeah, let him go to the ATM. I'll go with him."

We couldn't really send this guy to the ATM to get cash for a payoff. Could we? I decided we could.

Me: "Fuck it. Go with him."

Black Hank took him to the ATM, and during our late-night drinking session, he recounted to us how Bucho started sweating when he realized he'd already taken money out that day and the ATM wouldn't let him withdraw any more. Black Hank said he thought the guy was going to faint right there. Until he realized he had another card with him and withdrew the money. He said the guy thanked him and then hustled off into the casino.

After that incident, we saw Bucho in the club periodically. He was always very nice and came up to us to say hello. He was never again involved in anything that would require security. Except for the time he guided an intoxicated friend out of the club, thereby helping us out. He even showed me a picture of his kid. So in a sick sort of way, our shakedown was justified from the position that, even though it was dirty and illegal, it served to protect the club. Maybe it even helped Bucho get on the right path, though I doubt it. The ease with which we got paid and the fact that it was essentially a victimless crime, as Bucho couldn't tell anyone without incriminating himself, was not lost on us. This would pave the way for scores of future shakedowns. It also marked another low point on the continuing erosion of everything good in me.

When I started, my primary motivation was money, plain and simple. But the skewed view of living and working in an unreal environment, an environment that people wanted access to and just had to be a part of, an environment where I basically ruled and made the rules, served only to bloat my ego. The tradeoffs were becoming easier with each passing day. On a nightly basis, the security team was going to the after-hours party in the VIP area downstairs or to one of the other clubs in the casino. Everybody knew us there and we got the red-carpet treatment—it's common for clubs to show love to people who work in the business.

Normally, we took over one of the private booths and never paid for a drink, save for over-tipping the waitress. If we needed a drink at work, we'd simply get one of the waitresses to add it to a large tab or hit up one of the bartenders. The night would normally digress into getting drunk and bullshitting. As always with Black Hank, there were females around. I was left with a void in my heart from Shannon and I was seeking to fill it with something, anything. Even though I had Dana at home, it still wasn't enough. The outcome was simple math.

I put myself in a situation, time and time again, that fed the basest elements of human existence—vanity and ego. Add the free booze and easy money, and I soon came to find the parade of willing flesh irresistible. As I mentioned, Black Hank was a firm believer in the idea that you could say anything to a woman. He stuck to rudeness so that any woman willing to mess with him knew exactly what to expect. He should have been a psychologist because this worked without fail. Black Hank was never without female company. Quite frankly, I found my way into a lot of company merely as a result of collateral damage.

The girls Black Hank was talking to always had friends in tow. One night in the after-hours spot, I met two young ladies. The girls were Trish, a thick young brunette from the Bay Area, and Kelly, a thin blond student who hailed from Montana. I met Kelly first, early in the evening, around three in the morning, just as my buzz was beginning to take hold. We had a spirited conversation about politics, her studies, film, and other intellectual offerings. We hit it off well enough, and before she left with her friends, she passed me her number. I met Trish later in the evening, when my buzz had completely taken over. We shared a kiss and made plans to hang out at some time in the future. I made an attempt at a brief fling with Kelly as well. Even though, in our first conversation after that night, I got her mixed up with Trish and mistakenly asked her about San Francisco.

Kelly and I got together for dinner one night and she invited me back to her house to watch a movie. When we arrived, I felt like I'd walked into a horror flick. China dolls adorned the shelves and she had Lilliputian antique furniture everywhere. Her couch was a chaise that looked like it was designed for people in the 1800s, when it was hard to get the RDA of vitamins. I'm 6'4" and 215 pounds, so squeezing my frame onto this thing with her on top of me was all wrong. With the movie playing as a prelude to what was imminent, I found myself looking around the apartment and beginning to feel as though I was in a black widow's nest. *This is what Glenn Close's* Fatal Attraction *character's apartment looked like in college,* I thought to myself. By the time Kelly worked up the courage to make her move, I was so thoroughly creeped out, all I could think about was leaving. I begged off, citing fatigue. She and I shared an awkward kiss and that was the last time I ever saw or talked to her. But it was far from the last time I would step out on Dana.

Colette and I had exchanged numbers when I'd first met her, and she periodically came up to the room with clients. We talked a few times while she was in the room, and I had run into her in the casino a couple of times. She tried to turn me into a trick once, but I told her I didn't pay for sex. Despite my drunkenness that night, I remember very clearly a statement she made when I refused to pay: "Play your cards right and you might just get it for free," she said.

I called her one time on behalf of someone looking for female company, and when she came in to give me my kickback, the exchange was awkward. It was clear that Colette and I were attracted to one another in a nonprofessional way. When she invited me to lunch, I jumped at the chance.

We met at a Greek place on the west side of town. I had a first date, schoolboy nervousness about me and found it difficult to make small talk. I already knew what she did for a living, and since it wasn't a normal job, it negated a whole arena of talk. Still, there was electricity between us. I didn't care that she was a prostitute. I was intrigued and fascinated by her world, and to me, she was a youthful, free spirit. I found out quickly that I was her type. She liked tall, clean-cut white dudes. She had a daughter who was confined to a wheelchair as a result of a birth defect and the father lived out of state.

When I asked how she maintained that lifestyle, I learned that she kept a house where her mom lived while she cared for her daughter, and she kept an apartment just off the Strip where she could change, get ready for work, and then return to dress down when she had to take her daughter to school in the morning. I admired her effort to keep her life compartmentalized and provide an environment for her daughter that she obviously didn't have growing up.

We finished our lunch and said we'd see each other again. It turned out we saw each other again that night when Colette just happened to be in the casino around the time we were getting off work. She accompanied us out for a couple of drinks and Colette had no qualms about letting me know she was interested in hanging out with me on the regular. She became a part of boys' night out after work, and this was going to prove to be an extended courtship of sorts.

When I say that there was a parade of willing flesh, I mean exactly that. Las Vegas is the city where people drop their inhibitions and become anyone they want to be, if even for just a single night. In our typical fashion, it was late night at the after-hours spot. Security was there and in drinking mode. I was bullshitting with Cal when Black Hank walked up with a blond female in tow. Her name was Janie and she was an ER nurse from Chicago.

Janie was a cute girl in her early thirties, and her body had this Midwestern softness to it, probably due to good eating and long hours on the job. I introduced myself to her and struck up a conversation.

"What's it like working with trauma cases? Doesn't the gore get to you?" I asked.

"Not really," she said. "It's like working on a car—find out what's wrong and fix it," she told me.

"That's interesting. I never thought about it like that," I said, genuinely interested in what she had to say.

Black Hank was pawing her ass the whole time and looking at her like a piece of meat. She kept pushing his hand off and he kept putting it back.

"Yo, Hank, we're going to center bar to get a drink, then we're probably going to a strip club," Black Hank told me.

"Yeah, let's go to the strip club," Janie confirmed with enthusiasm. She was definitely up to party.

"Let's go. Bring her. She's going to suck some dick tonight," Black Hank said matter-of-factly.

"He's so rude and you're so nice," Janie told me.

I stood up and extended my arm. "Would you like to go for that drink?" I asked Janie, and she was all too happy to accept.

All of us went to the center bar and ordered up a round of shots, tequila for everybody. Janie was glued to my arm. My gentleman to Black Hank's scoundrel was working perfectly.

"I really want to go to the strip club," Janie insisted.

"Hey, Black Hank, you want to go to the strip club? Janie really wants to go," I said.

Black Hank had that look in his eye, the one that told me his buzz had taken hold and he'd be up for just about anything. "Fuck it—let's ride," he said.

The three of us walked to the parking garage arm in arm. Black Hank told her she could sit in front so she could suck his dick on the way to the strip club. The alcohol had fortified Janie, and she told us that we couldn't handle what she had to offer.

"I'll give you the Janie Special," she told us.

We piled into Black Hank's rental Chrysler 300. He had gotten it on loan from a friend at a rental outlet. He always had some scam or another in the works. Black Hank pulled his dick out and Janie started stroking it as he turned the ignition. "Let's see that pussy. Pull your pants down," He told her.

She obliged and shimmied her pants down to her ankles.

I leaned over the seat back to get a better look. Janie's body was in good shape—the softness was deceiving at first—but when she took down her pants, her legs were taut and gave way to her cleanly shaven nether region. I didn't really even mind the fact that there was a tampon string hanging out. Black Hank put the car in gear and backed out of the spot as Janie went down on him. I sat back in the seat and looked out of the parking garage at the waiting daylight. *Another day gone,* I thought when *BAM.* The car shuddered, as we had just struck something. Janie sat up as Black Hank pulled the car straight.

"What the fuck? Watch the road." I laughed.

"Fuck—I hit the curb. That's my bad," Black Hank yelled. "Don't stop. I just hit the curb," he told Janie.

Janie went back to working over Black Hank. We pulled out onto the street and steered towards the industrial area when the car began to vibrate.

"Hey, brother, I think you got a flat," I told him.

Black Hank pulled off into the unoccupied parking lot of an industrial park and we got out to survey the damage. The left front tire was completely pancaked. I helped Black Hank retrieve the spare and jack from the trunk. "You're on your own on this one. I'll check on Janie," I told him.

"Yeah, motherfucker, I bet you will." He laughed.

I climbed in the front seat and Janie was eager to greet me.

She unzipped my pants and went down on me with zeal. The head was sloppy, though, and I found myself wishing I had another drink.

Black Hank finished fixing the tire and watched for a moment as Janie blew me. "Motherfucker in here getting head while I'm out here sweating in a suit changing this tire," he muttered.

All I could do was shrug. Black Hank put the tools and flat back in the trunk and I zipped up my pants. The three of us proceeded to the strip club. Once inside, I ordered a round and we all took seats away from the stage.

We ran into Kirby, another bouncer we worked with. Kirby was a doughy, goofy sort of guy, the kind who played video games well into his thirties. He took a seat next to us and struck up a conversation with Janie.

Black Hank leaned over to talk into my ear. "Let's take this bitch back to your house and fuck her," he said.

"Yeah, I know. Dana is at work and we could do that. But that shit is all the way across town, and then you'd have to bring me back to get my truck," I said. I felt like the trouble of going across town just to double-team Janie wouldn't be worth the reward. The fact that I'd be violating the house that Dana and I lived in together played a huge factor. "Plus she's on the rag," I said.

This sealed the deal for Black Hank. "Yeah, fuck it. Let's go," he said.

Black Hank and I slipped out of the strip club, leaving Janie the ER nurse from Chicago in the capable hands of Kirby.

We later found out that Kirby had picked up where we left off. He took Janie back to her friend's house. They had a good conversation, then made out for awhile before she went in for the night, and that is a prime lesson on why you cannot kiss these broads on the mouth. Speaking from experience, women can be just as crazy and sexually reckless as their male counterparts—they just don't want to be condemned for it after the fact..

Pricks exist everywhere. I know this. But if you take your average, run-of-the-mill prick with a warped self-image and a gigantic sense of entitlement and you set him loose in Vegas, he becomes the king of the universe. All people are there to serve him and he makes the rules to which all others are subject.

One night as we were herding the last of the crowd onto the elevators, I was called to the lounge. When I arrived, Black Hank was standing over two nondescript, average, middle-age males. "What's the situation?" I asked.

"Dude's card was declined and this jackoff doesn't want to pay his bill," he told me.

"Sir, were there items on the bill you didn't order or consume this evening?" I asked him.

The smug prick smiled. "No, I'm just not going to pay. I feel I was overcharged for what I was given," he told me.

There it was—this guy looked at the menu, noted the price, ordered the bottles, drank the booze, and didn't feel like he should pay. He not only wanted to skate the bill, he was going to stiff the cocktail waitress in the process. The total of the bill put it well into the felony category for defrauding an innkeeper. "We'll just let you sort it out with Metro. How would that be?" I asked.

"Go ahead, do whatever it is you have to do. I'll wait," he replied.

"So this is how you guys do it in California? Remind me to never go there," I told him. You can't just let people like this go on believing they run the world. They must be shamed.

Black Hank followed me to the lounge entrance. "What are we going to do with these fucking clowns?" he asked me.

"Oh, this fucking asshole is going to jail. Keep an eye on them. I'll find Karim," I told him. Karim was our manager, but he spent most of his time enjoying the club. We loved Karim because he was the ultimate hands-off manager. The security team was free to do as they pleased as long as Karim was able to drink, chase pussy, and make connections that might be beneficial to him.

I finally found Karim in the back room drinking champagne. I explained the situation and told him I would wait as long as it took for Metro to arrive to punish this asshole. Karim looked at the bill and told me to comp it.

"Come on, Karim. Don't let this fucking jackass pull this. This is why people like him act this way, because people like us let him get away with it." I pleaded with him to make the asshole pay, but Karim won't budge—he didn't want the trouble or the paperwork, plus it would cut into his drinking time.

I walked back to the lounge with a sour taste in my mouth. I couldn't stand bending to people like this. I walked back in and saw the asshole taunting Black Hank.

"You want to hit me? Go ahead. Hit me. Right here," he said as he pointed to his face. "I've got a great lawyer."

Black Hank smiled at me and shook his head. I could tell he wanted nothing more than to tattoo this guy across the face.

An equation like this is simple, really—as a security guard, you have some limitations on the level of force you can use against someone. Now, you can't just go off handing out beatings to everyone who runs afoul of the club rules or acts like an asshole. Behavior like that would get you in all sorts of legal trouble and create huge problems for the club in general. But in special cases, like the one we were facing with this particular asshole, the potential legal situation was remedied by handing down said beating using a reasonable amount of force and then allowing your partner to slap you across the face hard enough to leave a mark. The story became that he assaulted you first and you used just enough force to stop further assault. The word of two soberish security guards became sterling against the word of two drunk, non-bill-paying assholes.

Unfortunately, the camera that they had just installed in the lounge that very week prevented us from doing what needed to be done and delivering this guy the beating of his life. He didn't know he had narrowly avoided getting his shit handed to him by the both of us. We escorted the men to the elevator and had to settle for a few parting-shot insults about their character and being human garbage. There was no joy taken from it, though, as the pricks had won this round.

The pricks weren't just from out of town—Vegas is full of wannabes and inflated egos. You don't necessarily have to be in possession of money or power or fame. You just have to want all of those bad enough to act like you're better than the rest.

A local club had a short-lived television show. It wasn't terribly compelling, nor very interesting, so it flopped. However, more than a few of the people who worked there felt it put them in league with other television stars and chose to act accordingly. We held the premiere party for the employees. I worked the rope leading to the media room, which held our projection screen so all could watch their follies and triumphs ten feet tall.

One gentleman approached the rope dressed in his best club uniform—two-hundred-dollar jeans and a striped button-down. He introduced himself as (insert name) followed by the name of the club. He punctuated the name of the club with a head nod, as though it were some universally accepted password. I couldn't help but smirk. I asked him what he did.

"Server assistant," he replied.

For those not familiar with what an S.A. is, I can explain in a word: busser. He picked up dirty dishes.

But that's the perspective at work in Las Vegas—the majority of us perform menial jobs and make an exorbitant amount of money. Naturally, that leads to the idea that we're actually accomplishing something, when in reality, we're just picking up scraps. But most people working in the service industry make fun of the guests constantly, as though we're not there to serve them. Now put that skewed perspective together with guests who are self-important and generally view us as the help. The potential for fireworks is amazing.

The crew continued on like this for a while. We were running fast and loose. I was hanging out every night after work, drinking, carousing, and taking advantage of my position wherever possible. Black Hank and I were like Butch and Sundance. I was really beginning to believe I had life by the balls, and there was no shortage of people out there ready to reinforce this idea. Monique was a regular at the club. She stood about six feet tall and had large natural breasts that accentuated her hourglass figure.

When she entered the room, she had the full attention of nearly everyone present. Men wanted her and women wanted to be her. She was from California and would come into town with her girls from time to time. She was sweet on me from the time we met and the feeling was mutual. She was pleasant and nice to talk with. We conversed about everything and regaled each other with our various and sundry relationship experiences. She was an admitted saboteur of relationships and thrived off dysfunction. I personally was too selfish to really care about anyone but myself and too self-absorbed to recognize this. Monique had made it known to me more than once that her affections were more than platonic. As one would expect, these confessions came when she had more than a few drinks. I deflected these advances without really being sure why.

The idea that I was being faithful didn't wash after the Janie Special and, like most cheaters, once is only the beginning. Still, I couldn't put my finger on why I wouldn't take advantage of the opportunity to be with a woman that men consistently fawned over in the club.

I ran into Monique one night after leaving our usual after-hours spot. I was pushing across the casino floor with a gait in my step that can only be provided by the right mix of beer and tequila. I passed the bar that lies about a hundred yards from the parking garage and there was Monique. She was all smiles, with a slight tinge of red ensconcing her beautiful brown eyes.

"Where you going, Hank?" she asked.

"Me? I'm headed home. It's late, well, early, anyway," I told her.

"Me, too—I'm going home. If I walk with you, could you drive me to my car?" she asked.

I recognized that this was where a man who was in a relationship should politely decline. I also recognized that this was where a man could get some head.

"Sure I'll drive you," I said.

We walked arm in arm to my truck on the sixth level of the parking garage and climbed in.

"Which level are you on?" I asked.

"Third" she answered.

Monique, once again under the influence, began making her affections known. I myself being under the influence found I was sufficiently loose enough to take advantage of the situation.

As we pulled onto the third level, Monique had already begun handling me through my pants. I backed into a space so that I could see security coming. Monique was all too eager to put her head in my lap. I wouldn't have seen security coming until it was too late. Luckily, they didn't, as that would be hard to explain, and even though I'm in good with casino security, there's always a bit of envy from the security guys who wear badges.

Monique worked and worked on me, her free hand sliding between her legs to get herself going. After a while, she sat up and looked at me like a piece of meat. "We are going to get a room and I am going to fuck the shit out of you," she told me.

It was now that I realized why I'd been deflecting her advances all this time—I was afraid. When I say this, be sure that I am not joking. While no stranger to sexual adventure—or misadventure, as it were—I was sure that Monique was one lady who could quite possibly tear me in half. The fact that she looked at me like a praying mantis that would devour me after the deed was done did nothing to assuage my fear.

"I can't—I really have to get home. I was on my way when I ran into you," I told her.

"Come on—let's just go upstairs for a little while," she coaxed me.

It struck me as funny that this scene normally played out the other way. But given the fact that attractive women coming in and making passes was a nightly occurrence, there was nothing lost in not taking advantage. In fact, knowing you could was almost as rewarding as doing the deed.

"No, I really have to go. Where's your car?" I asked.

Monique relented, and as I drove her to her car, I could tell she was disappointed. She bid me farewell with a kiss on the cheek and I started the long drunk drive home.

The next night, the crew and I were up to our usual. We'd retired to the after-hours for the usual parade of shots and beers. Black Hank sidled up to me and asked if I could give him a ride. He'd had to give the rental 300 back the week prior.

"Where we going?" I asked.

"I need to go to this broad's house," he replied.

"Fuck, man, I got to take Dana to work this morning. I don't got time for that shit. I'm half in the bag already to boot," I told him.

"Come on, man. Just take me over there. I have to get this money. She's going to write me a check for three grand," he told me.

My look at him landed somewhere between *You're full of shit* and *I'm not that fucking drunk.*

"Seriously, I been talking to her for a while. She's one of my girls—she's divorced and lives off alimony. Her husband was some rich dickhead." Black Hank continued the story, but I still wasn't convinced as I took another slug from my beer. Finally, Black hank delivered the coup de grâce: "Look, I'll give you ten percent and you might just get some pussy, too."

That sealed it for me—money and pussy. Historically, there hasn't been a combination that can compete with this one except maybe peanut butter and jelly, and then only if your mom made it.

"All right, I'll take you. But I got to take Dana to work first."

Black Hank and I climbed into my truck and started toward the west side of town. The sun was up and I briefly thought it foolish to be drinking from green bottles while the streets teemed with commuters on their way to work. I quickly dismissed this notion, as the necessity to keep my buzz going overrode the need for safety. We picked Dana up and dropped her off at work. She was a little perturbed by the scene, but she had become used to the drinking and early mornings from me.

Black Hank made the call, his voice dropping into low, seduction mode as he told her he was coming over with a friend. Listening to one side of the conversation, I think it went like this:

BH: "Hey, girl, I'm coming over. Me and a friend."

Girl: "What for?"

BH: "For what we talked about earlier."

Girl: "What did we talk about earlier?"

BH: "You know ... that. And to do that thing we been talking about, too."

Girl: "What thing have we been talking about?"

BH: "I'm coming over with a friend ... and we both going to fuck."

The rest of the conversation lasted about two seconds as she told him she had to take her daughter to school and then she'd see him there.

It was beyond me what kind of woman would want two six-foot-four drunken security guards smelling of smoke after a night of work to come to her house first thing in the morning, when she's dealing with the realities of her life, and pound her out.

We pulled into a gated community on the west side of town, replete with manicured lawns and undoubtedly deed restricted. We pulled into the drive of a tidy stucco house and got out of the truck. As we proceeded, I was in disbelief that this was really happening. My disbelief turned to complete shock when she opened the door.

Standing in the doorway smiling was a tight brunette suburban mom/kept ex-wife who couldn't be older than twenty-seven. She invited us in right away. The house was well appointed and decorated in a style that only a woman who doesn't work has time to accomplish. She apologized and explained that the only alcohol in the house was a weird cognac-liqueur mixture. At this point, I couldn't care less if it was moonshine that guaranteed I'd go blind after consumption. She poured us both a healthy dose of the dark liquor.

Black Hank took a seat on the couch and she sat next to him. I was standing there like the stiff white guy who just happened into a porn scene. I was just drinking my drink. Before I knew it, she was naked and going down on Black Hank. I was just drinking my drink as I watched what was unfolding. Black Hank put his hand on her hip to urge her to move onto all fours. She obliged and Black Hank took his shirt off.

"What's he doing?" She pointed to me.

"He might just get some ass. If he's ready?" He shot me a look and she pointed her ass at me.

Aaaah, fuck it.

I set my drink down and disrobed. I took a knee on the couch and grabbed her ass with one hand and played with her pussy with the other. I grabbed her ass with both hands and pushed into her. Now this was where the porn fantasy and real life collided.

I was pounding away and Black Hank was pushing her head down. In porn, the rhythm looks smooth and is enjoyed by all. In real life, the cadence was off and I didn't think any of us were enjoying the encounter. I certainly wasn't, and I was all too in agreement when she said she just wanted to fuck Black Hank. They retired to the bedroom and I was left to watch television. I poured myself another drink and sat on the couch.

I was looking around and spied her purse sitting on the kitchen counter. I availed myself of her cash—only about sixty dollars—and returned to my seat on the couch. I knew Black Hank wouldn't mind—he was turning her out to the tune of three grand. He came out a short while later.

"You ready?" he asked.

"Just waiting on you, man. Wait—shouldn't I say goodbye? I mean, after all we've been through." I smiled.

"Man, let's go. We got to go to the bank," Black Hank told me as he pulled a crisp check from his shirt pocket. It was made out to him in the amount of three thousand dollars. He even made good on the ten percent.

That's how it was—there were so many ways to make a buck in, out, and around the club. If it wasn't a handshake, it was a shakedown, or a kickback from a girl, or establishing an outright hustle.

Dolby came in one day and told us he was moving back to St. Louis. He said that his mother was in poor health and was soon to die. We all suspected it had more to do with his gambling habit. Dolby had it bad with the video-poker machines. We'd seen him playing his tip money from the pool after work, and there wasn't one of us who hadn't lent him money the day after we had a five-hundred-dollar split.

Our suspicions were confirmed when I saw him walking down the street near my house a full month after he'd quit and was supposed to be in St. Louis. Dolby did like to tell stories, though.

Dolby's departure left us a man down and Greasy was finally ready to come up. He had run afoul of one of the managers downstairs, and their revenue streams had crossed at a point. You always had to be careful with something like that. I'd learned enough to know that the no-tip-taking policy was a farce and that everyone was on the take—managers, security, hosts, everybody. If you were an underling, you had to make sure you weren't stepping on the manager's toes with concern to making extra revenue. They could cut your money off with one decision. After that incident, the manager moved Greasy out of his money spot and installed someone he liked better.

Greasy was happy to come upstairs. I knew he was trustworthy, since we'd first started making money together selling IDs back on the line, and I soon learned that Greasy had upped his hustle. In an entrepreneurial spirit, he'd started selling cocaine to the employees and patrons of the club. I told him there was no reason this shouldn't continue upstairs with me bankrolling the effort. We "stepped on" or cut our own supply so we could use without losing product. It also brought down the purity, which helped to ensure you wouldn't get too high while working, and we preferred that method to control our buzz. As a result, we always had cocaine, and this only served to add fuel to an already raging fire.

The addition of Greasy helped me tip the balance of the team towards a unit that would help keep the place wired up tight. Greasy fell right into step with the crew and it didn't take long at all for Greasy to show his mettle.

On a busy Friday night, Teague came out of the restroom and gave me a nod. This always meant he had a situation in the restroom. This was never an unruly guest, as Teague was always willing and was more than equipped to handle any drunk. I knew that it meant he had two guys in a stall. I called for additional security to the restroom and salivated at the potential opportunity to make some quick cash. Greasy and Black Hank showed up, along with one of our managers. This made for a potential complication, as we couldn't shake the tree if management was present.

The four of us listened to the sniffles and the witless banter about the make and model of their cars, what their wives thought about their trip to Vegas, and other assorted cocaine conversations. As soon as the stall door opened, I was on them.

"Gentlemen, let's have a talk outside."

We led them down the hall and I gave Black Hank a signal to get rid of the manager. Black Hank tailed off, asking the manager a question; in the process, the manager took the bait and hung back to answer his fabricated question.

Greasy followed me down the hall as I started my spiel.

"Look, gentlemen, there are only two things that two men could be doing in a stall together, and both of them can cost us our liquor license." I was just about to start with the zero tolerance part when I spied a huge patch of white powder on the end of one of their noses. "I don't imagine you guys were having sex, so you must have been using cocaine."

The protest began immediately. The men were vehement about the fact that they were not using coke.

"I'm going to need ID, gentlemen."

They pulled their identification branding them as foreigners.

"Fellas, before you lie to me again, I'm going to ask the gentleman to wipe the powder off the end of his nose."

The *Oh, shit—we're caught* look crossed both their faces.

"Look, I feel like you guys think we're assholes. I mean, you already lied to us and put our jobs in jeopardy here. Is that it? You guys think we're assholes?" I asked them.

The men looked down and counted their toes. They grumbled a collective answer before I cut them off.

"Guys, Las Vegas has a zero-tolerance policy when it comes to narcotics. You being from another country and in possession is a bad look for you continuing to remain in the country."

They both perked up at this. I could almost see the word *deportation* running on a ticker through their heads. I put in a fake call for Metro detail and told them that they were going to jail.

"I'm going to meet them at the elevator," I told Greasy as I left the hall.

A short while later, Greasy met me in another room. "They only had, like, four-sixty," he said with a broad smile.

"That's cool. You chucked 'em, right?" I asked him.

Greasy affirmed with a nod and we added the shake money to the pot.

That night, during our drink and bull session, it was decided that we needed a code for two in a stall so that we could avoid management presence interfering with a shakedown. We needed something that would blend in with all the shit-talking over the radio. A movie gave us our inspiration. "The Champ is here" became the call and that call was to be made many times.

I have never had much use for religion, mainly because it calls the behaviors nearest my heart into question. I did, however, find it a bit out of place when a young man in a yarmulke came into my section with another rotund gentleman and took a seat. I introduced myself in typical fashion, letting them know that I was at their disposal. The elder, portly gentleman was a gracious host and pressed a folded hundred into my hand. The yarmulke was the younger of the two and it seemed to be his first time in a nightclub. Their waitress arrived, bringing two large bottles of vodka. The men hosted a bevy of young women throughout the night. One group would arrive and have a few drinks and then leave, only to be supplanted by another group. There was no shortage of women to keep them company.

The older man proved to be a generous tipper and kept handing me hundred-dollar bills every time he wanted to talk to me, which was often. I handled my other tables economically, leaving my attention to the two Jewish men who were paying my bills for the next month. During the course of our conversation, I found out that they were diamond dealers in town for a show. He produced a slick-looking business card, which told me that he was in the diamond business. He asked me if I had done any personal security work and made it known that from time to time he was in need of a security detail to protect him while he transported diamonds. I thought to myself that certainly a man of his position had reliable, trustworthy, and bonded security.

Then I lied to him and told him that I worked personal security on a regular basis. I knew that this was a club conversation and any job offer made in a club evaporates more quickly than a line of cocaine. Nonetheless, I was intrigued by the idea that I, along with a few other armed men chosen by me, might be in proximity with an undisclosed sum of diamonds.

The young man was busying himself entertaining the young ladies who made their way through the section. I pondered the question of what an Orthodox Jew was doing in a nightclub in Las Vegas at three-thirty in the morning. A nightclub is no place for any person of religion. A nightclub is the antitheses of a church, and a nightclub in Vegas is one step away from the fiery damnation.

Still, he was having a good time, and given my predilections, I was certainly not one to pass judgment. If a young man wanted to get his chutzpah on in Vegas, so be it. That chutzpah was taken to a new plateau

118

when, late in the night, the young man began humping the ladies who would come into his section, full-on grinding his junk against them as they sat on the couch. He just grabbed hold, squatted over them, and furiously thrust himself upon them, sometimes pulling two women together in a sort of pre-pubescent dry-hump three-way.

It was so weird, I felt dirty just watching. I have to believe that someone who has a relationship with God that he recognizes by wearing special garb should not be humping drunken young ladies on a couch in front of three hundred strangers. God has to frown on things like this.

The climate in the nightclub was growing more interesting with each passing week. From a business standpoint, everyone was pleased with the success of the room. We'd been very successful in finding the right mix to fill the room on a nightly basis, and there was talk of expanding the Monday-night party even further. The management had the utmost trust in the security team, even though, unknown to everyone but the team itself, we'd grown volatile and reckless.

Black Hank had gotten it into his head somewhere along the way that others were skimming off the security tip pool. His "proof" was an instance where I had come out of the old managers' office, a side room that used to be, well, the managers' office. He went in after I'd left, where he'd found two crumpled twenties on the floor, and this had to have fallen out of my pocket. I told him this was ridiculous from a number of standpoints:

#1—Everyone was in and out of there all night. That cash could be anybody's.

#2—I was only in the old managers' office to funnel a beer and get back to my spot.

#3—I was the one who had established the tip pool in the first place, even though I had the most lucrative section in the nightclub.

#4—I'm certainly not dropping cash anywhere.

I let him know that I was not skimming and would be willing to turn my pockets rabbit ear and count up at any time during the night. I also reiterated to the team that I was the one who'd established the tip pool in the first place. I did it to ensure we all ate out of the same trough. This fostered a team atmosphere, and that was the most important aspect of doing the job—working as a team. Still, an alpha just won't let go of something because another man said to. That's the thing about alpha males all running together. Even with all the boasting and shit-talk, no one really wants to challenge one another. Even if you win, you might end up with an eye out of its socket. Black Hank held onto this and an uneasy truce was kept. Black Hank was still a soldier and he had everyone's back in a confrontation, but I sensed this was less a matter of honor and more of Black Hank having a hard-on to manhandle people.

Black Hank and I were escorting one half of an altercation out of the club—a skinny kid who was a few ticks away from getting his ass handed to him by a much larger guy. The kid was swaying and one-eyeing us as we put him on the elevator and got in behind him.

"What do we got here?" he asked.

Oh, boy—here it comes, I thought.

"It looks like we got us a skinhead …"

He was referring to me, as I keep my head shaven close.

"…And a Tyrone."

I suppose *Tyrone* was this kid's substitute for *nigger,* as actually saying *nigger* would surely result in pain.

"I can't believe you guys hang out together, a skinhead and a Tyrone," the kid continued his drunken tirade.

On the scale of insults I've received while working, this didn't even register. Though Black Hank was smiling, I could see he was growing angrier by the second.

Every time this kid said *Tyrone,* which was every other second because the preceding second was filled by *skinhead,* Black Hank moved a little closer to Mr. Insult. Thankfully, the elevator opened just as he'd come to stand next to him.

"Hey … Tyrone, get rid of his ass and let's go back upstairs," I yelled after Black Hank.

Black Hank smiled that *fuck you* smile and escorted him to the rope. Our doorman, Pauly, told the kid to shove off before he got his ass kicked. The night ended and Cal, Greasy, Black Hank, and I were walking through the casino when we ran into Mr. Insult. Being full of booze, as usual, Black Hank and I cornered the kid between some slot machines.

"Look who it is, Black Hank. It's Mr. Insult."

"What was it you said again, motherfucker?"

Mr. Insult looked sober now and completely scared shitless. He looked around for help, but he was sandwiched between two guys who dwarfed him and a wall of slot machines—daylight was nowhere to be found.

"Say it again, bitch," Black Hank goaded him. He slid his beer on top of the slot machine to free his hands.

My intent was just to scare the shit out of the kid. Now I was convinced Black Hank was going to drop his ass. I looked around for witnesses. Greasy and Cal were already scanning the casino for onlookers. None of this really mattered, as all of us were on camera.

"Bitch, say it again, motherfucker," Black Hank snarled.

The kid was thoroughly shitting his pants as he shrank against the slots.

"Fuck this bitch. He don't want none," I told Black Hank, recognizing the need to talk him down before he smashed the kid's face and we all lost our jobs.

Black Hank relented and the kid stayed where he was while we walked away.

Seldom do bouncers get to redress insults incurred while working, but when you do, it is ultimately satisfying.

The next night, I was standing on the perch watching the crowd. My boss, Danny, was standing next to me, and he and I were commenting on women as they entered the lounge. Teague rounded the corner and waved me over. I stepped down from the perch, and to my chagrin, Danny followed. I entered the bathroom and heard the men in the stall holding a conversation about the girls they were with that night. As soon as they exited, I stepped to them.

"Good evening, gentlemen. Let's have a talk outside," I said.

"Can I wash my hands first?" one of the men replied in a *fuck you* tone.

"Sure, no problem."

I called for security over the radio. I needed another member of the team to get rid of Danny and another still to take the hit, should we be able to shake them.

"Gentlemen, in my experience, there are only two things that could be going on with two men in a stall, and both of them can cost us our liquor license."

"Yeah, well, what are they?" Mr. Fuck You asked me.

"Well, you're either a couple of faggots or you're doing coke," I replied in a similar tone.

Now, I have nothing against any person's sexual orientation—the use of the word *faggot* is merely an attempt to illicit an emotional response from someone who's challenging me and therefore reestablish my dominance in the situation.

"What? Two guys can't make out in a stall? You have something against gays?" he asks.

"No. Not at all. I just don't believe that's what you were up to, seeing as how you were talking about females just a few seconds before we met you," I told him.

Greasy and Black Hank arrived just as Danny decided to step in to defuse the situation.

"Look, guys, we can't have anything—drugs or otherwise—going on in our bathroom," Danny said.

"We were not doing drugs," Mr. Fuck You seethed. He was getting pissed way too early in the game, the first sign of the guilty. "What? Do you want us to prove it? You want us to kiss and prove it?" Mr. Fuck You yelled.

His buddy pulled a funny face, which cemented the fact that they were straight.

Oh, hell, yes, I thought. *Make these assholes kiss in the men's room at a nightclub.*

Danny contemplated this. Now I really wished that he weren't there, just so we could degrade these idiots by making them kiss. That would be worth so much more than money.

He had to make them. It was the only right thing. I looked at the other guys, and even Teague was looking on intently with a sly grin at the corner of his mouth.

Danny finally spoke. "No, guys. I just want you to leave the club."

Damn it. The boss had just squandered a golden opportunity to punk two morons and chip away at their manhood by blemishing their hookers-and-coke Vegas trip with the memory of a shared kiss in front of four other men. This saddened me greatly as we escorted these clowns to the elevator. I hate losing, but I hate losing to jackasses even more. I suppose it's true that you just can't win them all.

With Greasy on the floor, the spiking business, and the money that came with, the team was running increasingly fast and loose. No one was going to rein anyone else in for anything. We just backed our teammates play. The mix of cocaine and booze certainly didn't help matters.

I was no stranger to getting impossibly intoxicated. I sometimes marvel at my ability to get completely, unequivocally bent and still function. I know this presents a huge danger to both myself and those around me. It would be safer if I were one of those people who would just submit to the substance and pass out or become incapacitated. It has happened to me a couple of times, and those times usually involved vomit. However, for the most part, I become an unreasonable beast with a voracious appetite for more substance.

One evening at work, I stepped onto the balcony to get some air. We had been drinking caipirinha at Greasy's insistence. A mixture of lime, cachaca, and sugar, it became the drink of the week due to the fact there was a case of free product in the storage area that security had claimed as the office. It was mixed inaccurately by our team bartender, Greasy, but it helped to cut the coke that had also become a nightly affair.

There were a number of attractive Asian women in the club that night. As I stepped onto the balcony, I saw one who had caught my eye when she walked in earlier. She was wearing an impossibly short skirt and it was that which drew my attention. But now she was like a limp noodle and was being held up by one of the young gentlemen who had accompanied the group into the club. I grimaced inside at the thought of such an attractive young sprite being turned into a slobbering goblin after imbibing too much. My inner grimace turned to outright horror when I noticed the stream of piss that was slowly inching its way toward the grate in the middle of the balcony after it had run down her leg. She was unresponsive when I got to her. The boyfriend was oblivious to the fact that his girl had pissed herself. He protested when I suggested that they had to leave, launching into a tirade about how she was fine and she was just tired. Embarrassed for her, I merely pointed to the piss that was now running down the drain in the floor. To his credit, he was immediately concerned after that and bid his friends farewell as they left.

The next night, all of us had more than a few drinks. Greasy and I had more than a few bumps of coke to even us out. The fellas exchanged farewells with the knowledge that we'd be right back here tomorrow doing the same thing. After the goodbyes, I found myself in a familiar place ... ready for anything. The tip money was good that night, and even after tipping generously at the bar, I found I had a few hundred left. Chance beckoned, and in my mind, the night still had much to offer. I headed off toward the poker room when I ran into Colette. Colette had been working that night and she had a few drinks on her.

Colette drank with an abandon I'd seldom seen in a woman. When she would reach drunk, she would speak with a Southern drawl that came out of nowhere. "Oh, hell—I ain't bothering nobody" was a favorite line.

I once overheard a prostitute tell a trick that it wasn't necessary to apologize after he spilled a drink on her. "No ... no, there are no sorries with me," she cut him off. It was as if it pained her for someone to show her the slightest bit of courtesy. Colette wasn't like this at all. She had been tempered by her experience. She demanded a certain amount of respect, and you could be sure that if she wasn't given this, she would let you know. I once had to stop her from firing an empty beer bottle off the back of a guy's head. The guy was a regular, a one-time pro basketball player, but Colette didn't give a shit about that. She had been trying to set the bottle down on the bar for proper disposal when he closed her out.

Mr. Pro Ball got his in the end. He was murdered later that night outside a local fast-food joint. He got shot a whole bunch of times while waiting for his food. I guess he insulted the wrong guy in the club. But it wasn't to be the only time I shook a man's hand on the night he was murdered.

That night, I suggested that Colette accompany me to the poker room and that I'd be happy to have the company. I sat down and immediately ordered a drink from a Russian girl who Greasy called Kamchatka. She knew I drank beer and soon had one in my hand.

The hands unfolded one after the other. I won some and I lost some. I enjoyed the company at the table and soon had everyone laughing. Colette sat beside me, resting her head on my shoulder and watching as I played. I figured she was glad for the company, too. Glad to be in the presence of someone who knew exactly what she did, exactly who she was, and didn't judge her. I enjoyed being around her, too. She had a good heart and was always good to me. She made me smile. I found her beautiful. Reagan, a bartender at the club, met Colette once. She remarked after meeting her that she looked tired, weary, and older. I found this surprising because in my eyes she was a beautiful young woman. Only after Reagan said this did I see where that could be possible. It still didn't matter to me. I liked being with her, spending time with her. I could be almost real with her, even if almost real was a drunken, drugged-out mess.

The almost comes in because she didn't know I had a girlfriend at home or that I would lay down with nearly any female that I pulled from the club. She didn't judge me either, but you can't judge what you don't know. We sat at the table and the men began to comment on Colette. This was common, as Colette dressed the part for her job and had the body to back it up. I took these comments in stride and Colette was without a doubt used to such things. They asked me who she was and I told them, "She's my sister."

Most scoffed, but a naive twenty-something asked the question, "Same father or mother?"

I guess he couldn't resist due to the fact that Colette was half-black and about three shades darker than me.

"Neither," I said with a shake of my head.

He got it and everybody had a laugh. Colette excused herself to the restroom and the men all congratulated me as they watched her walk away.

"Your sister got lipstick on your shirt."

I had removed my jacket when I sat down to play and Colette had been resting her head on my back. She had accidentally smeared her pink lipstick all over the shoulder of the canary-yellow shirt I had on. This was trouble. I had to go home to Dana. There was no explanation as to why I would have lipstick on my shirt. Well, there was an explanation, but not one any man wanted to give his girlfriend. I made my mind up very quickly. I would have to spend the night at Colette's apartment and go home after Dana went to work. Better to face the wrath of being out all night than own up to a lipstick-smeared shirt.

When Colette returned, I racked up my chips and said good night to the table. Colette and I went to her apartment just off the Strip on Flamingo, the place she kept to keep her job away from her daughter. While Colette's daughter lived with her mother in a house Colette had paid for, every night, Colette would head out dressed respectfully for "work" and stop at the apartment to get ready for her real job.

When we arrived, I hopped into bed. Colette excused herself to take a shower. A short time later, she stepped out of the bathroom. This was the first time I saw her naked. Sure, plenty of people had seen this before, plenty of people had sex with her before. She was by trade a prostitute and that opened her up to certain job hazards. But I didn't care. Colette and I had sex for the first time that night. I did not wear a condom, but then again, I never did. It was an undeniably careless action. But such was life for me, an endless chain of careless actions.

The age-old ritual of bachelor/bachelorette parties is a Las Vegas institution. They range from the terminally dull to the outright stupid. A few originals did occur from time to time, however. For instance, the ball and chain—a group of guys made the bachelor carry a fifteen-pound bowling ball connected to his leg with a length of heavy-gauge chain. My personal favorite was the group that had the bachelor wearing a designer wedding gown. If you're going to look like an ass, do it in style.

While bachelor parties have that *Let's get drunk, get stupid, and go to the strip club* mentality, bachelorette parties take on a whole different face. A group of women with a *Let's party!* attitude draw flocks of men. They all take their shot—the drunks, the frat boys, the old rich guys, the security guards, everyone. Most herds are impenetrable—they close ranks—and picking one off is impossible. Some are middle-of-the-road. They want attention and men to buy them drinks. They use the possibility of pussy (POP) to get what they want and then leave. The use of feminine wiles to get something is nothing new. The game is the same, and droves of men continue to fall prey. But this is the sinister difference between men and women and their pre-marriage parties. I can safely speak for the majority of men here … the last thing that a man about to get married wants is his bride-to-be and all her friends hanging around a bunch of sweaty dudes who are buying them drinks and have but one interest—screwing the bride and/or all of her friends. If your fiancée comes to Las Vegas and plans on going out to the clubs, this will happen.

One bachelorette in particular happened into the room with her friends. It was early still, but these women were already left-of-center and were definitely toying with men. The bride approached me with one of her friends.

"My friend is getting married," the friend said.

The fact that she was an attractive Asian girl compelled me to mask my contempt long enough to find out what they were about.

"Really? Congratulations," I replied. *No shit, bitch. Is that what the veil means?*

I quieted my inner voice. I hadn't even started drinking this evening, and this was what I had to put up with. I smiled a very warm smile at the thought of getting a drink right after I finished talking to these two broads.

My smile brought an even warmer one from the Asian girl. Body language being a large part of my trade, I could see this was going well. I opened my arms and leaned on the DJ booth. The bride ruined this moment by opening her mouth.

"Do you want to eat my candy?"

A repulsive thought, as she was nowhere near as petite as her Asian friend. The bride pulled at the candy necklace she was wearing and stretched

127

it toward my face. The double entendre spoiled my mood. I looked at the multi-colored candy stains on her neck and wondered if it was saliva from the sixteen other dudes who ate her candy or if it was just from her being a sweaty pig. I crossed my arms and politely declined, averting my eyes back to the crowd. The women walked away a little deflated, but this didn't last.

Throughout the night, they had a constant barrage of men assaulting their group and plenty ate the bride's candy. I got my drink and a few more after that. By the end of the night, the Asian proved to be a cold fish, or perhaps just a dedicated girlfriend of some man back in Pennsylvania. The bride, however, proved herself a bit of a whore. She was making out with a fat, bearded kid in a bad plaid shirt. My advice, if your fiancée is planning to come to Vegas for her bachelorette party: Send her and the girls to a spa somewhere, a beach somewhere, anywhere but here … even if it's on your dime. Your marriage will be all the better for it.

Stuff like this occurred because the club atmosphere is like a fantasy world where people go because nothing can touch them. It is a respite from the problems of the outside world. Many people feel as though, since it is their escape, they can do anything they wish. People's actions in the club vary from stupid to brazen to dangerous.

I was working my section when a VIP host brought a party to sit down. They were club people from San Diego. Club people were easy to work, even if demanding. They knew the drill and your night was bound to be successful so long as you catered to them. Made them feel as cool as they wanted.

I introduced myself to the two gentlemen who were hosting the party. With them were various and sundry females with that Southern California look. One of the men, an older gentleman, tipped me right off the bat. The younger of the two introduced himself as a club promoter. He handed me his card and let me know that if I was ever in San Diego, he could "hook me up."

"Cool, man. I get down there sometimes. Maybe I'll look you up," I said.

The night went well. The girls were of the loose, kissing-each-other, exposing-their-friends'-tits type, and this made the night interesting. I escorted a few of these young ladies to and from the restroom at the behest of the older gentleman, and there was always a crisp one-hundred dollar bill awaiting our return.

The two gentlemen held court and sat on the back of the couch. I stood a couple of inches behind them so as to ward off any of the other patrons who were but a few inches behind me. As savvy as these guys were, they got quite comfortable in a short amount of time. I watched as the older gentleman produced a bag of cocaine from his pocket. At a glance, it looked to measure well over an eightball. He pulled his black card from the same pocket and gingerly dipped a corner into the bag, retrieving a healthy bump. He lifted it to his face and as the card neared his nose and he was set to snort, I smacked his elbow, causing the coke to fall off the card. He turned around, no doubt miffed by the near nirvana moment he was just robbed of.

"What the hell are you doing?" he yelled.

"What the hell are you doing?" I shot back. "You're standing right in front of me. Have a little respect. This place is packed and you think you can snort coke wherever you please. We all know it's part of the game, but at least have the decency to blow it in the bathroom."

I was finished reading him the riot act. He apologized and pulled another hundred from his pocket. He may not have been that smart, but at least he knew the drill. There was no need or even value to be had from shaking these guys down. They were more than willing to fork over fistfuls of hundreds already, and I didn't want to throw them out because there's no benefit for the club in doing that.

In Las Vegas, there is a pantheon of guests who get to do this sort of thing. Of course, if questioned, club owners, management, et cetera will insist that this sort of thing doesn't occur in their club, or if it does, it is without their knowledge or consent, which is complete and utter bullshit. They're paying for the privilege, and this is something that takes place in every club everywhere. Well, any club worth going to, that is.

The business was growing so quickly that it became apparent we'd need to add yet another bouncer to the mix just to handle the flow. I had seen Johnny on Monday nights, when he came up with the support security from downstairs. He was a younger cat from New Mexico with just a few months on the job. He was a hard worker with a no-nonsense attitude. He could handle himself in a physical situation and had a Wile E. Coyote-style short fuse. The kid would get pissed off in a split second. But I liked that about him. I'd rather have someone who could be a liability for taking it too far than someone who wouldn't take it far enough. He also had that swagger that a young man should have, and he fit in with the team nicely. It was this mix that saw Johnny nearly stabbed to death in a drunken brawl outside a casino in Reno once. Johnny joined the team and the new blood solidified our team at five. His addition brought an even more wild personality to the squad. An edge we welcomed but certainly didn't need.

We were always ready for action. We waited for it. We welcomed it. Whether face-to-face or over the radio, there was a constant barrage of testosterone-laden barbs flying back and forth. No sooner would you be talking to a guest or a pretty young lady when one of the guys would let fly with an insulting observation about the person you were face to face with. With only your ears being privy to what was being said, you were prone to laughing at inappropriate times for no apparent reason.

The initial shot was followed by a string of comments from the rest of the team. Most times you could shake this off, and you could always take out your earpiece should they prove relentless. But for the most part, you would leave it in, as it was an occupational necessity and no one on the team would want their earpiece out if something were to jump off. A call would come in, and with some time on the job, you could hear the excitement in the caller's voice.

"FIGHT on the dining-room patio … it's BIG," Cal called over the radio.

Black Hank, Johnny, Greasy, and I formed a single-file line. We knifed through the crowd in the lounge, heading for the balcony, each one of us ready for what was sure to come. Looking out the window, I could see fifteen Asian males pushing and shoving each other. We knew that when we got outside, it was sure to be an all-out war, five on fifteen. We sprang through the door like gangbusters and fanned out. Then the weirdest thing happened—the Asians just parted like the Red Sea. Both of the warring factions just separated and stopped fighting.

They stood there looking at us and we stared back, partially in disbelief and mostly in dismay because the adrenaline coursing through our veins would sadly go unused. The lot of them went peacefully as we escorted them out. Some of them rode out on the same elevator without even so much as a stern look at one another. This was a strange occurrence in a nightclub fight.

It doesn't happen too often, but every once in a while, you get a contender, a prick so hard or so hopelessly stupid that they decide to challenge security to an all-out battle. The worst offenders are aging white males. It's usually guys in the late 30s/early 40s category, with their flagging testosterone and youthful dress. They're in a nightclub hitting on females twenty years their junior and trying to intimidate younger males. Dirk Clausen was one of these.

We were called to a section in front of the DJ booth. It seemed Dirk was trying to pick a fight with someone or anyone. Black Hank watched from the perch as Dirk made himself about a big a target as possible and shouldered people as they tried to make their way through the club. Dirk stood about six-two and looked like defensive lineman. A liability for obvious reasons, he had to go. I took a position off Black Hank's shoulder just as Johnny arrived. Cal was already standing behind Dirk. If there was going to be a confrontation, everyone wanted a piece. Black Hank spoke to Dirk calmly and asked him to leave. Dirk immediately complied, turning, and headed for the lounge door. He took two full steps and out of nowhere threw a forearm into Dani, one of our cocktail waitresses.

Dani went flying into the door and hit the deck. In unison, we pounced on Dirk. Black Hank threw an arm around his neck from behind. Cal grabbed his right arm and Johnny his left. I pushed the lot of them out the door and into the entryway to best avoid hurting any bystanders. Dirk was struggling to keep his feet and backed Black Hank against the wall.

Adrenaline took over for me and I tried to pick up and slam Dirk along with everyone else. My right shoe completely blew out and dropped me to a knee. Johnny, obviously in the grips of the adrenaline spike, was screaming.

"Let me in, Hank. Let me in," he said over and over, just wanting to get a bigger piece of Dirk than he already had.

I switched to plan B and grabbed Dirk's pant legs. I pulled his legs out and this helped Black Hank sink the choke. About five seconds later, Dirk stopped struggling and Black Hank let up.

"You ready to leave now?" I asked.

Dirk's face was beet red and sweaty. Through labored breath came the answer, "Yeah, just let me rest for a minute."

We led Dirk to the elevator, and on the way down, we became friends. Apparently, this was a measured testosterone engagement and Dirk had just wanted some contact. We were happy to oblige.

"How much you weigh, Dirk?" I asked.

"About 280," he replied.

"Jesus. I was going to slam your ass. I never would have tried if I knew that. Look at my fucking shoe." The sole had split from the upper and was flapping with each step.

Dirk just smiled and looked relieved when we let him off the elevator. We bid him good night and got back on the elevator, congratulating each other and reveling in the afterglow of asserting our dominance over another man.

Later that same night, a call came over the radio from Johnny: "Escorting one out from the patio door."

I descended from my spot on the perch and walked into the lounge to await his arrival. I saw the top of Johnny's head moving through the crowd, but I couldn't yet see the guest he was taking out. When they were about ten feet from me, the crowd parted to reveal a twenty-something male of a slight, lumpy build with sparse, odd facial hair. He was by all accounts a troglodyte. He looked relaxed and so did Johnny. This was new to Johnny, as he was easily and usually amped during an escort.

What occurred next, I will never be able to explain. I watched in slow motion as, without warning, the troglodyte balled his right fist, raised it up, and swung it backward to smash Johnny directly in the balls. The look that crossed Johnny's face was pure rage.

Unfazed by the cheap shot, Johnny engulfed the ball-smasher. As I hurried to help him, I watched Johnny control the wrists, then suddenly release them. He grabbed the guy around the chest in a modified reverse bear hug and was, I suppose, crushing his chest. In a split second, he let this go, and just as I reached them, Johnny finally settled on a choke. He wrapped his thick forearm around the neck from behind and started to squeeze. I knew I only had a few seconds to act. The ball-smashing troglodyte would be unconscious in no time, and some of the crowd had begun to watch. Witnesses to an act such as choking a guest out were bad news. Most would never understand that a guy who takes a cheap shot deserves what he gets.

With this in mind, I did the only thing I could. I picked up his legs up and we carried him towards the entrance to the lounge, where Johnny could choke the shit out of him with fewer witnesses. By the time we got to the lobby, we were nearly free from prying eyes. The only one out there was our maître d'.

The guy was spitting and trying to get air. There was none to be had. His spittle was dripping off the arm of Johnny's jacket. He became desperate for air and started bucking to get free. I dropped his legs to push the elevator button. I looked back and the ball-smashers face was purple. He was in pure agony.

This was a result of Johnny's trachea choke, which was much worse than just cutting off the blood flow and separating the guy from consciousness. His bucking was actually making it worse on him, because it was allowing SOME blood to get through, or maybe that was Johnny not sinking the choke so he could punish him. More than likely, it was the former, as Johnny wasn't always the clearest thinking during an altercation.

"Yo, Johnny, let up, man. The kid might break his own fucking neck."

Johnny looked at me and was having none of it. He was in full kill mode. He just stared at me and tightened his grip. I gave him an affirmative nod.

This nod is always 50%, *Keep choking the shithead if you really want;* the other 50% is, *I mean it—let him go.* We would fix any situation that arose from Johnny's decision. I was on his team and backed his play

133

no matter what. The guy had given Johnny a cheap shot and was now getting what he deserved. He was going to learn a very valuable lesson tonight.

All at once, Johnny pulled him up by his neck, dragging his limp legs nearly straight. I wondered for a split second if Johnny was going to slam him. Mercifully, he lets go, and the nearly unconscious ball-smashing troglodyte slumped to the ground. He lay there for a few seconds to get his bearings and wait for his eyes to reach true north. Johnny steamed off back to the lounge, most likely to get a drink.

"Not a smart move on your part, bro—I don't want to fight him, and I can fight. Now get up and get the fuck out," I told him.

He picked himself up on wobbly legs and wiped the spit from his chin. He looked like he wanted to say something to me but I cut him off.

"Don't fight security."

The DING of the elevator punctuated this for me and the troglodyte got on.

Johnny was a hothead, and when his blood was up, he could be a handful for anyone, no matter how tough. But that didn't mean he didn't meet his match once in a while.

It was a Monday, and the changeover between our regular clientele and our party clientele was starting. This time was especially dicey. Our regular clientele and the people up for just one night didn't always mix very well. There was a big-time Hollywood production in town and the stars of the film, along with the production team, liked to frequent our club. While we never saw the star of the film, her cast mates were in the club quite often.

This particular Monday, Johnny was clearing a section for one of the VIP hosts, who needed to seat a table for bottle service. He was asking a woman to get off the couch when he found himself under verbal assault from an actor largely regarded as a head case, who also happens to be a nominee for one of Hollywood's biggest awards..

"Big O is talking shit," Johnny's voice came over the radio.

There was a slight nerviness to his voice. This was unusual for Johnny. When Black Hank and I rounded the corner, we saw why. Big O was ripping into Johnny. He was physically worked up and looked as though he might swing on him right there, but Johnny wasn't backing down either.

A fistfight between an award nominated actor and Johnny would be about the worst press the club could get. But then again, maybe it wouldn't be—nobody in the media or the public at-large would be surprised by the fact Big O was involved in a nightclub fight. Hell, it would probably help sell the movie. Still, Black Hank and I stepped in between Big O and Johnny to create some space and redirect Big O's anger.

"He shouldn't be talking to a lady like that—that's pussy bullshit. A lady can't sit down?" Big O yelled over the music.

"Look, O, he's just doing his job. It's not an affront to the lady," I said.

Big O was having none of that. He was still pissed that Johnny had asked his friend to get off the couch.

"Fuck that guy. We used to rape guys like him in Liberty City," Big O said.

Black Hank and I smiled at this, not entirely sure that claiming to rape other guys makes you all that tough or not. Still, it's funny, because if he had said it to Johnny, there would most certainly be blows thrown. It seemed we'd gotten there just in time.

"Come on, O. You know how this goes. Just calm down and let us do our job. We're just working here. You know what that's like. Right? Let's not take it any further. We all know how that goes, too. He respects your friend, he respects you. We still have to do our job," I said.

I hoped this thinly veiled threat reiterating the fact that we'd kick his ass if he went too far, coupled with the idea that we respected him, would be enough to calm him down. I think if we had polled the security team, everybody on it probably loved this fucking guy. Not a man among us would want to kick his ass, but we'd have to. Security is a team sport. Johnny was on the team; Big O wasn't. That was the way it worked. Thankfully, raising the issue of a blue-collar approach to the job and letting him know there was no disrespect intended did the trick. Big O calmed down enough to escort the lady to another part of the club and we were left with plenty of ammunition to fuck with Johnny about. That was as close as he'd ever get to stardom and having "an award" shoved up his ass.

Confrontations are part of the job—shit, they are the job. I already told you that as security, we have to win. Now, while this doesn't make us right one hundred percent of the time, it does make it so that we have complete control over you while you're in the club. This is where our power resides, and we don't have to be right, we just have to win. That doesn't mean we relish kicking the shit out of people. I'd rather not put my hands on people if it can be avoided. A bouncer can always get hurt whenever there's a confrontation. But there are times when a man is standing up for himself, and there are times when a man is just showing his ass. The key comes in knowing the difference. Actually some of us do relish kicking the shit out of people who don't.

One night, a drunk was being escorted out by Black Hank. He was protesting the rough fashion in which he was being handled, and given Black Hank's penchant for escalating the level of contact, he may have had a point. I was standing in the lobby of the club when Black Hank entered from the lounge. He had the man by one arm and the back of his shirt and was moving quickly towards the elevators. I didn't see the initial exchange between them, but the man was offering little resistance. I did notice that his speech was a bit impeded and his protestations were growing increasingly vehement with each step. They reached the elevator just as Big Jim, the GM of the club, was emerging from the office.

"Are you the manager?" he asked with a slurred lisp.

"Yes, I am," Big Jim answered.

"This guy is roughing me up for no reason. He could have just asked me and I would have gone," he said.

This was a fair statement. Usually, one working in security would ask before forcibly removing a patron from the club. His point was an attempt for him to save face after being handled by another man. He was standing up for himself and merely trying to preserve his dignity in front of his girl, who was trailing behind with a concerned look. This was reasonable in any man's eyes.

"Sir, you're drunk and my security asked you to leave the club. You should do that," Big Jim replied.

As Big Jim moved past the man on his way to attend to the business of running a multimillion-dollar nightclub, the guest showed his ass. He decided to grab Big Jim. Big Jim was once a bodybuilder, and though he may have grown a tad soft from long hours spent working, he was still a formidable man. The man found he had made a poor choice as he found himself immediately throttled in a much more violent fashion than Black Hank had used.

"Oh, you're a tough guy. Here you go, tough guy," Big Jim said as he smashed the guy against the wall and slowly pushed him down.

Black Hank tried to take over, but Big Jim was reluctant to let Black Hank do the dirty work. We were left to watch as the man was pushed into a semi-crouch/squat position despite his best efforts to resist.

"You ready to leave now, tough guy?" Big Jim asked.

The man merely nodded affirmatively. I stepped forward and pressed the elevator button. By this time, his girl was in tears as she watched her man be emasculated in front of her eyes. It has to be tough for any woman to watch the man she loves get punked.

Big Jim handed the man off to Black Hank and we all got on the elevator. Black Hank followed with the man in a full nelson, and his girl, who was now crying uncontrollably, got on behind us.

"Real tough guy. How'd you like that, tough guy?" Big Jim taunted him. He just wouldn't let up.

The guy manned up for a second and a stream of expletives leaked from his mouth in one long, slurred string. His girl flew off the handle and she started slapping the shit of him. Black Hank had to wrench him away from her to get her to stop. She stopped sobbing.

"Would you just stop it? You're embarrassing me!" she screamed.

The man slumped in the corner because his girlfriend has just relieved him of his last shred of dignity.

The end of the year was nearing and my gambling activity had kicked into overdrive. The holiday months get lean in Las Vegas. I guess it's not popular to drink, party, and gamble when you're supposed to be with the family. One morning, after a thirty-six-hour poker session, I decided I was too drunk to make it home and I would instead head to Colette's apartment. She had given me a key, and I supposed that meant we were dating. We spent enough time together and treated each other like we were in a relationship, albeit a relationship compartmentalized by the demands of her other life and my other life. Our time together consisted of late nights and early mornings. Time I could easily explain to Dana, even though my explanations, excuses, and lies had become tiresome for her and I'm certain she didn't believe anything I said.

I was driving in a light drizzle, drunk and wired from drinking coffee and beer at the same time. One of the gentlemen I was playing with made a comment to the effect of me having a cast-iron stomach. I would soon come to find out what he meant. I arrived at Colette's and opened the door with the key she gave me. Colette was there and she was having a cup of coffee before she headed out to take her daughter, Mariana, to school. We had a short conversation that I didn't remember before she tucked me into bed and let me crash.

I woke some ten hours later in the darkened, empty apartment. I felt like shit. My head was pounding, but that was secondary to the near-rotted feeling that permeated my stomach. I headed home and Dana was there. She didn't really give me any shit about effectively going missing for two days. I guess she was over it all anyway. I crawled into bed and tried to rally. Moments after my head hit the pillow, I leapt out of bed and ran for the toilet. I began puking bile from the depths of my empty stomach. Yellow tinged with red swirled in the water. I wondered how I was going to make it in for my shift. I didn't really have a choice on whether or not I went. The poker session that made up my weekend had left me broke and I desperately needed the money.

I called my boss, Danny, and told him I was going to be a little late. I took a thirty-minute nap, brushed my teeth, ate two burgers from a fast-food drive-thru, and trudged into work. I was late and the team was discussing positions and the upcoming shift in one of the private rooms. I slumped down on the couch, a pale and shivering mess. While they all looked genuinely concerned for my health, it didn't stop them from raining down insults, calling into question my manhood and the ability to hold my liquor.

I pushed through my shift and worked my section. We made good money that night. This influx of cash was necessary, and each sweaty hundred that was pressed into my hand that night seemed to bolster me. When the end of the night came, my pockets were full again.

Colette showed up at the end of the shift to check on me and see if we were going out for some drinks that night, which, of course, we were. We headed to a spot just east of the airport to get something to eat and have a few drinks. My stomach was still in knots but that didn't stop me from draining a couple of shots and chasing them with a number of beers. After knocking around in the parking lot for a few with Johnny and Cal, Colette and I climbed into my truck and set off for her apartment.

I was speeding, but this was less a byproduct of being a little drunk than the fact that I was watching Colette finger herself. She had pulled her panties to the side and was rubbing her clit, looking at me with those blue-gray eyes. The blue lights on the motorcycle that pulled in behind me spoiled the moment. Are the cops ever there when you need them, or do they just show up when it's inconvenient? I pulled into a gas station parking lot and produced my papers.

"Have you been drinking?" he asked.

"Yeah, I had two beers."

I know this is the most popular answer when a driver has been drinking. But what can I say? I had a buzz on.

The cop asked me to get out of the truck and put me through the rigors of a field sobriety test. Whenever I'm interacting with a police officer, a laser-like focus takes over. It probably helps that I spent my life being raised by one. After the rigorous and ridiculous test, he let me know that he thought I was impaired but he was letting me go. This is what is wrong with cops—they can't really admit they made a wrong decision or that their course of action was flawed in any way. It's like the training overrides their ability to be wrong. If he really thought I was impaired, I wouldn't be going anywhere but jail.

I mainly passed the test as a matter of luck and timing. It was because my drinking had been slowed by my puking of blood and bile a few hours earlier. On any other night, he would have had an open and shut case the minute I stepped from the truck. It was just another instance of dumb luck and/or divine providence.

The drinking and drugging had reached a fever pitch and with that came the up and down emotions. I was disrespecting Dana at every turn. This was mathematical, of course. How can you care about someone else when you haven't a care for yourself? I was internally conflicted about hurting her but outwardly acting as though I had life by the balls.

Dana, by default, was a reflection of my own gross shortcomings. My inability to be true to her was a sad character flaw and my ego, though swollen, was fragile. Her very presence punched a hole through the illusion that I was living the dream. I needed her gone to preserve the illusion, but I needed her there to preserve my sanity. I convinced myself that I wasn't hurting her because I hadn't broken her heart all the way. I knew this wasn't true but my cowardice prevented me from facing that truth. I wanted her to leave me. Maybe so I could sink all the way down or maybe so I could blame her when I did.

I do remember glimpses of a morning that cause me to wince when I think on it. It could be that I blocked out the chain of events that led up to this or it could be the haze of the alcohol and pills that's played havoc on the memory. Whatever the case, the cause of my actions wasn't important. There is nothing Dana could have done or said to warrant me punching my rearview mirror off the windshield of my truck and then grabbing her by the back of her hair and screaming into her face, "Why don't you just go home?"

I was ashamed of my actions and the fact that I'd laid hands on Dana. I decided to break up with her, finally doing the right thing. Almost the right thing. We broke up, but not in a final *I'm leaving you, get over me* way. I left her dangling with the hope that we'd get back together after I sorted myself out.

Dana was going back to California and I was going to move in with Johnny. He lived in an apartment off Sunset, just east of McCarran airport. It was affectionately called "The Ranch" and had a string of male roommates who came and went, only to have another one take their place. It was the kind of place where the female conquests had a wall dedicated to them, which they signed. One night after work, Johnny was coming over to help me move my stuff. As usual, we'd had a few drinks before heading out to gather my belongings. Just before we arrived at the apartment Dana and I shared, I swerved into the parking lot of the bar up the street. Johnny followed in his Jeep.

I wanted to wait long enough for Dana to go to work. I told myself I wanted to avoid the awkwardness, but really, I just wanted to hide from her. I parked the truck and Johnny and I walked into the bar. It was a locals' joint, a gaming bar popular throughout the valley. Johnny and I bellied up and ordered shots, beers, and food. The bartender was an attractive brunette named Taylor with an electric smile. We got to see that smile quite a bit as Johnny and I, when drunk, are pretty much the foremost authority on everything. This can be entertaining for the bartender, especially when you're the only two degenerates half-cocked and still drinking at six in the morning.

Taylor seemed to warm to me and I noticed. Now, I've never been particularly smooth with the ladies—I typically eschew pickup lines in favor of being the strong, stoic, and very silent type. But I do have one line that works every time, and here it is: "Girl, when are we going to have, like, ten genetically superior babies together?"

Go ahead use it and see what happens. Yes, it's ridiculous, but it works because of these reasons:

#1—It makes them laugh. The idea of having ten babies is ludicrous and funny.

#2—It's complimentary. I'm saying their genes would make a superior baby.

#3—It's alludes to sex in a nonthreatening manner. Because that's how you make babies.

#4—It tells them you want children. A lot of women do want children.

So I started into my we're-going-to-have-like-ten-genetically-superior-babies routine when I noticed the ring.

"Oh, no, never mind, darlin'. You're married," I said to her. Not that it mattered to me, really. That agreement was between her and her husband. Still, I read something in her body language. "Happily?" I piqued.

The frown that formed in the corners of her mouth said it all. Taylor and I continued to chat and she gave me her number before we left. Johnny and I walked out to the parking lot. We talked and threw punches at each other for a half hour before deciding to move my stuff another day. I returned to the bar to talk to Taylor and have a few more drinks. Taylor told me she didn't even know I was drunk until I fell asleep at the bar.

A couple days later I went to visit Taylor at her bar. She bought me a few drinks as we chatted and then she said she could take a break. We went outside, where she then suggested we get into my truck and talk. The talk consisted of her trying to convince me to screw her in the parking lot while she was on break from her job in a busy strip mall off Tropicana. Naturally, I gave in.

I sandwiched my move in between working, partying, and avoiding Dana. When I finally moved into the Ranch, Johnny's other roommate had moved out and was replaced by JT. JT was a bouncer at another popular club on the Strip. The atmosphere was charged with raging testosterone and reckless possibility. Dana had moved back to California, but I made no time to dwell on my mistakes or the way I'd handled things. It was easier to cover them over, replacing them with distractions, of which there were plenty.

I was carrying on pseudorelationships with Colette and Mandy. I was seeing Taylor on a semiregular basis, when she could steal away from her husband. Angie had happened back into my life on regular basis as well. I'd also slept with Dani, a cocktail waitress at the club. It was easier to move on to the next distraction or take part in an old one rather than examine my life too much. The only one I felt bad about was Colette. The others were based on mutual benefit and feelings for one another that didn't reach far past the physical. But Colette was different.

Collette and I would do average things together like going to the movies. I didn't judge her, even though I knew she was a prostitute. I was flawed much deeper than she. She brought me into her real life. She let me meet her daughter, Mariana. Mariana was bound to a wheelchair, but her smile was bigger than she was. She gave me a glimpse into a part of her that no one who paid to sleep with her was given, and that was the important stuff in life.

I will say that I have met scores of women who I have far less respect for than Colette. Yes, Colette was a whore who took money from men for sex. I'm sure she was degraded further than I will ever know. In the course of a few conversations with her, I became sure her profession scarred her psyche on a level I couldn't possibly fathom. But in terms of purity of heart and being a good person, I have met few women who compare. I have seen married women and men sully their unions time and time again for a fleeting one-night stand. And they press on as though they are essentially good human beings. Few, if any, would put themselves in league with a whore. These people, including me, are far worse. We have dirtied things that cannot be cleaned—love and trust. Just because your payment comes in the form of a diamond necklace instead of a grip of sweaty hundreds, it doesn't make you any less a whore.

It was New Year's Eve and the security team assembled at full strength. A huge crowd was expected and the throngs of people that streamed through the doors after we opened did not disappoint. The well-dressed dinner crowd was docile and the early evening was uneventful. As the midnight hour approached, people flooded the balcony to watch the fireworks. I moved through the crush of people and watched as they grew more and more agitated. One gentleman stopped me.

"Could you help me out? This lady won't move out of the way."

He and I were standing nearly chest to chest.

"Where would you like her to get out of the way?"

He looked around and realized the stupidity of his question as I walked away.

I neared the lounge door just as a struggle broke loose. A mass of people shoved away from each other and a group was crushed against the balcony rail. I was convinced someone was going over the side. I pushed through and seized the first person I saw involved—a man in a tuxedo had a woman by both arms and was yelling in her face. I gripped his elbows. "Let go of the lady."

He didn't comply.

I torqued his elbows and squeezed them toward one another. "Let go of the lady."

The man made a futile attempt at resistance and finally relented.

"In the lounge—let's go," I told him.

"But the fireworks are about to start."

This is what annoys me about people. His concern was the fireworks.

This guy had started a confrontation with a woman in a confined space filled with people to get a better view of fireworks. Concerned with only himself, he failed to recognize the potential for injury or death should a melee break out. When finally confronted with the fact that he was endangering people, his defense was that the fireworks were about to start. I realize that my working philosophy is in direct conflict with the way I directed my personal life, but that was the job.

"You should have thought of that before you started shit. You're definitely leaving right now. Now, hurry up. I have to get back to watch the fireworks," I told him as I pushed him into the lounge through the wall of people trying to get out of the patio door. As he and I rounded the end of the bar, a woman came crashing through the crowd, cocktail in hand.

"Get out of the way. I've got to watch the fireworks," she slurred. She pinballed off a couple of people, tried to turn the corner, and tripped over a velvet rope.

The next few moments unfolded in a Matrix-like sequence of events. The velvet rope was pulled in front of a two-hundred-pound ice sculpture of the club's logo. The woman tripped and fell over the rope. Her cocktail flew, spraying a group of people standing nearby. Her head and shoulder smashed into the sculpture where the base met the logo. The logo toppled and all two-hundred-plus pounds fell right on top of the woman.

"We have a problem in the lounge," I called over the radio.

The woman shoved the shattered blocks of ice aside and sprang back up. "I'm okay. I've got to watch the fireworks," she said.

Man, these fireworks better be fucking awesome, I thought to myself.

I stopped the woman just as our boss arrived. "You okay? Are you hurt?" I asked.

"No, I'm all right. I was just trying to get to the balcony," she replied.

"Okay, go watch the fireworks. I'll catch up to you in a minute." I sent her off so I could go over it with Big Jim.

"The lady is shithoused and fell into the ice sculpture. The big part landed right on top of her," I told him.

"What do you think?" he asked.

"Well, if we toss her for being drunk and she gets pissed, she could get it into her head we were negligent and make trouble," I said.

"Yeah. We don't want that," Big Jim replied.

"I think the best course for us is to track her down, apologize, offer medical attention, let her refuse, and then bring her a fresh cocktail. She's on her own after that," I offered up.

"Do it," Big Jim told me.

Just as I thought she would, the woman declined medical attention. She did accept the cocktail I brought her, though. Even though the woman could have an injury that we couldn't see, I was effectively doing my job, which is to protect the nightclub.

Now, I knew she could, most likely, seek out a lawyer and bring litigation against the club anyway. But I was trying to smooth things out in the now and keep the money moving for the club and for security. Filling out paperwork and taking the proper precautions with this lady would have eaten up precious time, and we all know time is money. We all had a position to fill that night and mine was the upstairs man in our service-elevator hustle.

The management said the club was full but we knew better. All night, the security team had been bringing loads of people up the back express elevator to enjoy the open-bar package the club had in place. Greasy rode the elevator down and went into the casino to gather the group that had assembled. He called me on the radio with the code word and I pressed the button to bring them up. You needed a key to reach our floor from the bottom. But I could call the elevator up with one push. We charged them one hundred a head for the package that the nightclub had been selling for $250. It was a windfall for the security team, and the hustle had us flush with cash to ring in the New Year.

SPADES

For me, it was a new year in a new world. The place we'd found ourselves in was better than one we could construct. When I stepped onto the perch, surveyed the club, and saw that the crowd was frenetic, the bass was throbbing, and the drinks were flowing, I felt like a Titan. I was in charge of security for one the hottest clubs in the nightclub capital. While I wasn't actually in charge, I still made and enforced the rules. When the rules I couldn't change didn't fit what I wanted, I simply circumvented them to get what I needed done. The team I had built was more than happy to follow my lead. This was less because of my leadership skills and more because I gave them plenty of leeway to do whatever they felt like. We had carte blanche to avail ourselves of all the privileges that the rich usually paid for, while we got paid to do so.

The craziness was snowballing. Not only did I not want it to stop, I wanted more. It seemed that as it grew, so did the business of the club. Booze, broads, dope, and dough were all there for the taking. These things brought their own brand of trouble, though real trouble never seemed to touch the team. It was as if an aura of invincibility surrounded us. This kind of freedom would prove to be the most dangerous intoxicant I have ever experienced. While not particularly religious, I felt like I was being protected by the hand of God, and I would continue to act accordingly.

The year opened with more celebrities than ever. It was early on a Monday night and a group was having a late dinner in one of the private rooms. I was called in early to oversee the privacy of the group and basically watch the rope leading to the private rooms. I was well familiar with the spot, as it was mine when I first moved up. The dinner party consisted of an ex-heavyweight champion of the world, an American football HOFer who struck fear into the hearts of opposing quarterbacks with his pass rush, one of basketballs great enforcers, and the last guest was the goat—he was arguably the best basketball player of all time.

The men enjoyed their dinner as the typical Monday-night crowd began to file in and fill the room. The night was just getting started and the celebs would periodically come out to take a look at the action. It wasn't long until Max came by to say hello and see what he could see of the group. Max was a magician who worked the room and entertained the guests. He would say he was a mentalist, as his trickery was more cerebral than slight of hand, but whatever you called them, his tricks were amazing.

It was then that the enforcer, The 3X champ, and the goat all stepped into the cramped hallway leading to the private rooms. Max offered to show them some tricks. The 3X champ and enforcer were all for this, but the goat was acting like he couldn't be troubled. When Max asked him to initial a playing card for part of the trick, the goat looked at it like a cheap ploy to get an autograph. What the goat didn't know was that the card was going to end up in his jacket pocket without Max so much as touching him. I'd seen the trick countless times and I still couldn't figure out how the hell he executed this.

Luckily, the enforcer was much more down to earth and jovial. He signed the card and the show went on. Max pulled out all the stops during the short time he entertained them. The enforcer and the 3X champ were amazed, and even the goat warmed to the experience. Max's tricks were that good. He was well on his way to being a star if he hadn't passed in his sleep just a short time later.

The men retired to the private room for after-dinner drinks and I returned to watching the rope. I was anxious to get on the floor and make some money. It was fine entertainment to get to meet and watch celebrities, but for the most part, they were notoriously cheap. They were used to getting taken care of and seldom took care of the people taking care of them. This night was to be no exception.

The 3X champ came out and he was obviously feeling his buzz. He wanted to talk and get some stories from me on the Vegas action. He and I exchanged a few stories specific to our lives. I asked him about his hardest opponent, what life was like after boxing, and what it was like running in the circles he did. He wanted to know as much about me as I did about him. He was convinced that I should be a cop due to the way I looked.

"You look like a cop. Man, you should be a cop," he said.

I asked him to write me a letter of recommendation. He got a great laugh off this and said he would—this was definitely the liquor talking.

He was a three-time heavyweight champ with celebrity friends and he was talking to me like we'd been friends forever. As the club got crowded, the celeb dinner group decided they should take off. I shook hands with 3X champ and the enforcer, but the goat and the HOFer couldn't be troubled. This just solidified what I already thought about celebs. They're just like everyone else—some of them are cool, and some of them are assholes.

The next morning was to be the first time I bounced the border of the United States and Mexico with the intention of bringing back drugs. It was with Johnny. He had done it before. It's simple, really—buy steroids in one the many pharmacies there, secret them away in your luggage or on your person, and make your way back to the U.S.

We set out on an early morning after shutting down the club. Johnny and I drove the six hours to Tijuana, partially drunk from our after-work ritual. We pulled across the border in a Jeep owned by Johnny's old roommate, paying no mind to the fact that two white boys going into TJ at eleven o'clock in the morning on a Tuesday would raise all kinds of red flags. Add to that the fact that the vehicle we were driving was registered to a person who lived in another state and it was a recipe for disaster. I didn't care—my nihilistic mindset just had me ready to do the next reckless thing. That was the juxtaposition of my life at the time, one night handling some of the biggest celebrities in the world and the next preparing to smuggle drugs out of Tijuana.

We pulled a right off the freeway. First stop: Revolución. Revolución is the famed boulevard that is the nerve center of tourist TJ, although the entire city seemed to embody the recklessness that was in my heart. We went into a pharmacy just off Revolución recommended by Flanagan. Flanagan was a friend of Johnny's, an expat Scotsman who had been deported from the U.S. for selling drugs and had lived in TJ after his deportation. He was well connected down south and smoothed us out at this pharmacy.

The guy who ran the counter was a portly Mexican we called Tio. We told Tio that Flanagan had sent us. In a scene out of the movies, Tio looked around and then pulled out a spiral notebook. He flipped to a page with Flanagan's name scrawled across the top, then turned it around and showed us a list of prices for preferred customers. We shelled out and bought six hundred dollars worth of junk for around twenty-five dollars a bottle. Not bad considering each bottle would be worth an additional hundred dollars back in Vegas. Tio bagged the junk in a black bag.

We walked, black bag in hand, to the truck and stashed it in the only piece of luggage we'd brought—Johnny's bat bag. Then we headed back up the street to have a few cervezas. Our buzz had long since waned.

On the streets in TJ, they have these plywood boxes that stand on the sidewalk. A makeshift shed, if you will. It is here that they handcuff troublemakers to a metal pipe that they have running through the box. I wondered if this was where we were to end up. I also made a mental note for next time to wear a handcuff key around my neck, just in case. Handcuff keys are universal. If you're going to do illegal shit, get one.

Johnny and I made our way up the street and headed upstairs to Carnales. Carnales had the loudest music and seemed like the place to be. I was content not to go wandering very far as this was my first trip down and I was convinced that anything could happen around the next corner. There was a special on Corona for lunch, so we ordered a bucket. Then IT came.

IT was that uneasy silence punctuated by forced conversation. It is the byproduct of the moments before you are about to do something very illegal. This is natural. But it is important to get yourself in check. It can make the difference between handcuffs and sweet freedom. I use the forefather's method. I find it calming to remember that all those guys who signed the Declaration of Independence, because they were girded too tight by the government of England, were basically outlaws. They struck out to do something they knew was illegal because they did not agree with the rules that governed them. We celebrate these men. So I just imagined that I was doing what John Hancock would do. This didn't just calm me. It swelled my heart with the same fervor they probably had—it made the powers that be my sworn enemy as I upheld the memory of our forefathers. Wasn't that the spirit of America? Maybe it was a stretch, but it worked for me.

Our waiter returned with a bottle of some rotgut tequila and a whistle. I had only seen this phenomenon on spring-break travel shows. But in TJ, Tuesday is just as good. He did the whole thing, pouring the tequila into my open mouth for as long as I could bear. He shook my head and blew the whistle. It was ridiculous, and I found myself wondering when the last time the grubby towel he pulled from his belt and used to prevent a spill was washed. Johnny followed suit. We ordered a couple more shots and another bucket of beer. We crushed these and decided it was time to go. The mood on the walk back to the truck was jovial. It seemed that liquor worked for Johnny. Johnny drove and we pulled onto the ramp leading us back to the 15 and back home. The flashing lights behind us, however, signaled that the shit had just gotten deeper.

A fat Mexican police officer with a dirty uniform ambled up to Johnny's door. His accent was thick. "You know why I am pulling you over?" he asked Johnny, who looked a little shook.

"No," came the answer.

Short and sweet. Don't talk too much. These are two very simple rules when talking to cops.

"You didn't use you blinker to get over."

Johnny quickly apologized, and the cop informed us that it was going to be an eighty- OR eighty-five-dollar fine, and he'd be right back. I didn't realize municipal fines in Mexico were negotiable, but I recognized that he was shaking us down and I loved him for it.

"Give me the money," Johnny said.

"Talk him down—tell him we only have forty," I said as I fished a wad of cash out of my pocket." I was fucking with Johnny because he was nervous.

"GIVE ME THE MONEY AND LET'S GET THE FUCK OUT OF HERE."

Johnny was not amused. He was pretty much the craziest fucking guy I'd ever met, but the idea of getting busted in TJ had him on edge like I'd never seen.

The cop returned while I was leafing through cash. I quickly dropped my remaining money between the seats, as I didn't want him getting any bright ideas about the amount of the fine.

Johnny handed the money out the window and the cop pushed his hand back in. "No, put it in this," he said as he shoved a filthy-ass envelope that had no doubt seen its share of dirty money through the window.

Johnny made the deposit and the cop told us to drive safely.

We waited in a relatively short line and made the border. The guard was extremely personable, but he held us for a minute. Our shakedown story was the saving grace. I did most of the talking from the passenger side. Being shaken down was extremely rewarding for me, and I wanted to tell the guard. He said we should have refused to pay and asked to be taken down to the station, and that's how he would have played it.

I stroked his ego. "It's a little easier when you can pull a business card that says you work for the U.S. government. Speaking of … do you have one I can borrow for next time?"

This elicited a chuckle from the guard. He told us to take it easy, and just like that, we were back in the States. Johnny and I were in high spirits after a successful trip. It was time to celebrate on the six-hour drive home.

We stopped at a convenience store and bought a twelve-pack of beer and two giant cups. We rapidly consumed the beer, using the seat belt to pop the tops. Johnny hit the wall just before Barstow, California, and I was left to navigate through the high desert while he slept it off in the back of the Jeep. I finished the beer and listened to the same CD again and again. By now, I had been up about thirty hours, which wasn't a big deal except for the fact that I had no cocaine to keep me going. All

151

that got me through the drive was the combined excitement of the trip to Mexico and the sobering up I did while driving.

Johnny woke up as we arrived in Primm to resume driving. We talked about the easy money we'd just made and exactly when we were going to make our next trip to Tijuana. Both of us failed to see how close we'd come to getting pinched on multiple felonies and how that could ruin everything. The near-fresh lessons of just a couple years prior were lost to me.

The very next morning, I lay in bed enjoying a nice drug-induced sleep. I had begun taking Seroquel, an antipsychotic, and Noritryptiline, an antidepressant. Two of Dana's prescription bottles had made it into my toiletries. While they weren't prescribed to me by a doctor and the two probably shouldn't have been taken together, I still took them. I'm certain they shouldn't have been mixed with cocaine and booze. But at the time, it was a wonderful cocktail that helped me sleep.

I was jolted from my peaceful rest by Johnny when he jumped on my bed. "Hey, wake up—Maria just called. She said Blake just won seven grand and she wants us to go take care of him, keep him out of trouble."

Maria was a hot cocktail waitress who worked with us at the club. She was a part-time model and fitness competitor and she was Blake's wife. Blake was the owner of a software company that worked with the casinos. He was affluent, and seven grand wasn't a great deal of money for him. But Blake, like us, was one who got fall-down drunk. When Blake and I met, we hit it off almost immediately. Sure, he was rich, but his mom and dad were hardworking blue-collar-type folks, and Blake got his work ethic from them, so he was a down-to-earth guy. Maria trusted me to keep him out of trouble.

"Fuck, man, I was sleeping so well," I yelled at Johnny. I closed my eyes and weighed the options. We had to go to work that night. I knew we'd be up to our late-night antics once again and sleep was very necessary. On the other hand, no adventure was to be had by lying in bed all day, and I really liked hanging with Blake. The decision was simple.

"Fuck it—let's go," I told Johnny. "Only one stipulation—no drinking."

Blake was with two of his employees, friends of his from back home. The mood was celebratory, and we killed our first shots of tequila after a short protest that went something like this:

Blake: "Shots for everybody. I'm buying."

Me: "We really shouldn't—we have to work tonight."

Johnny: "Well, we have to stop drinking at six so we can make it to work."

The idea that we wouldn't drink was highly unlikely to begin with and was all but dashed to bits when Blake offered. We hit every bar in the place and Blake was buying. I guess it was amusing to attempt to get the two guys that had to work as drunk as possible. I was in the midst of my first cycle of steroids at the time and I was weighing in around two hundred forty pounds. Blake handed Johnny his wad of winnings, a fat stack of hundred-dollar bills, as he'd decided he was too drunk to handle money.

As the day wore on, I suggested we get something to eat. We chose an Italian place in the casino. More tequila, bottles of wine, and after dinner drinks had us all on tilt. The melee that was the meal saw me come out on top by managing to get the least drunk of the bunch. I was restrained a bit, as I felt responsible for getting Blake home. Maria, who was a bit of a wild chick herself, was known to have a fiery disposition, and I had no desire to betray her trust.

It was now 7:00, and Johnny and I had violated our 6:00 p.m. drinking curfew by an hour. I gathered the crew and we all piled into Blake's SUV. I drove the crew back to Blake's house in Anthem and made sure they made it into the house. They passed out rather quickly, leaving Johnny and I with a dilemma. Should we take Blake's $80,000 dream car to work? Of course we should.

We sped back to the Ranch and Johnny was fading fast. The after dinner drink was working on him.

"Get your ass in the shower—you'll feel better," I told him.

Johnny and I had to get our game faces on, as it was sure to be busy. We had two DJs working that night and the back room was open. Once he was showered and dressed, Johnny looked like he'd rallied a bit. A suit gives even the most heinous drunk an air of respectability. We hustled to work and dropped the Range in valet. We walked through the casino and Johnny's second wind blew through quickly. He was looking rough.

"Tighten up, ho," I chided. I absolutely couldn't let the opportunity to break his chops pass. The code of foolish bravado that governed two reckless idiots willing to show up to work fully cocked wouldn't allow for coddling. "Don't worry," I reassured him. "Greasy is sure to have some get right. A couple bumps will straighten you right out. Personally, I could use another drink. My buzz is waning."

We arrived at work and set up the room. A couple of trips to the bathroom had Johnny back in the game, at least for a while. About 11:30, the club was packed and Johnny joined me on the perch in the lounge.

"Bro, you've got to put me in the back room. I can't handle the patio door. The fucking people are getting to me," Johnny told me.

The patio door was a high-volume pathway to the balcony. The cocktail well was there and there was a constant crush of people trying to get outside or to the bar. It required constant supervision to keep traffic moving. This was Johnny's normal position, but in his half-drunk, fully-coked state, the constant interaction was a hazard to his mental stability and possibly his employment if he popped off in the wrong spot.

"No problem, man. Get back there and send Greasy up. Get Colby to pour you a drink. You're looking a little wrought up. Balance, man … the key is balance," I told him. Blake and the crew showed up around 1:00 a.m. looking rested and refreshed. For a moment, I thought he might be pissed that we took his cash and car. I pulled the valet ticket and tried to hand it over.

"Hold onto it. We took a limo. We're heading to the strip club in a little bit. Call me after you get off and you can meet us over there to pick us up," Blake told me without a hint of being put out in his voice.

The rest of the night went well and we left the club with beers in hand on our way to meet Blake. We had a stop to make at home first to change our clothes, though. There was no telling what the night would bring.

I was bolstered by the white mouse in my pocket. But Johnny was having none of it. "I can't go," he told me.

"Fuck that. Get dressed and let's go. Blake and them are already there," I protested.

"Dude, I can't go. I'm done. We've been drinking all fucking day. I'm wasted. I need to go to my lady's and crash," he replied.

"You can't tap out now. Come on. This shit is just getting good … fuck. Let's ride." I employed everything from my bag of tricks to get him going. From insulting his pride as a man, to offering him narcotics to keep him going, to reminding him he started this shit twelve hours ago while I was sleeping peacefully. This was all to be in vain, as Johnny was really done. He was tapping out for real.

"Well, fuck it. Go get some rest. Be safe," I told him before I hopped in the truck and headed off.

I called Blake and he told me that they were at some shithole strip club that I'd never been to. But he couldn't tell me where it was. He handed the phone to a bouncer and the bouncer proceeded to give me the most fucked up directions ever. He sent me to wrong side of Interstate 15 and had me driving around an industrial area looking for the club. I was convinced that he couldn't be that stupid so I drove around for an hour. In that time, I called Blake a couple more times, none of which he answered. I asked three cabbies where the fuck this bullshit club was and none of them knew. I finally stopped to bump up and Greasy called.

"Where you at?" he asked.

"I'm fucking driving around an industrial park looking for this bullshit strip club," I told him.

Greasy let me know that the strip club in question was about five minutes from where I lived. Isn't that always the way?

Greasy agreed to meet me over there. I called Blake again and he answered.

"Hey, Blake, I'm about five minutes away. The bouncer gave me shitty directions," I said.

"Hey, don't bother. We got the strip club limo and we're heading to the house with a couple strippers. Just meet us there," he told me before he hung up.

Fuck. This is getting live and I'm missing the shit, I thought to myself.

Greasy met me at the strip club but declined the invite to go out to Blake's on the grounds that his house was too far. Now all I could do was shake my head. My alcohol buzz was all but gone, having been edged out by having to stay straight in order to drive, and completely flattened by bump after bump of cocaine.

I pulled into the convenience store on the corner of Sunset and grabbed a 22. The sun was coming up and I desperately needed to get my buzz in order, like some alcoholic vampire needing to feed to bolster myself against the sun. I popped the top with the seat belt and put the truck in drive. I pulled my phone out and dialed my boy Sasso, a friend of mine from Florida. It was at least 8:00 a.m. there. To my surprise, he was awake.

Sasso and I talked about God knows what until I pulled through the gate and into Blake's driveway. I sat in the truck for a minute or two and we finished our conversation. I jumped out and headed for the front gate. I opened that and closed it behind me. I pushed up the sidewalk and headed for the front door. I could only imagine what manner of debauchery was going on inside the house. In my mind, it was a wild, naked freak party complete with strippers and blow, a Las Vegas classic.

I opened the front door and expected to be awash in revelry. But nothing was going on. The house was empty. *Fuck,* I thought. *Where have they gone now? No big deal. They must be out by the pool.*

I strode across the kitchen and deposited my beer on the island countertop. I walked to the sliding glass door and looked outside. Nobody was out there. This was puzzling. *Where the fuck could they be now?* As I mulled this over, a few questions popped into my head. *Wasn't Blake's pool on the other side of the yard? And where was the putting green?* I spun and looked around the room. It hit me like a ton of bricks. I was in the wrong fucking house.

In the cookie-cutter land of stucco and model homes I had made a crucial mistake and walked into a stranger's house. I beelined for the island and scooped up my beer. I tiptoed for the front door just as I heard the stirrings of whoever lived there.

"I think someone's out there," a male voice floated through the silence.

I heard a muffled female reply.

"Who's out there?" the male spoke again.

I took two giant steps for the front door, not wanting to get caught inside. As soon as I touched the knob, I spoke. "I'm sorry, sir. I'm in the wrong house." I pulled the door shut and ran down the sidewalk. I jumped in the truck and threw it into drive. I whipped into the street and pulled some four houses down to Blake's actual residence.

The strip-club limo was backed into the garage and the front half was sticking out. I parked the truck on the street and hustled into the house. I was greeted by a drunken crew, two coked-up strippers, and the black limo driver, who was sitting on the couch watching television. I was explaining to Blake and the crew that I'd just walked into the wrong house when the doorbell rang. Blake answered and I heard a familiar male voice.

"I want to know who was in my house."

Blake invited the man inside and I approached the front door. "I'm sorry. It was an honest mistake," I began. "But you can see that the house is laid out the same and the door was unlocked."

The man surveyed the scene that was in front of him: two coked-up, tattooed strippers dancing; a brace of horny, drunken squares cheering them on; the black limo driver, smiling away; and me, standing there like a fucking asshole.

"What is it that you people do?" he asked.

I produced a business card and led him back to the front door. We stepped outside and he handed me his business card. It read *United States Secret Service Special Liaison, Las Vegas Metropolitan Police Department.* A lump gathered in my throat. With a pocketful of coke and my fingerprints inside his house, I was certain I was going to jail. "I'm sorry about this, sir. It was an honest mistake. I had no intention of walking into your house. I work in the security field and definitely don't want any trouble." I was dancing, trying my best to sell the sincerity. I truly didn't give a fuck about anything but staying out of jail.

"Is this your car?" He pointed to Blake's SUV.

"No, sir. I picked up the owner of the house's car because they had been drinking and took the limo," I said. *Please don't call more cops,* I thought.

"I'm going to need your ID," he told me.

Fuck—I'm going to jail.

I produced my ID and he jotted down the information.

"I am going to run this," he told me.

Right, as though I have a fucking choice. "Please do, sir."

"You know you could have gotten shot?"

I was well aware that a Secret Service agent could have put a pill in my head without much effort. He would have been fully justified to do so, as I was an intruder in his house.

"Yes, sir. I'm counting myself lucky this morning. I'm sorry to have startled you," I apologized again.

The man finally, reluctantly relaxed. "You have a good morning," he bid me farewell and walked back up the street.

It was official—my buzz was completely gone. Not even the strippers and blow could provide a rush equivalent to that which I'd just experienced. I made the crew breakfast and went home. I pulled the blinds and ingested a handful of pills. I sank into the safety of my own bed and pondered just how close I'd come to death or worse.

Every so often, someone on the staff would get out of line with their intake. We had to take a drug test as a pre-employment stipulation; after that, all bets were off. It's the nightclub industry—no one really cares. One of the best examples I worked for is now a high-ranking manager with one of the nightclub groups in Las Vegas. He said to me, "I don't care how fucked up you get while working, as long as you can do YOUR job. The minute you can't handle it, you're gone."

He drank quite a lot on the job and was always glad-handing guests, making sure all were having a good time. He led by example, and this bred extreme loyalty amongst his employees. He knew we were going to play anyway and understood that better it be in the open and modest than in the shadows and rampant.

I listened to this advice, but there were plenty of people who didn't. Usually it was one of the cocktail waitresses getting too smashed while drinking with the guests. You'd see them at the end of the night too blotto to handle their paperwork. Those were the ones who ended up fired and looking for a job. Then the management would have to tighten the reins as a show for the HR department. We'd sit in our preshift meeting and listen to how there was a zero-tolerance policy when it came to drinking. They'd tell us how they didn't want to see us with a drink in our hand for any reason and we were to let the bussers and porters clean the joint up. This, of course, was a heaping load of steaming bullshit.

It was Monday night and we were up to our usual. The club was slammed and we were exploiting every opportunity to make money. These nights had a wonderful quality to them, and something just coursed through the club. I personally couldn't wait for Mondays.

It was my Friday and was the best night in the club. Women were all over the place and a buzz, should you want one, could be had simply by asking. On an uncharacteristic sober night for me, I was asked by my boss, Kalil, to stand in for his reprimand of a security guard from our sister club. The guard in question was a bottle blond and rumor had it that she had done a few porn films. Amongst the security team upstairs, she had garnered the nickname "Suck-A-Softy" for her willingness to suck a limp dick. Greasy had first-hand knowledge of this and bestowed the name upon her.

Suck-A-Softy was thought to have been drinking on the job because a plastic bottle of vodka fell out the security jacket she was wearing. The club was rife with on-the-job drinking, so reprimanding someone for this when nearly all of us drank on a nightly basis was straight hypocrisy.

But Kalil had merely asked me to stand in and therefore saved me from being a hypocrite, at least in this case. When he first asked me to be present, I noticed his eyes were a bit bloodshot and thought he might have had a couple drinks on him. By the time we actually pulled Suck-A-Softy aside to give her the reprimand, I was positive.

"Now, why, when we told you pacifically not to drink on the job, would a vodka bottle fall out of the pocket of the jacket you were wearing?"

I was thinking I must have misheard him when he said "pacifically."

Suck-A-Softy offered a weak rebuttal and Kalil cut her off, saying, "But we pacifically told you. Pacifically not to handle alcohol."

159

Now I was getting more and more uncomfortable with every slur. Kalil was smashed and reprimanding an employee for drinking. *Please stop trying to say* specifically, I thought to myself.

Suck-A-Softy tried to rebut and Kalil cut her off again, showing just how unreasonable his drunk ass has become. "Why would you do that?" he asked. "When we pacifically told you not to?"

Now I just couldn't take any more and had to turn away from them to hide my smile. *If he says "pacifically" one more time,* I thought, *I may just lose it all the way.* Luckily, he ended the reprimand and left Suck-A-Softy to fear for her job. Though she would never get fired for that, as it would have cast suspicion on drinking at large in the club, and we couldn't let that ruin the fun.

"I think that went well," I told Kalil. "Let's go get a drink."

Greasy later admitted that it was his vodka bottle that he had stashed in the jacket earlier that night as a means of evidence disposal and to throw anyone off his trail.

But that's how management worked—they were in it for a good time and to make a name for themselves so they could advance to the next hottest, up-and-coming place. During the five years I was there, we went through five GMs and a host of support managers. No sooner did they get there, than they moved on. That's how I was able to get and keep the place wired—by the time they learned the ropes, they were moving on. They simply didn't have the time or the inclination to care what we were doing in the security world. The rest of the time, they were having fun or worrying about making their side money.

If you were in the club, knew the drill, and could be trusted, you were golden. Shit, most of the time, if you helped the managers, they'd help you. Naturally, they couldn't make it blatant, so they could preserve plausible deniability. But I remember sitting with Kalil during an after-work drinking session. He started in all serious about how he and the big boss, the one who crunched that kid into a little ball, knew what Greasy and I were doing. I wasn't foolish enough to play stupid with him—that's how you got your ass in real trouble, playing people for fools. I knew he meant the coke. I was almost certain one of our barbacks ratted out after he lost all his tips for the night playing C-LO with security after the shift. But the thing is, when you're all dirty, you're all clean. No one wants to mess it up for anyone.

"What do you want me to do about that?" I said.

"Just keep it quiet. If we can hear it, other people might hear it, too," he told me.

I confirmed that I could do that with a simple nod of my head, and that was good enough for him. "Shots," Kalil called out and I knew we were good.

Sometimes the management even got you laid. I was in the club one evening when one of our managers, Karim, was hitting on a couple of attractive females in their mid-thirties. I was nearby and Karim waved me over.

"You're going to go with him," is all Karim said.

Now, as much as a lothario as Karim could be, I didn't think that a simple command from him would make a woman who looked like Liz do what she did. Liz was a pharmaceutical rep from the South. She had the drawl that melted me and she was built like a brick shithouse. She accompanied me to my truck that night and I had the full intention of taking her back to the Ranch. Liz had different plans. She unzipped my pants, freed my dick with the hand she wore her wedding ring on, then fucked me in my truck in the parking garage of the casino. I came inside of her and she assured me that it was fine.

"What do you want from me?" she asked all of a sudden.

I wasn't sure what she was looking for from the bouncer she'd just met and screwed in his truck in Las Vegas. She collected herself just as the real emotion welled in her eyes. She told me she was going to bail on her morning meeting and I could meet her in her room around 9:00 a.m., after her roommate left.

I went home, drank beer, snorted a few lines, and awaited her call. She called just as she said she would. I hustled back to the hotel and knocked on her door; she answered without a stitch of clothing on.

I suppose I gave her just what she was looking for, an escape from that boring, mundane existence she faced as a wife and mother back home in Mississippi. It's a story told over and over on a nightly basis in Las Vegas. Later that day, I walked her to a taxi, but I couldn't say goodbye as one of her colleagues came over to ask why she'd missed the meeting.

Liz called me during her layover in Texas to tell me her bottom hurt from me banging her. Then she poured her heart through the phone, telling me she would move away to be with me and she'd hop a plane back if only I'd ask her to.

"We had fun, didn't we?" is all I could say.

I heard her start to cry as she hung up the phone.

The very next night, a few of Johnny's female friends from Arizona came to the club one evening. One of them was a friend of a friend from Oregon. She was young and in shape from her duty in the Air Force. She and I hit it off immediately and she and her friend accepted the invite to have a couple of drinks at one of the 24-hour bars up the street from the Ranch. We were already half in the bag and Johnny was heading to all the way in as fast as he could get there. I was attempting to maintain at least a modicum of sobriety.

I was sure the deal was closed after Miss Air Force asked me when the last time I had sex was. Of course I lied and told her two weeks ago.

"That long?" she asked.

Drunken conversations about sex are seldom subtle, but she was leading, so I ventured the question, "When was the last time you had sex?"

"Last night before I left," was her answer.

Perfect. This girl was right up my alley. The drinks were flowing at the late-night spot. All was moving along smoothly and the Ranch was but a short, drunken drive up the block, where no doubt another name would be added to the wall.

Johnny sat down with two shots of tequila. "Here you go, bitch," he said as he slammed the glass on the bar in front of me.

"I'm not a bitch," Miss Air Force replied.

Johnny was drunk, and since he was talking to me, he looked puzzled by her response. The puzzlement was soon replaced with a smile. "That's debatable," he told her.

"You don't even know me. I haven't talked to you all night," she shot back.

Reasoning with Johnny when he's had as many drinks as it took to get almost home is worse than impossible. I saw my chances to split Miss Air Force's legs evaporating with every slurred exchange.

"You don't need to talk to me for me to know you're a bitch. I see 'em all night long." Johnny nodded his head, affirming his answer.

I slammed the shot he'd just handed me and prepared to step in.

"You're just rude," Miss Air Force said, standing her ground.

"Bitch, that's because I don't even like you." Johnny sealed my chances of getting laid with this statement.

Miss Air Force gave her friend "the look." She gave me her number and the girls left.

"Thanks, dick. Real smooth. Now I have to go home with just your ass," I told Johnny as I ordered two more shots.

"What? She was being a bitch," he protested.

"No, she wasn't. Your ass is drunk."

Johnny took a listless pause as his mind worked on this. "I didn't want to listen to you fuck all night anyway," he told me. "Just drink your drink, asshole," I told him as the bartender set us up.

We drank every single night and as such we rotated through a plethora of bars, clubs, and strip clubs. We had a few that were our regular spots, though, and one such strip club was a favorite destination for Johnny, JT, and me. It was THE strip joint in Las Vegas. More than a few times we ended up there to blow our hard-earned tip money. While I'm not an aficionado of lap dances, there are few better places to drink than a spot where titties are out. Johnny, JT, and I were in our usual booth.

Now, while I usually don't get lap dances, I do like the company of the dirtiest, most white-trash-looking strippers possible—it's the Florida in me. I'm talking gutter trash, heroin chicks, and there was a Russian girl there that fit the bill. We had drinks and JT ordered a meal of chicken wings, French fries, and a club sandwich. Girls were stopping by and plying their trade. I bought Johnny a lap dance and looked around for a substitute for the Russian. Another girl had stopped to sit on JT's lap and their conversation up to that point found her with her top off.

"Oooh. Can I get a chicken wing?" she asked.

"Girl, you the one making all the money around here. You should be buying me a chicken wing," JT said as he stripped another bone clean.

"Well, how about some fries, then?" This stripper was full-court pressing JT for his food.

"Hank, do you believe this bitch?" he asked me.

"What? With all that dancing, you know she works up an appetite. Give her some food. Give her some club sandwich," I told him.

JT deposited the stripped bone on the paper. "All right, girl. Get you some club sandwich," he told her.

The girl reached for a quarter of the sandwich, spilling lettuce as she lifted it to her mouth. The vision of a topless stripper sitting on the lap of a 6'5" black man in glasses while eating a club sandwich is something I had never seen before or since.

JT reached up and tweaked her nipple with his greasy, wing-sauce-covered fingers. He squeezed and pulled it until his fingers slipped off.

I couldn't take it. Later on, some poor sucker was going to pay this girl to take her top off, and while she ground on him with her titties in his face, he'd be sucking on a nipple covered with hot-wing sauce.

I left JT and Johnny at the strip club and headed home. High and drunk, I climbed into the driver's seat and started the short drive home. The streets were eerily empty as I tried to beat the sun home. It was just starting to rise, and one of my favorite sights in the world was the early morning haze visible on the mountains that lay to the west of town.

I was alone and completely hammered. Sunrise or later was the best time to drive if you were going to drive drunk. Early risers were just starting to hit the road and the infrequency of police sightings made it seem as though cops were on a shift change, or maybe they were just banging on the windows of the local donut spot.

When I was a block from the Ranch, I failed to brake for a red light in time and pulled well into the intersection that sits at the east end of Casa de Shenandoah. It has a high block wall to keep out trespassers. It is well known for housing animals of all kinds, even a giraffe. I know this to be true because, while you can't see the animals, you can smell the piss and shit from outside. At any rate, I realized I was in the middle of the intersection and for whatever reason, I decided to adhere to traffic laws instead of running the damn thing. I checked all my mirrors and looked out the rear window of the truck. There wasn't another car in sight, so I threw it in reverse and backed up. I heard a CRUNCH.

I looked out the back window to see what I'd hit but nothing was back there. My stomach sunk when I realized I'd hit a person. I was going to jail for real this time. I was drunk and high, and that made it even worse. Thoughts of ruin raced through my mind. Court dates and fines followed by jail time could be seen on the horizon. These concerns were secondary to idea that I'd just hurt someone because I was being careless with my life. The person I hit could be broken somehow and that was on me.

I threw my truck into park and prepared to get out, ready to face the music. Suddenly, I saw a head pop up on the right side of my truck. The head was wearing a helmet. The man began moving, kind of rolling up to my passenger-side window. When he reached the window, I already had it rolled down.

"Hey, bro, I'm sorry. You okay?" I said.

He was sitting on a motorcycle and messing with the side mirror, which was hopelessly bent.

"Hey, bro, are you okay?" I asked again, hoping he wasn't in shock.

The rider turned his attention towards me and stared at me with a listless gaze. As I stared back, I realized that he was more smashed than I was. This motherfucker was riding a motorcycle and he was completely wasted.

I quickly produced a business card and handed it out the window to him. "Hey, man, this is my card. Call me in the morning and whatever it takes to get your mirror fixed, I'll take care of it. Let's just get home," I told him.

He just stared at me and blinked. He checked back in after what seemed an eternity and handed me a business card. He was a mortgage broker.

"All right, bro, cool. Call me tomorrow," I told him.

I pulled off from the light, leaving the man sitting at the intersection. I watched in my rearview mirror as he gassed the bike and took off, making a right turn. He never said a word to me. He also never called. I do hope he made it home. Las Vegas is probably the only place in the world where you can get into a drunk-driving accident with someone who is more drunk than you.

It was a big weekend—a diminutive member of rock royalty was set to begin his residency at another casino-hotel, and we were hosting the after-party. Events like this always took a great deal of planning to preserve the privacy and level of service that celebs had come to expect. Since we were great in these respects, we'd become a destination for celebs.

This guest had private security who came in advance to coordinate. We had a private room set aside at his request, and another smaller room was prepared to receive him and his wife. It all had to be meticulously planned, right down to the special bottle of port that was to be popped and ready in the smaller room. He had a star-studded guest list and was very particular on how they were to enter. We were also instructed that he didn't like to be looked in the eye. That's celebrity for you.

Events like this, while they helped us maintain a high profile and kept us aloft in the increasingly competitive Las Vegas nightclub market, proved to be problematic when it came to making money. Celebs are notoriously cheap. Clubs typically comp their entire bill just for them to appear, and save for the Pop Princess' security guard handing me three grand, I never received tips from any of them. I once had to shut down the club and turn the lights up on an alliterative comedy movie superstar because he had a brick of cash out and refused to take care of anyone. The planning and handling that went into getting them into the club and managing them while they were there pretty much put a damper on making any other money.

Everything was ready and our guest was set to arrive when Greasy walked up to me as I was making my final checks.

"Hank, I got to hit the parking garage and pick up our package." He was referring to our cocaine delivery for the weekend.

"Seriously, Greasy? They're due any second and you're supposed to be working the door for this thing," I said.

"You want to get paid or not? We ain't going to make any dough off this clown anyway," Greasy said, stating what I already knew to be true.

This still created a giant pain in my ass. The management expected the handling of these things to go smoothly. You botch something for someone as high-maintenance as the coiffed little man we were set to receive and you could guarantee he wouldn't return. Clubs kill for high-profile celebs and this cat was stratospheric in terms of exposure. I was supposed to be concentrating on not looking him in the eye, and now I was going to be a man down when they arrived.

"Fine, I'll bring him up. Go ahead. Go get our package. Then hustle your ass back up here and get on the door to his room," I said.

Greasy took off for the parking garage and less than a minute later, the call came from Pauly: "They're being dropped out front."

I hopped on the elevator and headed downstairs. My timing was perfect, as I saw his lead security guard walking at the head of a phalanx of large bodies. I opened the rope and they rushed past me and into the waiting elevator. I climbed on behind them and hit the button.

With all the bodies packed in the elevator, our guest of honor was hard to see. Finally, one of the guards shifted on his feet and I spotted him leaning in the corner next to his wife. *Man, he's smaller than I imagined,* I couldn't help thinking to myself. I was staring when the little man looked up and right at me. I'd be goddamned if I was going to avert my eyes, and he didn't seem to give two shits about the fact that I was looking right at him. Who knows if this was a baseless legend that followed him around? Such is the mystique around celebrity.

We got off the elevator and I led them to the hallway, where his security took him the rest of the way to the larger reception room. I closed the small set of doors leading down the hall and his lead guard returned with the guest list.

"He's asked that you don't let anyone back until I come and tell you to. He wants to DJ a little bit before they arrive," he said.

I looked at the guest list and the names on it gave me pause. Being the guy telling music industry award winners and rock legends that they couldn't get in somewhere is not the place you want to find yourself.

"It's whatever he needs. I'll hold the door as long as he wants," I said. There was nothing else to be said. I was not in the position to make the call and ultimately, it was his decision. Still, it sucked. The big-time guests on his list—they weren't going to blame the eccentricity of our guest of honor—they were going to blame me and therefore the club I worked for. The potential for flaring tempers and bad publicity was all too real. I found myself wishing Greasy would hurry up and get back so he could man his position.

I heard the music fire up from the back room as our guest of honor started spinning. I listened for awhile, realizing he was better than a lot of DJs I'd heard. But I guess when your life is music, your talent stretches beyond the obvious.

Greasy finally arrived, a bit more wild-eyed than when he left. I could tell he had tasted the product.

"Really, motherfucker?" I said.

Greasy just smiled sheepishly. "I had to make sure it was real."

This statement was pure bullshit, as we had been dealing with this guy forever and we sold plenty for him.

"Just get your ass on the door. Here's the list. No one comes back until they tell you. I'm going to tell them about the switch on the door," I said.

Greasy took his place at the door and I headed down to talk to our guest's lead security. I entered the room, which contained our guest of honor, his wife, his manager, six security guards, and our bartender. The guest of honor was DJing and no one was dancing. Everyone stood by as if they were awaiting the next order.

In a surreal turn and as if on cue, his wife started twirling about in the middle of the room. *Their home life has to be fucking weird,* I thought as I approached his security.

"I've got to run the room," I said, "but I've put my guy Greasy on the door, so you're in good hands. Just have him call me if you need anything he can't handle."

We shook hands and I headed back into the hall.

The door was unmanned and Greasy was nowhere in sight. The list I gave him, slid into a crack in the wood trim, flittered lightly in the breeze of the AC.

"God damn, Greasy," I muttered under my breath as I headed up to take command of the door. As I did, I passed the smaller private room set aside to receive our guest of honor and his wife, the one with the special bottle of port. In the room, I saw Greasy with the port wine tipped up, and he was drinking directly from bottle.

"What the fuck are you doing, dude?" I hissed, trying not to alert anyone else.

Surprised by my entrance, Greasy jumped and some of the port escaped his mouth and spilled onto the table. "What, man? I need a drink. This coke got me in the upper room. I need a little comedown," he told me. Greasy obviously didn't care that this bottle had been specially ordered, corked, and set aside for our guest.

"Stop drinking his shit. Put the cork back in, clean that shit up, and get your ass back on the door. Quit fucking around," I said.

The potential for a major incident was gigantic. If anyone on our guest of honor's team caught Greasy lipping his special bottle before he and the wife sat down to enjoy it, it would be a black eye on the club. Luckily, it was me who caught him. Greasy did what I told him and our guest of honor was none the wiser when he and his wife retired from their star-studded party to enjoy a nice glass of port as a nightcap.

This wasn't the only time shit got pulled on celebrities—they were fair game, too. We threw out a famous comedian's sidekick for being a habitual line-stepper when it came to smoking weed. I watched as Karim served a famous poker player a $13,000 bottle of super premium cognac that was filled with regular cognac ... twice. One of our guys manhandled a guy who starred in some of my favorite family shows as a kid. The thing was, he let him back in the club because he hadn't realized who he was.

Celebrity encounters weren't all about us getting over and acting a fool without them knowing. Some were a learning experience. Most people have a fascination with celebrities, only to have it knocked down a peg when they finally get to meet or see them. The real thing seldom lives up to the oft-retouched media image. I learned this one night when a Hollywood starlet came up with a famous magician. The magician was flexing his pecs and acting like a jackass so much so that I couldn't avert my eyes, until our starlet finally removed her mask and her skin was terrible. But one night, an award-winning actress was having drinks with her friends in one of our private rooms and I found myself hoping to see her.

It might have been because I loved her movies or it could have been because she was America's sweetheart at the time. No matter the reason, I couldn't very well intrude on their private party, and stars usually kept to themselves. My chances of seeing her were slim. But as fate would have it, I would get my chance. I was at the entrance of the bar when she came down from the private rooms. She was wearing a hat and probably not wanting to be noticed; she kept her eyes low as she made her way through the bar.

I found myself staring at her as she approached. I wanted to catch a glimpse of her to see if the real thing measured up. As she got to within three feet of me, she looked up right into my face, made eye contact, and smiled. I'm guessing she felt my stare. I'm certain she was used to that sort of thing. The fact that she looked right at me and that she was every bit as beautiful in person as she was on the big screen had me feeling like a ten-year-old boy. My eyes darted nervously down as I immediately felt like I was in grade school again. She made me, the thick-necked tough guy who would say anything to anyone, walk the line immediately, all five-foot-one of her. One look was all I needed to be smitten, and I'm still a fan of hers to this day.

Other celebrity encounters were benign and some were merely socially interesting. I watched as a famous tennis player and her singer boyfriend had their first married fight, months before it came out in the tabloids that they were married. I sent a chick to broken-promise land when I took hundreds of dollars from her to let her sneak into a rock star's private party, only to have to throw her out seconds later when she immediately made herself a nuisance. We all got to see real power as the head of an automotive industry giant told America's favorite spy to smoke his cigar outside. Celebs are certainly a different breed and Las Vegas will continue to be their playground. If you meet one, just don't bow down all the way.

While the recklessness and risk-taking was at an all-time high outside of work, once we clocked in, the team moved like a well-oiled, precision machine. Shakedowns were a regular occurrence and a major source of income for us. Whenever we caught someone doing drugs or even in possession of narcotics, we went into our routine. I was normally the bad cop, the setup man. By the time I'd finished building them up to the fact that they were going to jail, they would do nearly anything. I walked out and the good cop walked in. This was usually Black Hank or Greasy. Both had an easygoing way, and by the time they were finished, the money was in hand, followed by a bunch of apologies and thanks from the guest.

One night, we'd been summoned to the bathroom by Teague. Two men were in a stall and the sniffles followed by witless banter were echoing off the walls. We waited until one of them opened the door and we pulled them quick. I walked in front of them with the smug satisfaction of someone about to get paid for doing nothing. Black Hank followed behind. We entered one of the private rooms off the hall.

"IDs, gentlemen," I told them.

The men produced their identification—one of them was from Cali and the other was from Washington.

"Where's the coke?" I asked. There was no reason to waste time. Their sniffing could almost be heard in the lounge.

"We don't have any coke," came the weak protest.

"Look, I don't care who has it. One of you can go to jail or both of you can. It doesn't matter to me."

I fake called for detail. Neither man flinched.

"Look, guys, make it easy on you. Do we really need to involve Metro and make trouble for everyone?" I asked.

Still, the men were not swayed. They were definitely doing coke. I'd heard them. I was sure of this. I knew they didn't flush it. They had to have it on them.

"Turn out your pockets, gentlemen. Do it now."

I was entering new territory here. We were certainly not allowed to force people to turn out their pockets. Search and seizure were certainly in the realm of the police, but even then, it was only permissible under circumstance. But most people in an authority/subordinate situation react as they are taught, and these men willingly complied. They rabbit-eared their pants pockets and I reached in their back pockets myself. No coke meant no payoff for us.

"Get 'em the hell out of here," I said.

Black Hank escorted the men toward the front door.

I went over the scenario in my head while I walked the hall. I was convinced they'd been doing coke. My gut told me so. They moved like cokeheads and there were only seconds in which they could have freed themselves of any evidence. I retraced our steps and cursed myself for walking in front of them. My smugness had probably cost us money. My gut proved right as I pulled back one of the double doors in the hallway. Behind the door on the ground was a fat baggy of coke all twisted up and tied off. I picked it up and hefted it in my hand. It felt like it was around two grams. It wasn't a few hundred dollars, but since we used coke all the time, free product was never a bad thing. I dropped the baggie in my shirt pocket and made a call over the radio: "Greasy to the old managers' office." We needed to taste the product.

I know a certain hypocrisy exists in being an avid user of cocaine and shaking people down for the same thing. I'm sure I've shaken people down while I was high. It happened so frequently, it would be impossible for me not to have been. But the club life is full of contradictions. We want everyone to buy bottle after bottle, but don't drink too much. Don't let in underage people, but let's not ID the young girls who are coming in with that roller. Don't take money, but everyone does. You learn to live with the compromise, and incrementally, each one gets easier and easier.

One night, Black Hank called me over the radio. He had been watching one of our VIP hosts enter and leave one of the adjoining private rooms. It was Black Hank's job to watch the room and be abreast of who people were. He knew that the party in the private room was a special client of the VIP host due to the amount of time the host had been spending in the room. He also had a hunch that the VIP host's comings and goings were tied to drugs. By the time he radioed me, he had confirmed this hunch by peeking through the curtain and watching as the group snorted coke.

"They're in there doing it. The dude in the yellow shirt is in charge of the party," Black Hank told me.

"You ready to get paid?" I asked him.

Black Hank flashed his trademark smirk and I knew he was down. I pulled open the curtain and Black Hank followed me inside. There were about a half-dozen men and a couple of younger women in the room.

"Gentlemen, we have a problem. We cannot allow the use of narcotics in our nightclub," I said.

The women beat a hasty line to the door and we let them pass—fewer witnesses. The man in the yellow shirt tried the same, and I extended an arm to keep him from passing.

"Hold on. No one is going anywhere until we ascertain who is holding the cocaine. Then that person gets to talk to Metro," I told him.

"What is Metro?" Yellow Shirt asked in a distinctly British accent.

"Metro is the Las Vegas Metropolitan Police Department. Clark County has a zero-tolerance drug policy, and that means someone gets to leave in handcuffs."

The spiel was always the same, and it fell out of my mouth in such a believable cadence that you could feel the tension rise with every word. Always looking to up the ante, I added a twist: "Cocaine possession is a felony, gentleman. That's bad news for you guys, being from out of the country and all. I figure the worst that could happen is deportation."

Yellow Shirt's face went pale at this. Well, at least we knew who was holding the coke now. I put in a fake call for "detail" and stepped just outside the curtain so Black Hank could work his magic. The VIP host hurried up to the curtain; apparently, the girls were hookers he'd put on the men, and they went to get him when they saw the heat they were catching. Everybody was just looking to get over any way they could.

"What's going on?" the host asked.

"Your guys were doing cocaine," I told him.

"Come on. Just let me talk to them," he said as he tried to push past me into the room. I stepped in front of him. "They said you sold it to them," I said, playing off Black Hank's hunch that the host was involved.

The host's body slackened and I knew he did sell it to them.

I don't normally play people that I like, but the host was fucking with our money. He was getting paid from his guys, the hookers, and the coke sale without sharing any of the revenue. The fact that he was doing this on our watch was unacceptable.

"Look, bro, I don't want to make this any louder than I have to, but this sort of thing can get us fucked up. Just let us do our thing and get them out of here discretely. How's that sound?" I asked.

The host finally buckled and walked away. He knew that we had the authority to get him fucked up in more ways than one. I stepped back inside. The Brits were arguing over whether or not to pay.

"What's the problem?" I asked Black Hank.

"Yellow Shirt wants to pay, but his friend is drunk and thinks he's tough. He don't want him to pay and refuses to go get the cash."

I needed to hurry this process. "We've got to get this done. Too many people involved already," I told him. I stepped forward. "Fuck it, guys—don't worry about it. Black Hank, go ahead and escort the rest of these gentlemen to the elevator. I'll wait with our friend until Metro arrives," I said loud enough for everyone to hear.

With the only option other than jail being taken off the table, Yellow Shirt asserted his authority.

"GO GET THE FUCKING MONEY NOW," he yelled at his friend, who tucked his tail and headed downstairs to retrieve our cash.

The shakedown netted us a quick seven hundred. At the end of the night, the VIP host came to me and tried to smooth things over.

"You know I like all you guys and I wouldn't do anything to cause a problem," he told me. He was almost contrite, and VIP hosts are NEVER contrite, especially with security. He pulled out a wad of cash and leafed off a number of hundreds. He pressed them into my hand. "This is for you and the guys. For the trouble, I mean," he said.

I failed to close my hand around the money, letting him dangle with the idea that he couldn't trust me, and he'd always have to watch his step around my team. I stared at him for a moment. He was twisting inside. If security wasn't on his side, his life had just gotten a whole lot harder, and he knew this. Finally, I let him off the hook.

"We know how to play the game, man. Don't worry about us," I said as I took his cash. I didn't bother telling him that security sees everything—he already knew.

174

Not all of the relationships I formed in the club were predatory and superficial. While most of the people met in the club were acquaintances born out of the artificial club life, a few were nice and genuinely interesting. Motorcycle Ken was one of them. I met Ken when I was first working the pay line at the club. He would come in for the Sunday-night party and from our first meeting he was cool. He had an accent that I mistook for Southern, though he was actually from North Carolina. He was a blue-collar guy and though comps were generally reserved for the rich and famous or those who were connected, I still took care of him and his friends when they came to the club.

I took care of him because he was likeable and real, two qualities in short supply in Las Vegas. When I went upstairs, he made that his new hangout and would bring in his friends who were also riders. They dressed in motorcycle gear, and though one would think they were out of place in a club like ours, the novelty of having people from the motorcycle culture added another facet of cool to the room. I would comp their beers and he always "took care of security," even if it was just the odd twenty or forty bucks. From time to time we would hang out after work and Ken would hang as well. One such evening, Johnny and I watched as chicks were coming up to him and his rider friends and chatting them up. Time after time, the women would walk away, never to return.

When Motorcycle Ken was left by himself at the end of the night, Johnny and I took him along for our customary post-work mayhem session. We vowed that night to get him laid. Colette met us downstairs—she had begun working more frequently at our casino in particular and always found herself with nothing to do around the time we were getting off work. We all sat down to have a drink at the casino bar. We all surveyed the bar and finally spotted two above average girls who weren't prostitutes and decided they were the ones to hit up. He invited them over for a drink and they accepted.

Colette, being as intuitive as a woman with her life experience would be, made the first move. She immediately began putting the girls at ease. She knew just how to speak, just what to say and when, all the time leading the conversation toward the goal of getting one or both of the women interested in Motorcycle Ken.

Motorcycle Ken verbally blundered again and again. Each time, the women turned away to talk with Colette or me or Johnny, anyone one but Motorcycle Ken. It was like a verbal chess match, with all of us steering the girls' interest back to him. I found myself wondering if it was the liquor or just his personality that rubbed girls the wrong way. Johnny and I ordered a couple of rounds of shots to further loosen the girls' grip on reality.

Finally, the booze and psychobabble took hold and one of the girls became mesmerized by Motorcycle Ken. Johnny and I smiled at one another and then took over the job of distracting her friend. Aided by Colette, this was the simplest of tasks. Most girls felt more comfortable around men when they were already in the company of a woman. I sensed Colette was enjoying the opportunity to "turn one of these girls out" for the benefit of Motorcycle Ken. When the girl sat on Ken's lap, we knew the deal was all but sealed. Another round of shots hit the table to celebrate a job well done. We clinked our glasses and then, to our horror, Motorcycle Ken gave a toast.

"Tonight was awesome, guys. You know, usually, I'm like pussy repellant. But you guys set me up nice on this one," he blurted out before anyone could stop him.

In one statement, all of our hard work came crashing down around us. All the drinks we bought. All the verbal wordplay went for naught. Motorcycle Ken had stripped bare the reason for our interest in the girls. All but the dumbest girl who's told that her only value is that of a mattress-back wouldn't be offended.

The women put down their drinks and stormed off. Johnny and I took our shots, then chased them with the shots left by the girls. We jumped on Motorcycle Ken, who was grinning sheepishly, as though he'd proven himself right and therefore kept some measure of pride. Except pride and pussy have nothing to do with each other.

Later that week, the boss had called me into a meeting. It seemed that the casino had gotten a complaint from a girl who had been staying in the hotel with some friends of hers. She had been looking for one of her friends when she saw her disappear into a side room with a security guard, or at least someone in a suit. When she tried to open the door, it was locked. She went off in search of her other friends and when she came back, the girl she was looking for had reappeared, looking a bit disheveled and definitely worse for wear.

The story was that the girl questioned her raggedy friend at length, and after a time, she disclosed that she had in fact had sex with the security guard while another one watched. The raggedy exhibitionist chick wasn't even the one who lodged the complaint—it was the friend, who was apparently trying to preserve the raggedy chick's virtue. So for what was otherwise consensual sex, the bosses wanted me to put the team on notice to keep the shit above board and stop taking chicks off into side rooms. Since that wasn't my thing, it wasn't a big deal for me. It took time away from making money and could be potentially hazardous for the other guys if I wasn't available and some shit went down. Plus, I was the man in charge and had to be available to get the whole story straight if something were to go down. I couldn't exactly do that if I was getting a blowjob in the broom closet.

But I hated to begrudge the other guys an opportunity to steal a nobber or quick bang on the side if that was their thing. I know the management was concerned with the potential for a sexual-assault situation and the accompanying bad press. But the reality of that was that there was never any need to take it that route. On any given night, there were scores of females just waiting to bang a bouncer, whether that was at their house, in a hotel room, or in the goddamn broom closet. The idea that one would have to strong-arm any woman was ludicrous.

Now, sure, the guys in question shouldn't have been doing that shit on the clock. They were at work and that was not what they were being paid for, banging out chicks in broom closets or side rooms while other guys watched. But on the scale of bad shit we were doing in the club, this scored very low.

Still, I had to do my due diligence and take it to the guys. Of course they all feigned ignorance. But I knew that Black Hank and Greasy both had the proclivity to get at girls and whisk them away. Black Hank wasn't ashamed of the way he did his business; in fact, he was proud of being a dog. But Greasy was a more undercover-type dude. One day, while moving chairs, we found a pair of panties in one of the storage rooms on the roof. They had been ripped off and discarded, left there for us to discover. It was only later, while he was drunk, that Greasy told me how he had taken this broad he'd always wanted to have a shot at into the room and she had jumped on top of him in a chair.

"I ripped them shits right off, Hank. Riiiiipppped 'em right off," he said.

Of course Greasy was also a hypochondriac, and every time he had sex without a condom, which was a lot, he thought he'd contracted AIDS or hepatitis. Every time he did this, we were his confession booth.

"I know I got something this time," he'd say. "The Lord is going to strike me down this time. I just know it. I can't keep doing this," he'd tell us.

Still, that didn't stop him from getting into situations like the one I just described time and again. I left the meeting with the boss and I did my job, giving all my guys a warning. But I knew it wouldn't take. I was surrounded by alphas who followed my lead because I'd been there the longest and put them on. But as far as taking orders, that just wasn't going to happen. Alphas don't take orders.

The club was dialed in, and except for the consensual-sex complaint, things were running smoothly. Our daily life was a party with very little worry. Our only concerns were how to make a buck and where our next buzz was coming from. In the club life, there is no shortage of solutions to either of these dilemmas. We only worked four days a week and this left plenty of off time for leisure pursuits, like drinking, lifting weights, and travel for the purpose of drug smuggling.

We decided to go back down to Tijuana. Johnny and I had been cycling on steroids since we'd gotten back. I was initially turned off to the idea by an aversion to stabbing myself with a needle, and Johnny had to help me out by doing the deed for me. But once I saw that I could become a giant, no-neck, two-hundred-sixty-five-pound beast who could bench-press a dump truck and pretty much overwhelm any challenger, my reservation about needles faded.

I wasn't noticing any ill effects, save for one instance of "roid rage" in which I told a woman that I would kill her after she flipped me the bird. She was in the wrong to begin with, as she had mistaken me for some asshole who had honked his horn at her. The snap had felt like an out-of-body experience. I'm usually very calm, and it takes a lot to get me boiling over. I soon tied this to Deca 300, as it was the newest in a cocktail of steroids that I took twice a week.

The hunger for more took over and Johnny had filled my head with dreams of adding Anadrol and Winstrol into the mix. We headed out from Vegas with one planned stop in California to meet Johnny's boy, Flanagan. He was the one who had set us up in TJ in the first place. He had the day off and was going to accompany us along with his girlfriend, Jerri. Flanagan was happy to go down with us, as he had business with his man, Berto. Berto owned a number of pharmacies, including our steroid superstore. Flanagan was heading down with a load of Oxy-Contin and was set to hand it off to Berto. Apparently, the market for Oxys in Mexico was better than in the U.S.

We set out early in the morning and tried to keep up with Flanagan and his lead foot. We stopped for gas and as Johnny and I emerged from the station, we saw Flanagan screaming at a guy who was sitting in his car near the gas pump. The guy looked genuinely frightened as Flanagan pounded on the roof of his vehicle and screamed obscenities. When Johnny and I rolled up to flank Flanagan, the guy nearly shit his pants. He barely waited until Flanagan was out of the way before he hit the gas, missing him by the smallest of margins as he screeched out of the station.

Me: "What the fuck happened?"

Johnny: "Who was that guy?"

Flanagan: "Some fucking cunt that tried to cut this lady off at the pump."

Flanagan pointed to a lady parked next to the pump—she had just collected herself enough to actually pump gas. She looked petrified, uncertain as to what she should make of the two guys with cartoon muscles and shaved heads who had just joined the crazy fuck with the accent who was threatening to kill some guy. She smiled weakly and mouthed the words "Thank you" to Flanagan.

Since we'd just narrowly avoided beating the shit out of some oblivious square at the gas station, I knew we were in for a fun day. Just a short while later, we were involved in a car chase when two Asians in a tricked-out import sped after Flanagan after he cut them off. Whether Flanagan cut them off on purpose or by accident didn't really enter the equation for Johnny and I. Two men were chasing friends of ours and felt they had the upper hand because Jerri was a woman. When we finally caught up to them, Jerri got their attention and simply pointed so the Asians could look behind them. Their anger turned to fear when they saw how close I was to their car and that Johnny was hanging out the passenger window screaming for blood. This was enough to dissuade the men from chasing Flanagan and Jerri any longer. We hadn't even made it to Mexico yet and we'd been involved in two altercations while transporting drugs.

We finally pulled across the border and, oddly, I felt safer than I had in America. At least we could drop off the drugs, only to pick up some more and do it all over again, this time in reverse. Flanagan took a back way and parked us next to a weird market/bazaar-type place. He stepped out of his car and flagged down a Mexican with a spray bottle and a handful of rags. He handed him ten dollars and told him to wash both cars. As we made our way through the winding corridors of the bazaar, Flanagan explained that the Mexican would have both cars sparkling by the time we got back. He would also wait by them and ensure their security because he was hoping for a payoff when we got back.

We walked for what felt like forever through the bazaar, taking twists and turns. Flanagan was giving us a TJ education and the lesson was simple: take the back way in and walk through to shake anyone who could be following. He also explained the way the police worked. The brown uniforms could be counted on to be mostly crooked—city cops on the take and narco employees. The darker-uniformed officers were for the most part straight-up cops—federal police who would break your ass if they caught you working. We popped out of the bazaar and onto the street. A couple of turns and we were walking into our steroid spot.

"Como está, Tio?" Flanagan greeted the man behind the counter.

Tio broke into a wide smile and hugged Flanagan. Then Tio called into the back room and a small man in a black designer pullover stepped out with an even bigger smile—this was Berto. Flanagan introduced us to Berto and he shook my hand with all the vigor of someone genuinely pleased to meet you.

Though it was never confirmed, I was convinced at first meeting that Berto was big-time cartel. You don't amass the holdings he had in a Mexican border town without being connected. I was excited because we were in tight since Flanagan had come down and made the introduction to Berto in person. Now we were cartel connected—that meant we could get work any time, and white faces that are willing to work in narco are priceless.

For all the we-don't-profile talk that comes out of law-enforcement circles, it was certainly easy for guys who looked like us to get by without so much as a couple of routine questions. It didn't hurt that we looked like we were in the military, either. It was different on the Mexican side, though. The profiling worked against us. The authorities knew why we were down there, and it was most likely because we were up to no good. That was why we got shaken down the first time. Nobody was going to raise a stink if they were committing crimes. It was the same laws that governed the nightclub shakedowns we were notorious for.

Now we could get anything we wanted, any time we wanted. So Johnny and I shopped like kids in a candy store while Flanagan stepped into the back room to handle his business with Berto. The transactions were short and sweet and Berto and Tio bid us a sincere farewell as we left. Berto told us to come back with or without Flanagan and that we were welcome any time.

We took it across the street and sat down for lunch. After more than a few Coronas, we took the winding path back through the bazaar and reached the cars, which were still be attended by our Mexican car attendant, and another ten-dollar bill sent him away all smiles. We got in line to head back across the border and the mood was relaxed. Johnny wasn't showing any sign of nerves—the beers were working on him. I didn't have nerves because I just didn't care.

First off, in order to be nervous, you have to think you're doing something wrong, which I did not. The hypocrisy with which the people who make the laws operate was enough for me to justify what

I was doing. Sure, there would be consequences if I got caught, but for me, that was part of the juice. Was I better than they were today? Too many people set out to do wrong and then when they get caught, they're sorry. Well, fuck that.

Smuggling dope isn't tourist shit. It's one of the few authentic experiences that money can't buy. Rich folks go deep-sea fishing and trekking through the Himalayas and shit like that. But anyone with dough can do those things. Hell, if you're rich enough, you could probably get a Sherpa to carry your ass up the mountain. But bouncing the border with your car full of illegal drugs and putting your future life on the line is as close as you can get in terms of purity of experience. No amount of money can give you that. No one can do it for you. The price of admission is having the stones to pull it off, and the rush of a successful crossing is undeniably amazing. The juice is in the gamble.

We headed back to California with only a cursory few questions and a glance at our identification at the border. When we reached Flanagan's house, he immediately hopped on the phone and started pushing juice. Johnny and I were going to head home but the decision to stay the night came when the painkillers and Xanax came out. After washing a few down with a number of beers, I drifted off into a contented sleep on the couch.

After returning from Tijuana with a full complement of juice, we were looking to unload and make some quick cash. Johnny had people in Arizona who were always looking. We bagged the juice and hit the road for Kingman. Once there, we made a deal with one of his boys for a quick buck and headed back home. We came across the river through Bullhead City and decided to stop for dinner in Laughlin. We stopped at the brewery in a casino and had a couple of steaks and a few beers. We weren't ready to go home just yet and decided to head for the arcade to play some video games. Just as we arrived, the young attendant was pulling down the aluminum gate.

He refused to take money to keep it open and we were left to hit the casino floor. We stopped to play roulette and in true cosmic fashion the cocktail waitress seemed to be laying in wait for us. We hadn't even been issued chips when she sidled up to the table and asked us if we needed a drink.

"Shot of tequila and a beer," Johnny blurted out reflexively.

"Sure, me, too. I guess we're staying here tonight?" I asked.

"Yeah, we'll just get a room up the block," Johnny replied.

We played roulette, winning some cash that was quickly turned into a few rounds at the bar.

Upon our arrival at hotel up the street, I dropped my truck with the valet and grabbed our only piece of luggage, a shoulder bag that held the steroids. We checked in, dropped the bag in the room, and headed for the bar. After a couple rounds at the hotel bar, we decided we'd head back up the block to play poker. Johnny had never played and after a brief explanation, he was ready to get in the game. We took a taxi to one of the run-down casinos and headed for the poker room. Their only game was 4-8 limit, which was sparsely populated, and we were seated immediately.

We called for the cocktail waitress and ordered another round. A large tip upon her return kept her lurking around our table and we gathered a good head of steam very quickly. We were well into the evening when a thin, stringy-haired white male sat down. Think Jesus if he were addicted to meth. This guy thought he was a pro and took a great amount of time examining the board and his hole cards and took an equal amount of time deciding whether he should bet, fold, or raise. While this is an annoying trait in a player, it was his money and he should be allowed to take a reasonable amount of time to make a decision.

At one point, Johnny was excited about his hole cards and raised out of turn. While this is a breach of etiquette in the world of poker, it's certainly not a crime. Meth Jesus acted as though it were punishable by death. He was wound up and confronted Johnny, who was confused, as he didn't know he'd done anything wrong. I explained to Meth Jesus that he was a rookie and didn't know the etiquette.

"Maybe you should teach him before you take him to play," he said.

This was a shitty comment and his tone was just as shitty. Being the cooler head, I apologized to Meth Jesus and explained to Johnny that he had to bet in turn.

We ordered some more drinks and all was good until Meth Jesus opened his mouth again to call Johnny a rookie. Now, since I was down with Johnny, I could call him a rookie—it was me just stating a fact, and there was no malice when it came from me. But Meth Jesus used the word like a dagger and his tone just pissed Johnny off.

"You just can't let it go, can you? I guess I'll just have to kick your ass," Johnny told him.

Meth Jesus weakly called for the floor, aka the poker room boss, and I immediately started the damage control.

"Did he threaten another player?" the floor asked me.

"Yeah, he did, but only after he made another comment about a dead issue. Just tell him to leave it alone and things will be fine," I implored him.

Thankfully, he saw the reason in this and let us off with a warning. He left and I addressed the table.

"Look, fellas, we just came out from Vegas to blow off a little steam. We work security out there and just came here to get drunk and lose some money. Can we do that?" I asked.

The table at-large responded positively because we livened up their rock-dead game with laughs and drinks, but Meth Jesus sat in the seat just simmering. The confrontation really soured Johnny's mood and he upped his drinking. I solidified my play and my stack grew to three times its original size.

What happened next was a perfect storm of events. The waitress, in taking advantage of the drunken revelry to pad her wallet, brought drinks at a blistering pace. I was drunk. Johnny was smashed and pissed off. Then Meth Jesus opened his mouth.

I will admit I don't even remember the comment he made, but it was the last straw.

I looked at Meth Jesus. "You just couldn't resist, could you?" Then I turned to the dealer. "You better call security." Then finally, I addressed Johnny. "Fuck this dude up. I'll hold off security."

The card room at this particular casino bottlenecked at the entrance because it was surrounded by a wooden fence of sorts. You couldn't go under the fence, only over, and the only clear way in was the four-foot-wide break. I imagined that I could hold off security long enough for Johnny to truly hurt Meth Jesus. The late-night security staff that I had seen earlier was a collection of old men. It was also quite possible that they didn't have the manpower at that hour to control five hundred pounds of drunk, pissed-off, steroid-rage-filled white boy.

"Don't do this, fellas," the dealer said as he tried to calm the situation.

Meth Jesus realized he was in trouble and was now facing serious bodily harm. He immediately backtracked. "I'm sorry. I'm really sorry. So you guys are from Vegas?" he said. The pompous, shitty tone had been replaced by real fear.

This placated Johnny enough, and since we were both blind drunk while nearly touching off a brawl, we decided to call it a night. We took a taxi back to our hotel and crashed. We both woke the next morning with serious hangovers.

We checked out late and jumped in the truck. I pulled out and immediately pulled back into the valet circle, as we had forgotten our only piece of luggage, the bag with enough junk in it to get us both matching sets of handcuffs. Johnny hustled to the room and retrieved the bag while I waited in the parking lot.

We hit the road and I was driving as fast as possible. My hangover was of the tremendous, skull-splitting variety and I just wanted to get home. We stopped for gas and mulled over getting a couple deuce-deuces of Heineken for the road. For reasons unknown, we decided against this and were back on the road.

We had nearly reached the junction for the 95 when I saw a Nevada Highway Patrol car pull out from behind a guardrail. I attempted to slow down as much as possible, as I now realized I was speeding in excess of one hundred miles an hour. The officer hit his lights and just pointed at me to pull over. He walked up to the passenger side.

"You know why I'm pulling you over?" he asked.

"Yes, sir. I was speeding," I answered.

"The plane clocked you at 103. What, do you have a hemi in this thing?" he asked.

"No, sir. You really think I need one?"

He got a good laugh at this and that was just how I wanted things. There was a bag of steroids just sitting on the seat between Johnny and I. It wouldn't even take a thorough search of the truck to ensure us a trip to jail.

He took my documents and returned a short time later with a ticket. "You guys drive safe, now," he said.

The decision not to get beers during our gas stop had proven to be one of the best decisions ever. If we'd had the open containers, we would have been cited. This would have resulted in a vehicle search and additional felony charges for the possession of steroids. Again, I ask: *Dumb luck or divine providence?*

After our busy weekend, it was back to work, and on Saturday night, we were slammed. The lounge was bursting at the seams and I was in my usual spot on the perch overlooking the mass of people. Black Hank was standing next to me when I got a signal from one of the bartenders. This usually meant some drunk or rude guest giving the bartender or another guest a ration of shit. We pushed through the crowd and met the bartender in the service well.

"What's going on?" I asked.

"This big guy on the other side of the pillar is holding his ground at the bar. He's not letting anyone else to the bar in that spot," he told me.

Great, a territorial dickhead. These guys were the worst. They thought they owned the bar or the couch or whatever spot they were standing in at the time. At least we'd get to knock an asshole down a few pegs. Black Hank rounded the pillar first and the bartender pointed out the culprit. It was Dirk Clausen, our two-hundred-eighty-pound defensive lineman with a penchant for shoving women, the one we'd choked out a number of months prior.

Black Hank stepped in to talk to him. The conversation lasted about fifteen seconds, until Black Hank withdrew and that familiar smile crossed his face. "He said he ain't leaving," Black Hank told me.

The lounge was packed with guests, and the last thing we wanted was a physical confrontation with five very large people battling for supremacy. I stepped in to talk to Dirk.

"Look, Dirk, we've already been down this road," I told him.

You could almost see the recognition of what happened last time cross his face. He complied and calmly walked to the elevator. A buddy of his wearing a ridiculous fedora followed close behind, and he was running his mouth the whole way. We all got on the elevator and Greasy followed us. The fedora talked shit for the entire elevator ride, while Dirk remained agitated. Black Hank called Dirk out for staring at him.

"You look like you still want to do something. Well, go ahead," Black Hank told him.

Normally, you wouldn't taunt someone who was leaving voluntarily. But the clown in the fedora was exacerbating the situation by talking shit and trying to get a rise out all of us. The fedora took Black Hank's challenge of Dirk personally. Even though he was the smallest guy on the elevator, he stepped between Dirk and Black Hank. I put myself between him and Black Hank, and this primed the powder keg. Luckily, the elevator door opened just in time.

The fedora had begun to step off when he threw a half-hearted punch that glanced off my chest. I set upon him and Greasy followed suit. We slammed him onto the bench in the entryway.

"Calm down. Quit struggling," I told him.

He relaxed, apparently satisfied that he had gotten his shot in.

"We're going to stand you up, and when we do, do not start fighting us. You understand?"

He nodded affirmatively. Greasy held fast to one arm and I, the other. No sooner did we stand him up, then he pushed back against us.

I pulled his arm up to force his head down and Greasy swept his legs out. With no hands to break his fall, his face slammed into the marble. I also felt his arm bend at an unnatural angle.

"Owww," was all he could muster.

"You done now?" I asked.

"Yes," came the meek reply.

Greasy and I stood him up. Greasy held him while I retrieved his stupid hat off the floor. We opened the rope and I smashed the fedora on top of his head and gave him the customary shove into the lobby. The aftermath brought a threat of litigation from the fedora.

Allegedly, we had broken his arm when we slammed him on the marble. He quickly withdrew his claim when it became apparent that he could face assault charges for striking me in the chest. I will give him this—at least he had the balls to take a shot at me. He's only one of two people who ever did.

The demise of Black Hank came much as I thought it would. I warned the guys to stop taking females off into the side rooms. So when Black Hank got busted getting head in the old managers' office, it came as no surprise. To his credit, she was a hot-ass schoolteacher, a local, no less. She had made it obvious that she was available and looking. I had been talking to her earlier in the night and gotten this much from our conversation. Her breath was rank, though.

Black Hank at least attempted to hide his indiscretion. He had locked the door to the old managers' office, which had become a storage area for the barbacks. It was never locked unless someone was doing something that they didn't want anyone else being privy to.

One of the barbacks needed something for the bar and, upon realizing it was locked, summoned Kalil to open the door. When Kalil opened the door and saw Black Hank at attention and the schoolteacher on her knees, that was the end of the line for Black Hank. There was very little that the managers wouldn't overlook or ignore. But blatant disregard for something they'd told us not to do, something that could get the business fucked up, just couldn't be tolerated.

We needed a replacement, and on Johnny's recommendation, I brought up Crow. I called him the knight in shining armor because, compared to us, he was a monk, robes and all. He was intelligent, good looking, and tall. Crow had a calm way about him that comes with being self-assured and not willing to give an inch on your convictions. Good or bad, an alpha is an alpha, and Crow fit in immediately.

After a short training period for Crow, it was time for his initiation party. The training was cursory. Whether or not you could handle a guest or monitor the place was not the truest test of one's qualifications. Whether you could drink till the sun rose was the surest way to gain acceptance to the team.

We all headed to our after-work spot on Sunset. It was a 24-hour bar across from McCarran airport and was our haunt, as it was on the way home for Johnny and me. We proceeded to get mashed up. Johnny's girl, Reagan, who came out to drink with us every once in a while, asked me at one point why we drank the way we did.

"We drink the way we do because we're just out here in the desert waiting to expire," I said.

She was put off by this but it didn't make it any less true.

I had surrounded myself with a bunch of like-minded knuckleheads, a few of them probably crazier than myself. I loved the guys for this. Not everyone was on the same fatalistic track I was, but I sensed that they enjoyed the ride they were on just the same.

We'd been drinking hard since we'd gotten off work, with the most serious drinking coming between the hours of 6:00 and 11:00 a.m. The Ranch was close and I told Crow he could crash there and turn around for his shift at 4:00 p.m. that day. I jumped in my truck and Crow followed me on the short drive up the block. When we arrived, he said I was swerving, coming dangerously close to hitting the curb more than a few times. Then he realized HE was the one swerving, and it just seemed like he was watching me. Truth be told, we were both probably swerving out.

When I got home, I called Colette. I wanted to see her for the obvious reasons, but I also wanted something to drink and we were out at the house. Rather than risk another drunken drive to the store, I asked her to bring something over. I then proceeded to pass out. When Colette finally arrived, Crow answered the door in his tighty-whities and ushered her in. I woke up awhile later, parched and still drunk. I headed down the hallway and went to my room, where Colette was asleep. The look of her naked mocha skin against the white sheets is still etched in my mind. I crawled into bed beside her and went to sleep.

Later that afternoon, I was in the kitchen when JT came out of his room. He asked me who the tall-ass guy who had made an erroneous entrance into his room early that morning was. It turned out that Crow had gone looking for someplace to sleep that wasn't in the common area. He was afraid to sleep in Johnny's bed, as it was often used by Greasy as a smash pad for his side chick. Many were the nights I would listen to Greasy and his side chick in the next room playing out the rape fantasy she was into.

Needless to say, I wouldn't want to sleep in that bed either. Crow was so drunk, he went into the only other room available and that was JT's, where he promptly tried to get into bed with JT. JT liked to keep his business tight and was worried about unfamiliar faces being in such close proximity, so I attempted to put him at ease. That was Crow and he was one of the boys. He was on our side, one of the good guys.

No sooner was Crow in and settled than Cal decided it was time to move on. Cal had recently been the victim of a divorce. His relationship went the same way mine did with Shannon. Cal's wife had made the decision to step out on him, since he wasn't home at night. She did this even though Cal went home every night, didn't drink to excess, and had stayed true to her. To me, it seemed that, unless your significant other worked in the industry, your relationship was most likely doomed. Hell, it was most likely doomed if your significant other did work in the industry. There was just too much temptation, too many pitfalls, too many beautiful people, too much money, too much shallowness.

In the ultimate slap in the face, Cal's punk-ass wife got the house and her lover moved in with her. I helped Cal move into a shit-box apartment on the east side of town. It looked like a reclaimed motel that was being sold as a studio unit. I felt bad for him moving into that situation. Cal was a good dude with a good heart. He was a hard worker and put his family first, over all the club bullshit. Cal was done with the industry and done with Las Vegas. He entered school, trained to be a truck driver, and hit the road. I was sad to see him go.

On Monday night, Johnny was working the lounge in his usual section. This section was adjacent to mine and was one of only three in the lounge. I saw him talking to a couple gentlemen—one white and one black. He was holding a box of mints in his hand and they were obviously discussing the contents. I walked over to find out what was going on. He opened the box and showed me what was inside—right next to the white mints were a dozen little blue pills with neat stars stamped into them.

"Gentlemen, we have a problem. Come here," I told them.

We walked into the hallway that ran behind the lounge and provided a sprawling view of the south Strip. I took another look at the pills, as I wasn't completely sure.

"Is this ecstasy?" I asked.

Their confession was the surest way to hurry along the proceedings.

"Yeah, that's ecstasy," Johnny reassured me in his customary overzealous fashion.

"Thanks, Johnny."

I began the Clark–County-is-a-zero-tolerance-county bit. By the time I finished, the white kid looked petrified. But the black kid piped up, his voice surprisingly calm, with an ice-water accent from across the pond.

"Come on, mate—there's no need to invite the authorities. We can work this out on our own. What's it going to take?" he asked.

I didn't even have to mention a bribe—he offered one up with no coercion.

"How about five hundred?" I said.

The black kid cracked a broad smile. "Come on. I'm a geezer, mate. How about you keep the pills? That's worth at least a few hundred. You make something. We get a break. Everyone makes out," he said.

This kid actually impressed me, and I felt like I was standing in the middle of a Guy Ritchie movie. I smiled when I realized I was talking to the black, British version of myself.

"What do you think, Johnny?" I asked.

"Fuck it. Keep the pills. It didn't cost us shit," he said.

"All right, fellas—you're off the hook. Just keep it cool and enjoy your night," I told them.

"Thanks, gents. You're all right."

The Brit collected his friend, who still had that deer–in–headlights look; after all, they were his pills and therefore his felonies. He had failed to be discreet when taking one, and Johnny had spotted him. The Brits had a good time that night, though. Take it from me—nothing heightens a rush like an escape from trouble.

Johnny and I wound up splitting the pills with Greasy. Crow had no interest in using or even handling drugs.

The next night was a Tuesday, my night off. I was still dealing with insomnia. The only sleep that I could get had to be aided by chemicals—booze or pills—usually both. I was on my way to bed after drinking a number of beers. I wasn't quite there and went looking for a friend to rock me to sleep. I opened the small wooden box that housed my narcotics. There, amongst an assortment of Mexican Valium I'd gotten from Johnny, were four of the tabs of ecstasy we'd taken off the Brits.

I pulled a blue pill from the box, popped it, and washed it down with the last of a beer. I counted up the Valium I had left and realized that I was counting red pills. The Valium Johnny had given me was red.

Now, I had spent some time working as a pharmacy clerk when I was younger, and of all the sleeping pills and painkillers I'd encountered, none of them were ever red. So it was a knee-jerk reaction to take the blue pill. This error in judgment was no doubt aided by the fact that I was liquor-sharp.

At any rate, I realized that sleep wasn't going to be found. I was flying a solo mission on ecstasy, a drug I hadn't taken in years. It was good fun, as ecstasy can be, and when the first pill wore off, I found myself in familiar territory with a waning buzz. I took another pill and snorted the last two. Ecstasy really isn't a solo drug, and most of the time I was rolling was spent furiously masturbating. I heard someone arrive at the house around eight in the morning. I peeked out my door to see who it was.

Johnny stepped to the end of the hall and saw me. "What are you doing?" he asked.

"What are you doing?" I asked back.

He smiled because my answer meant only one thing.

"What the fuck are you on?"

I told him how I'd accidentally taken the blue pill and he could only shake his head. Johnny summed it up very succinctly: "Nice job, you fucking dumbass."

When you're cranked up, your weekend goes fast, even if you had an extra day to binge. The cycle of make-it-and-spend-it was never-ending for me, so by the time the weekend was over, I was ready to get back to work.

I reported to start one evening and there was a buzz already rippling through the place. I put on my radio and went into the lounge. "What's going down?" I asked one of the bartenders.

His reply stunned me: "Some guy jumped off the balcony."

I immediately went to the balcony.

It was still early and there were few guests to contend with. My boss let me know that the police forensics team was on their way up. I blocked off the area where the man had leapt over the rail. One of our waitresses had been on the balcony when he jumped. She said she saw him standing there. She turned around to set out some candles and she heard running footsteps behind her. When she turned back around, the man was gone.

Greasy joined me outside. "So this dude Fosbury flopped it off the goddamn balcony?" he said.

This made me laugh. His insensitivity to this somber situation was par for the course. For us, the human side of the situation was moot. It was true that someone had just died and all he had was gone, a sad end to one person's life. But in true Darwinian fashion, a weaker specimen had just erased himself because he decided his burden was too much to carry. Why argue with that? What his death represented to us now was a pain in the ass. The place was crawling with management and cops asking twenty million questions and watching videotape. It was cutting into our time to make money and get a buzz on.

We were truly becoming callous, though we'd never think we were. You see, the moral erosion is gradual. It washes away grains of you without you even really realizing how much of you is being lost every day. When it's your job to deal with the sickening things people do to themselves and each other, and the rest of the time you're immersed in your own struggle, you lose respect for the human condition.

The problem with lunacy on this level is that, even if you're into it, even if you enjoy it, eventually, it takes a toll. Most of us believe we're here for a higher purpose—we're here to do something right and good and true, something pure. As the long, hot, and dry summer swept into Las Vegas, I began to feel the walls closing in. This could have just been the drugs getting to me. It could have been the fact that I was three months behind on most of my bills.

I was in the grips of my lowest point, my rock bottom, to use an addict's term. I was finally in a spot where the liquor had ceased to help mask reality and the pills didn't feed me like they used to. But still I battled insomnia with pills and booze, continuing to pollute my system and my head. I gambled recklessly. I thought this would rescue me from the hole I'd dug. Deep inside, I knew it wouldn't. I gambled until I couldn't anymore, until the money was gone, and then I sat at home, alone. I sat there shivering though it wasn't cold. The usual cocktail of Seroquel and Noritryptiline washed down with a dozen beers failed to make me drowsy. I was raw like an open nerve. I felt the tears coming.

I felt alone and afraid. I went out to my truck and climbed inside. I didn't want JT to hear what was coming. Then I wept and wept. It was the guttural sobbing of a man lost. I found myself wishing I had the strength to take it all away. But I knew that I wouldn't, nor did I really want to. I wept for my own weakness. I cried myself to sleep that morning and slept it off in my truck. I woke in the heat of the day, climbed out of my truck, and fell into bed. I finally managed to get a decent amount of sleep after this "bottoming out." I woke up and felt a new resolve take over. I was going to right this ship no matter what it took.

Even though I had this newfound resolve, I retreated into a shell and began staying home. No more going out except for work—that was to be my source of entertainment. No more gambling; that was a start at least. I was at least going to be able to eat and catch up on my bills. That's the good thing about taking in cash every night—it doesn't take long to catch up. I was convinced I could fix the situation with even the smallest amount of effort, which was good, because putting out maximum effort had only applied to mayhem. I stayed home at the Ranch, watching movies, playing video games, and whiling away my time with whatever intoxicant made its way through the door. People were always over and Greasy practically lived there.

One night, I was channeling my energy into draining a twelve-pack and guiding my basketball team to victory on Xbox when Greasy happened through the door with his side chick, Lolita. Yes, Greasy was married. Yes, he slept with other women. Yes, he, too, carried on a pseudo-relationship with Lolita. I imagine we fell into these things as a result of poor character and personal weakness. But as a wise man once said, "When pussy's chasing you, you can't run that fast."

Greasy brought Lolita to the Ranch regularly and the two of them could be heard screwing in Johnny's bedroom. More than a few times, I was awakened by Lolita's screams: "No, Greasy. No. Noooooo. Noooooo. Noooooo. You bad man."

I knew from the first few times that going back to sleep was impossible. Lolita was on some rape-fantasy-type trip, and as Greasy would tell, she would make him hold her down while she struggled to get free. Whatever gets you off, I guess? When they walked through the door, they had a full complement of booze purchased at the local convenience store, and on this particular night, we set about the task of draining all the liquor in the house.

After we had consumed nearly everything, I produced a bottle of absinthe that Stu had brought back from Austria. It was my first time consuming the stuff, and as we poured the first glasses, we marveled at the way the bluish liquid ate away the ice cubes. The first drink of the stuff was uniquely black licorice and an hour later the bottle was gone. I was on a complete clarity of mind head-trip, or so I thought, and Greasy had a different sort of buzz. One where his legs would give out and he would suddenly go crashing to the floor. I suggested he sit down and we play video games. Somewhere along the way, Lolita engaged me in a philosophical conversation about the nature of a relationship between a man and a woman and whether or not there can be friends after romance.

It seemed she was looking for me to be an ally to her after she had hung out with an ex-boyfriend and Greasy had gotten miffed about it. I personally believe there are no friends after romance, especially if you are carrying on a relationship with another person. She and I went back and forth in a verbal sparring match. I set up the conversation to guide her to a point that would ensure her no escape.

"Well, there is obviously something you appreciate about that person that you are not getting from your current relationship," I said. It's hard for people to admit these things, especially when they are on the spot.

"That's not true," she said, playing right into where I was going.

"Well, so why do you hang out with him, then?" I queried.

No answer.

"There must be something?" I rephrased the question.

"Well, there's not." She maintained her position.

"Well, good—it's settled, then. My boy doesn't have to get upset anymore because you just admitted there is no real reason for you to be around him. Shit, I missed a layup."

Lolita was now sufficiently cornered and I had defended my friend. I could get back to the task at hand, which was kicking Greasy's ass at video games. She should have let it rest. But she couldn't.

"That's not fair," she piped up.

"What's fair about it? You admitted there is no real reason to hang out with the guy. You know that when you do, it upsets Greasy. What's to be fair? He's old news. Greasy is hot off the presses," I told her this to give her an out. She didn't take it.

"It's just not fair," she said, desperately trying to hold an indefensible position.

I tired of the conversation and went for the jugular. "What's more important? Hanging out with him or the way Greasy feels?" I asked.

She paused, and this was enough for Greasy.

"What in the hell? That should be an easy answer," he yelled.

Greasy was right, and she should have taken the out. They had a back and forth and retired to the bedroom for a while. The conversation ended with Lolita's exit after their breakup, though they would still see each other for sex and continue interrupting my good night's sleep. The entire conversation was pointless anyway because Greasy was married. It was more than bit hypocritical to be angry at your side chick for hanging out with her ex when you have a wife at home.

But logic seldom governed our world at any point. If it did, we would have seen the madness in our daily behavior and run away screaming. It was only later that I thought about why I had argued with her. I could have just avoided the conversation entirely, begged off drunk, or simply ignored her. The best explanation I could venture was that I like wordplay, and verbal sparring keeps one's powers of manipulation sharp. I thought it would be a benign conflict. I didn't think it would cause heartache, but that's one thing I'd become very good at—causing heartache.

If I was going to right the ship, then cash was paramount. I was going to do WHATEVER it took to fix this situation and start heading in the right direction. Greasy called me to the hip-hop room one evening and told me he had just sold an eight-ball to a party in one of the private rooms. This was good for me because I was bankrolling our distribution efforts and shared in the profit. It also ensured that I always had coke.

"You should shake 'em, Hank. We know they got it," he said.

"You're telling me you just sold coke to some of our guests and I should go in and put the squeeze on them?" I asked.

"Yeah, we know they got it, and they got dough. I need it," he told me.

"Yeah, I need it, too."

I thought it through for a minute. If these guys wanted to raise hell at any point, now or in the future, it could put us on the radar as being crooked. But we were good at what we did. The good cop/bad cop routine Greasy and I had been running for years, since our days selling IDs on the line, it always worked. Still, it's a sticky spot to be in, selling narcotics and then shaking them down for possessing narcotics. It's a hazardous double-dip, but boxing people in was our specialty.

"Fuck it. Let's get paid," I said. I radioed Crow before I entered the private room. I swept back the curtain and stepped inside.

"Gentlemen, we have a problem." I pulled the curtain closed behind me. "You cannot use drugs in our club. Now, before you say anything, we have it all on camera." I pointed to a spot on the wall that held a fixture that wasn't a camera at all. "Clark County has a zero-tolerance drug policy. Now, one of you can go to jail or all of you can go. It doesn't matter to me."

Crow arrived as I put in a fake radio call. I stepped into the hallway and waved Greasy down. "They're all set up. You can see the nerves on these clowns. All you have to do is knock them down," I said.

Crow and I made ourselves scarce and went into the hip-hop room to have a drink.

A couple of minutes later, Greasy came in a with a handful of crisp one-hundred-dollar bills. "They paid the check and I let them escort themselves out. They left their bottles and all," Greasy told us.

"So that means we can sell the room again?"

Greasy nodded.

"More money for the club. More money for us. Scruples not included," I said. This added a new wrinkle to our particular brand of mayhem—sell it to 'em, shake 'em down.

There are a million reasons women flock to security guards in a nightclub. We are the safe choice to converse with as we are working and, in her mind, probably sober. We have a job that requires us to be tough guys and some are attracted to this. Most of us are larger and taller than the average man. Finally, most of us look good in a suit, and women love a man who looks good in a suit.

On one particular evening, the leader of a pack of older women was talking to Crow. Crow's being tall and polite as well as intelligent meant he attracted female attention all the time. She had four friends in tow and one could immediately recognize that these women were trophies. All were older but still attractive. Elegantly dressed, their trophy status was solidified by their jewelry—the diamonds were huge. We all hung out in the lounge and talked for a while. They said they were from Texas and their husbands worked in oil. This explained the diamonds and designer clothes. These ladies were looking for a good time and no doubt were the class of women that only wanted to hang out with men that looked the part. You could get away with anything in a suit. They invited us up to their room after we got off of work.

Being a sucker for Southern belles, I was game. They were staying in the presidential suite. Being blue-collar guys, we would have accepted the invitation to see the room alone. But the opportunity to party with five Texas trophy-wife MILFS just sweetened the pot. We all tossed back a number of shots and beers before we headed up to the room. We arrived in the lavish suite and the party's beginnings had a distinctly middle-school dance feel. Crow broke the ice and suggested we order some booze from room service. The ladies ordered us a case of beer for $240 plus tip. The other liquor they ordered pushed the bill well over a thousand dollars.

"Your husbands are cool with this shit? I can't imagine you ladies drink much beer," I said. Their Pilates-toned frames made this obvious.

"Honey, they're doing the same shit right now," she said.

This highlighted what I'd thought about older, married, moneyed couples. Monogamy was a poor man's game. While probably not true in every case, the rich stayed married because the family name was at stake. The potential for disgrace and scandal, especially in the genteel South, was a price not willingly paid. So the couple just did what they wanted, each forgiving the other their transgressions. That was just fine with all of us.

Crow continued to make himself right at home in the suite and wandered through the rooms with the matriarch of the clan showing him around. Greasy took a seat at the piano, fingered the keys, and, being a talented wretch, he went into Beethoven's "Moonlight Sonata." The booze arrived and shots were poured. We tried to give the ladies cash for the booze, but they refused. Everyone loosened up and before long a round table had been swept clear and the shortest of the women jumped on top and was dancing.

Our doorman, Pauly, was playing the cut and when no one was looking, he disappeared with one of the women into a rear-room bathtub. He came out a short while later half clothed but refusing to divulge what, if anything, had happened. More libations were had and the drunkenness reached a crescendo. I excused myself to the bathroom and Shorty, the table dancer, offered to show me where it was located. I thanked her and went in. She lingered as I closed the door, leading me to think she might burst in at any moment. The bathroom was strewn with the women's toiletries and travel bags. Jewelry was everywhere. I spied a diamond ring that looked as though it might have gone unmissed in the tornado that was the bathroom. I pocketed the ring and went back to the party.

Everybody was laced up. The ladies were beginning to pair off, with the shortest one taking a liking to me. By this time, my mind had shifted from pussy to cash. I winked at Greasy and shot a quick glance at the women's purses, which were all over the room. Without exchanging a word, we knew what was about to go down.

"More shots," called Greasy.

Shorty came up to me hardly able to stand under her own power. "I want you to take me to bed and fuck the shit out of me," she said.

Normally, this sort of thing was just my game. I would take her to her the bedroom and treat her like a farm animal, trying to shape her into all sorts of things. But she was beyond drunk and these women were society broads.

Should Shorty wake up and regret what she'd done, as she surely would, the potential for me seeing real trouble greatly increased. I already had a stolen ring in my pocket and the potential for a payday was still in sight. I told the matriarch of the clan what she'd said and that she probably just needed to be put to bed.

"I'm sure she didn't say that," the matriarch said.

I was taken aback by this—it was her tone that sucked. The ladies had shown us hospitality and their genteel way up until now. It was the first air of superiority that had slipped out.

"Oh, she definitely did. Look, I'll put her to bed if you really want me to prove it," I replied smugly.

"No, I'll take care of her."

With that, she took Shorty to bed with another of the women helping out. I was incensed by her superior tone and the booze no doubt heightened my outrage. I was determined to jack these broads for as much as I could get. I was going to steal from them anyway, but this show of attitude made me relish it all the more. Who the fuck did they think they were, anyway? They were married and hanging out with security guards in a suite paid for by their husbands. Drinking booze paid for by their husbands. Real superior.

The women returned and the party continued. The attitude never resurfaced, and it may have just been the reflection of this particular woman. But still, I'd glimpsed it.

Maybe "slumming" it" was their thing or maybe they just got caught up in Vegas. Maybe they were getting a thrill and a little attention partying with younger men but still wanted to go home with no regrets.

We all got smashed up, and one by one, the boys dropped off. By the end, I was too smashed to leave or to steal anything else. I slept the night on a couch in the suite. I rose around 11:00 a.m. and cracked two lukewarm beers to combat my hangover. I said goodbye to the Texas dilettantes and thanked them for the good time. I shuffled off down the hall, a little pissed at myself for missing a potentially huge payday. At any rate, I still had the diamond ring sitting securely in my pocket and there was no time to lament missed opportunity—it was Saturday and we had to do it all again.

My experience with the Texas society broads touched on a phenomenon that thrives in Las Vegas—the indecent proposal. Whether it's hookers and johns, dealers and junkies, or simply an extramarital affair, indecent proposals abound in Vegas. Should you want to find your way into one, just wait around one will present itself in a matter of time.

There was short Cuban guy who always came into the club. Berto was from Florida and had long money. Where that money came from was a source of much speculation. He kept houses in both Florida and Las Vegas. When he was in town, he would call me personally to set his table up. He was always very generous and constantly offered to take security out to, as he put it, "party with him before he died." He always had a couple of beautiful women in tow, mostly Latin girls. I received a call from him one night as Johnny and I were fully cocked and heading to another bar.

"Hola, Hank. What are you doing tonight?" Berto asked.

"A friend and I are heading to the last stop to have some drinks. What's going on, Berto?" I replied.

"Well, Hank, I have a couple friends over here in the hot tub and they are looking to get fucked."

I could hear a couple of girls speaking up in Spanish and they both started laughing.

"Seems like you're in pretty good company, then," I told him.

"Yes, Hank, I am. But we could always use more good company. We took a little bit of the ecstasy and we are just partying here in the hot tub. You should come over and bring your friend," he told me.

"Yeah, I don't know, Berto. It's late and we're drunk. You should just handle that," I told him.

"Tonight, Hank, it is not my thing, I think. I just want to watch you fuck them. What will that take?" he asked. After this statement and given Berto's flamboyant way, it occurred to me that he was bisexual.

One of the girls took the phone. "Hello, Hank," she said.

"Hello, who is this?" I asked.

"This is Araceli. So are you coming over? I think you should," she told me with a laugh as Berto took the phone back.

"So, Hank, come over. You do a little of the ecstasy, the girls will entertain you, and I will just watch. What will that take? I want to hang out with you before I die," he said.

I could hear his smile over the phone. I mulled this over for a moment. The invite to fuck the shit out of Araceli and her friend, who were no doubt two hot Latin girls, was quite enough. But being an opportunist in the land of opportunity, I settled on a figure for stud services rather quickly.

"I don't know, Berto. How about a thousand dollars?" I asked him.

Berto answered without hesitation. "No problem, Hank. Are you bringing your friend? Because that will be two thousand, one for you and one for him," he said.

Fuck, I should have asked for more, I thought. I had ventured the shit as a joke, but he was serious.

"Just a minute, Berto. Let me ask him. Hey, Johnny—Berto wants to pay us a thousand dollars each to fuck these broads while he watches. You want to go?" I asked.

Johnny shot me a look because I knew he couldn't. He was very much in love with Reagan, and despite the constant advances from other women, he remained true to her. I admired this in him. Don't get me wrong—I thought it was doomed, as most industry relationships are, but I admired him for trying. Now, without a partner in crime, I couldn't go. I already didn't trust very many people in Las Vegas, and I imagined a scenario in which I got there alone and a gay sex rape took place with my ass as the guest of honor.

I was not entering a dicey situation like that—narcotics and paid sex with hot Latinas while other dudes watch—not without backup. A lot could go so right. But if it went wrong, it would be amazingly bad. At least if we had to fight while we were butt-naked with dicks swinging, there'd be two of us.

"Nah, sorry, Berto. It's too late and we're too drunk—maybe next time," I told him.

"That is too bad, Hank. I will see you in the club. Bye-bye."

I hung up the phone and looked at Johnny. "God damn it, Johnny. That would have been the easiest two grand we ever made and I need that money. Way to take the moral high ground on this one," I told him.

"Fuck, I know," was all he could muster.

Taking advantage of all the opportunities to make cash while staying home, not gambling, and spending very little had me on the comeback financially. Gone were the days of having to borrow a few hundred dollars from Johnny, which he kind of owed me anyway after he cost me a G with his cavalier attitude about having sex with Latin model chicks.

Johnny's girl, Reagan, was a bartender at our club. She'd convinced him that becoming a barback was the way to make it out of his dead-end security gig and into something potentially more lucrative—bartending. I couldn't argue with her there. Our bartenders made buckets of cash. It was nearly impossible not to clear over 100K behind the bar.

Johnny decided that was the avenue he was going to take and made the transfer to barback. With Black Hank getting fired, Cal taking off for a new job, and now Johnny moving on to a different position, it seemed like the team was coming apart at the seams. The team I built was coming apart. I suppose everyone needed a change, whether they chose it or not. I knew needed a change, too. But first I had to finish digging out of the hole I'd created.

It was Monday night. The club was crawling with people and we were sharking for dough while trying to keep a steady buzz going. I got a call from one of our part-timers, one of the security guys who came in just for Mondays.

"Hank, come to the dining room—some people are having sex," he said.

"Where the fuck are they having sex?" I called back.

"Just come to the roof door."

In the dining room, there was an alcove just behind the bar. It was very small and was nothing more than a vestibule for the door that led to the roof of the hotel. There was only a curtain separating the vestibule from the wide-open space filled with a few hundred people. I pushed through the crowd, pulled back the curtain, and ducked into the vestibule. I saw a skinny black kid dressed gangster. His partner was a white girl in a skirt who was still lying on the service table with her legs splayed out.

One look and it was obvious that these two were from different sides of the tracks. Both had no idea who the other one was before tonight.

"All right, let's get dressed."

The black kid was already in the midst of pulling up his pants when I entered the space. The girl, though, looked like she was going to have some trouble composing herself. Not only was she completely wasted, with her eyes having a difference of opinion on which way to look, but the black kid had somehow popped up between her legs while she still had her panties around her ankles, so he was effectively surrounded. He dropped to one knee and kind of half threw the girl's legs over his head. This showed us exactly how drunk this girl was, as it nearly carried her off the table and onto the floor.

The girl struggled to balance herself as she stood and then tugged at her panties, trying to get them up while maintaining some sort of dignity by holding her skirt down with the other hand. This ended in defeat as she slumped to the floor, once again putting her on display. The part-timer helped her up and the black kid helped her with her panties. He offered to take care of her.

"That's more than generous, but we'll help her find her friends," I told him.

By now, a few more security guards were on hand to watch the scene unfold. I employed one of them to escort the gangster out of the club.

"Will you help this young lady find her friends?" I asked the part-timer.

He did so, and I told the rest of the guys to go back to their positions. I surveyed the scene to make sure nothing was left behind. On the light-gray service table, I saw a few dark specs. *I know this bitch wasn't on the rag,* I thought to myself. The foulness of the thought had me shaking my head. I pulled my flashlight and hit the table. The girl's wetness was still glistening on the table. I took a step closer to get a better look.

Those spots are brown, I concluded, again thinking to myself. The horrible realization that this girl was being fucked in the ass by a guy she hardly knew washed over me. *Fuck, how low do people sink in the name of a good time?* Though I full well knew exactly how low people would go in the name of a good time. I followed the trail of spots across the table and up onto the wall, with my flashlight finally illuminating the three fingers outlined in shit on the wall—this girl's shitty handprint. This girl had her hand in her own asshole while she was being fucked without protection by some dude she had met in the club. It was in this exact moment that I realized I had to get out of this job.

I still had a great deal of work to do in order to facilitate getting my shit straightened out, or at least achieving a degree of straightness. In reality, my shit was so crooked, it wouldn't be straightened out for ten lifetimes, but I could at least do my best to get it bent back into some semblance of shape. The next step in doing this was continuing to exploit the Tijuana connection. There was no problem getting work down there, and I'd already been given the best safety net a dope smuggler could hope for.

On an earlier solo trip that had gone smoothly and therefore doesn't bear inclusion in this tome, Robledo told me that if I found my way into trouble in the States, I could come down south and work. I didn't really know what this meant, but I knew that he'd given Flanagan work after he'd been deported from the U.S. and he'd come through the other side no worse for wear. So that was good enough for me to not really care about the risk of smuggling. I was disappointed about losing Johnny as my riding partner, though. It was always a great deal more fun when I had him to roll with.

But he was trying to make good with Reagan, and she was taking good care of him. She was responsible, hard-working, and beautiful. Despite working as a bartender, she didn't party too much, and as far as I could tell, she was without any limiting or dangerous mental problems. So in Las Vegas, she was basically a unicorn. I respected Johnny's choice to give a healthy relationship a go and for him to try and better his position. But that meant I was making a solo trip, and it was the worst possible time to be going. Any move born out of desperation is usually the wrong one. My insomnia had returned with a vengeance and I was plagued by dreams of sharks and plane crashes. As a result, I'd slept only thirteen hours that week.

It was a Tuesday morning when I set off to meet Flanagan in San Ysidro, a U.S. border town. Now, I'm sure San Ysidro is a nice place, full of nice people. But the time I spent there made me feel like it's basically the asshole of California. Flanagan owed Johnny and I some money. He'd been doing some business south of the border and I was meeting him to collect, then continue south to make our biggest buy to date.

On the way down, I had a sickening feeling that something was going to go very wrong. Like a big gray cloud, it crept closer with every mile that ticked by on the odometer of my truck. I tried my best to push this out, as confidence is key, especially if trouble does arise. The last thing you want to do is sweat. The premonition was lasting, though, and would not be ousted from my head. I felt like I needed to take an extra level of precaution to conceal the smuggled goods.

This idea was so well entrenched that I stopped into a local sports shop to prepare myself further. While I was there, I purchased a set of soccer shin pads and a pair of compression shorts. My thought was that I would wear them and conceal the product on my person. While this wasn't exactly a cutting-edge smuggling technology. or concealment method, it was a far cry from the IDGAF method of just putting it in the side door compartments of my truck in plain view. This wasn't foolproof by any means, but it helped to lessen my feeling of impending doom.

I got to San Ysidro in the early afternoon and then spent the rest of the day hanging out at a mall I'd found, waiting for Flanagan to arrive. We played phone tag for a while and I waited well into the night for him to get there. When he finally got into town, he gave me the name of a motel he'd checked into and I set off to find him. Shortly thereafter, I found out there was no such motel and Flanagan was suddenly unreachable. Naturally, I was pissed because he owed us money. I was more pissed because he'd wasted my whole fucking day at a shitty mall in San Ysidro when I could have bounced the border and been well on my way home if he hadn't fucked me around all day. It was late and I needed a place to stay, so I called Dana. She was cool with me coming over.

I left Dana's house with a plan to return so we could hang out. I promised to grab her some asthma inhalers while I was down there. I think this was her insurance that I'd make good on my word and deliver on our plan to hang out.

I hit the highway and headed for TJ. The sickening feeling was invading my guts again and I just wanted to get the trip over with.

The minute I pulled over the border, I was red-lighted and made to go into secondary. This had never happened to me before on either side of the border. I pulled to the right and stopped at the red light in front of a guy who was sitting in a lifeguard chair. I stopped for about ten seconds, just long enough for the Mexican sitting in chair to get a good look at me. He was looking at me so intently, I knew it was so he could give a description. I pulled away and knew the game was on.

I immediately changed profile. I pulled off the short-sleeve green shirt I had on and donned a dark-gray flannel. Now I was pissed off. I was pissed at Flanagan for jerking me around the day prior. His bullshit now put me at risk and had me playing the game on a level I didn't really want to engage in. I was so pissed that I completely disregarded his lessons. I pulled into the first pay parking lot I saw and parked. The parking lot was behind a restaurant and pretty much right across the street from Robledo's. I was also pissed at the Mexican in the lifeguard chair. He'd profiled me. A white dude heading into Tijuana by himself on a Wednesday at 10:00 a.m. is about the biggest red flag you can wave.

I should have just stood in the street with a sandwich board that read, *I am here to smuggle drugs.* He knew this and he was challenging me. I could bail out. I hadn't done anything wrong yet. I hadn't purchased or taken possession of any drugs. I was free and didn't have to put myself at risk. But this was the game, and you're either a full-fledged, dedicated participant or you're fucking chum. Remember, there are no tourists in this shit. He thought he could play the game better than me. He thought he could beat me. Challenge accepted, motherfucker.

I moved between the grocery store and the restaurant, looked both ways, and crossed the street.

"Hola, Tio," I said.

That wide smile crossed Tio's face. I made the buy and went across the street to deposit the product in my truck. I changed back into my green shirt and went into a pharmacy up the street to buy Dana some inhalers. After that, I proceeded to Carnales to have a couple beers.

I was the only one upstairs in Carnales that morning, just another red flag. The bartender approached me with a bucket of beers and sat down across from me. He told me his story about how he'd been deported from the States for smuggling and distribution. He and I drank the beers as we talked. I ordered another bucket and we drank those as well. He asked me if I needed work. What kind of product I wanted and how much.

"I can get you anything you want, man. Just let me know," he said.

I thanked him but told him I had my own work. There was no need to lie to him. He knew what I was down there for and I welcomed the opportunity to make as many connections as possible down south.

It wasn't that serious down there yet. The mass killings hadn't started, at least not to the level they'd reach when the cartels went to war with the state. There was an idea of fair play. You either were a participant in narco trafficking or you weren't. At that time in the game, there were civilians and noncivilians, combatants and noncombatants. If you weren't mixed up in narco, you wouldn't just all of a sudden find yourself in danger. I was mixed up in it and never felt like I was in danger. America liked to talk about the mayhem and chaos that exists in Mexico as though death lurked around every corner. While that may be true now, that wasn't my experience. I just relaxed, ordered some lunch, and drank some more beers.

After lunch, I sat and read a book for a long time. I couldn't just drop down and then immediately cross the border again. I then proceeded across the street, and as I climbed in my truck, a police car pulled up behind me. It wasn't blocking me in, though, and I pulled out and quickly stuffed the compression shorts and shin pads full. I was about eighty yards from the border when a cop rode up next to my truck on a bicycle. He motioned for me to roll down my window and I knew my actions over the next few moments would make all the difference in my life.

Mexican cop: "Where are you going?"

Me: "I'm in line for the border. So I'm heading back to the States."

Mexican cop: "Is the truck registered to you?"

Me: "Yes."

Mexican cop: "What were you doing in Mexico?"

Me: "I came down with some friends for lunch and to hang out. They stayed and I have to go home."

Mexican cop: "You came down for lunch?"

Me: "Yes."

Mexican cop: "Where did you eat?"

Me: "At Carnales. I have my receipt right here. You want to see it?"

Mexican cop: "Did you purchase anything?"

Me: "Yeah, I purchased lunch."

Mexican cop: "Did you purchase anything else?"

Me: "Yes, I purchased some inhalers for my girlfriend."

Mexican cop: "Are there any drugs in your car?"

Me: "Other than the inhalers, no."

This bullshit questioning was all a setup. I knew they were on me from the border. This guy didn't just happen to pick my truck out from the thousand or so cars waiting to cross the border.

Mexican cop: "Do you have any problem if we search you and your car?"

Me: "No ... No problem whatsoever."

I opened the door and climbed out. He made a call over the radio and the only Spanish word I could make out was "nervioso." He was trying to scare me up and it was working, sort of. A situation like this was a chess match. A cop, whether foreign or domestic, has a certain amount of moves he can make. I, in turn, had a certain number of moves I could make. He could ask questions and probe, trying to make me nervous. By answering these questions, I could affect what move he made next. If I folded up, I lost and got to go to jail. This was not an option, since being arrested in a foreign country while attempting to smuggle drugs was not what I wanted to happen.

If I answered his questions without an inordinate amount of nervousness, he would back off. Most normal people were nervous when talking to the police. They would contend that only the guilty need be nervous, but we all know that's not true. By and large, most people only talk to cops when they're in trouble or getting a ticket. Both are bad experiences, and who really wants to talk to a cop when the outcome is usually bad? At any rate, I was leaning against the concrete guardrail trying to appear as relaxed as possible. Three more cops showed up to start tossing my truck and he started back in with the questions.

Mexican cop: "So you didn't go into any pharmacy?"

Me: "Yes, sir, I did. To purchase the inhalers."

This was a very weak attempt to get me to contradict myself and therefore open a crack that would allow him to ratchet up and heighten the stress level. Wasn't going to happen.

Mexican cop: "Where are your friends?"

Me: "I don't know exactly. They said they were going to watch the movie shoot."

I'd seen a the grip truck and lighting rigs being set up off a side street and assumed there was a shoot going on. I fed him this fabricated nugget of truth, or what I call a legitimizer, giving my fake friends something real to do. Because real people do real things, but in the world I was feeding him, so did fake ones. You didn't need an elaborate lie, just a believable story that was rooted in possibility.

Mexican cop: "All right, wait here."

I was relaxed as I sat against the barricade waiting for their next move. I knew they wouldn't find anything in my truck. I did, however, contemplate what to do if they told me to turn around for a pat down. I could run for the border, an eighty-yard dash. They would impound my truck, which I'd probably lose, and who knew what charges I'd face on the American side when they stopped me and searched? But if I allowed the pat down, they'd impound my truck anyway and I'd be facing charges in Mexico.

This was the only prisoner's dilemma I would ever play with the authorities. Prisoner's dilemma usually dictates that a criminal will usually select the least worst outcome. I enjoyed freedom, so I didn't play this game. But we'd reached a point where the game was unavoidable, albeit in a modified scenario. Since we were already playing, if I was facing charges, I preferred to do so in my own country. If facing a personal search, I decided I'd bolt and try to make the run. I thought I could make it unless the fat one got a hand on me. This thought made me smile and shake my head. It is important to find the humor in situations with potentially life-changing consequences.

The cops tossing my truck found nothing and closed its doors. Then they went to the most basic play in the Cop 101 handbook—good cop/ bad cop. The first cop had already established himself as my adversary through his aggressive questioning. He let the guys toss my truck while he squawked some shit over the radio and let me sweat it out on the side of the road a bit. Then he sent in the good cop, a short, thin man of unimposing stature.

"Hey, man, if you have anything you need to tell us, let us help you," he said.

This was an appeal to the human side that we all possessed. Everyone just wanted a little help. A friend when they were embattled, like I was now. Under stress, manipulations like these made emotions well up and the wrong emotional response was what they were looking for to make their next move. I took the emotions that welled inside me, looked him right in the eye, and told him the best lie I had: "Help me what? I don't have anything."

The hint of anger in my voice sold this point. A normal, nonguilty person, when detained for an unreasonable amount of time, will be angry. This is natural human behavior. Guilty fucks will talk in circles and answer questions till doomsday just hoping the cops will let them see the light of day. They prattle on, not knowing that each bullshit question they answer in a calm fashion leads them down a path that has the cops branding them guilty, twisting them up until they crack. Innocent people crack the other way first. Cops will fuck with your head. You have to fuck with theirs back.

The Mexican cops conversed for a few more minutes. All the while, my lane was backing up and causing a traffic cluster-fuck. Time was now on my side. Every lane change, every blow of a horn further agitated the situation and puts them under a microscope. They couldn't impound my truck for a teardown search without causing delays at the border. They weren't sure they'd find anything if they did a teardown, and if they didn't find anything, they'd look like assholes. They'd questioned me and I wasn't giving them anything. I'd already decided my path if they escalated, and I was resolute to sock one in the face and run for the border. I sat, relaxed, until the first cop came back.

Mexican cop: "Sorry for the trouble."

211

Me: "No problem. I understand. You guys have a tough job."

I climbed in my truck and waited for another ten minutes to cross the border. No doubt the U.S. side was watching the proceedings and were satisfied enough with the Mexicans' thorough search not to hassle me. I finally exhaled when I crossed the border and drove for a while without blue lights behind me.

On the ride back, the juice I felt from this encounter was as close to nirvana as I'd ever been. It coursed through my veins. I'd just come as close to ruining my whole life as I could, but I felt alive and strong. I bested them even though they KNEW I was dirty. All their training, all their resources meant jack shit. I'd won. But something else happened on the ride back—I blinked.

After I came off the adrenaline high from the closest of calls at the border, I had hours to reflect on what getting caught would have meant. The stark realization that I was attempting to "right the ship" while simultaneously putting myself at risk of ruining my entire life finally slapped me in the face. The hypocrisy of my situation attacked me from all angles. This single idea caused me to step back and look at the scope of my life and just how out of control I'd become. I had money, drugs, booze, women, and a solid job at a high-profile club in Las Vegas.

This is the dream, I told myself. The people who paid top dollar to visit the club, they just got to taste what I gorged myself on every night. Of course, the morning after brought the harsh reality into the light. I was a late-twenties drunken sodomite with no respect for himself or anyone else. I was putting myself and everyone around me in danger. Worst of all, I didn't care. This lack of care raged in me like a runaway blaze, threatening to consume what little soul I had left. I knew I had to beat back the flames and then try to rekindle something good inside. What I didn't know was just how hard the bad would be to snuff out.

When I returned to work, I vowed to try—to try and clean things up for real, to try and make better decisions, to try and care. Since resolve is always best when fresh, I'd managed to avoid drinking all weekend. By the time Monday night rolled around, I was in a great mood. The club was packed and I was actually enjoying conversing with my guests past the cursory greeting and subsequent request period.

Now, when you work in a nightclub, you just get a feeling for what is going on. You develop a "sixth sense" of sorts when it comes to the mood of the room. You will only understand after you've worked in a room filled with drunk and drugged-up herds of people for a long time.

On this particular night, all was going well until I spied a young woman sprawled out on a couch in the section adjacent to mine. The security guard who was on the perch that night was a grunt from downstairs and these guys typically couldn't see past the pussy that walked by their face every other second. I watched for a second to see if the young woman was just reclining, resting, or if she was passed out. As the other guests in that section stood up and sat down, her body just slid around. After nearly being sat on a couple of times, her friends made the effort to move her errant limbs, but she made no attempt to gain control of them. I moved towards the couch and radioed for Crow.

I tried to rouse the woman but she was altogether unresponsive. I lifted her eyelids and the eyeballs were fluttering in their sockets, the milky white part momentarily giving way to the bottom of her iris, only to move back again. Crow arrived just as her boyfriend realized what was going on.

"She's in bad shape, Crow. Let's get her up and to the office," I said.

Before we lifted her, I hit the radio. "We're going to need an EMT. We're taking one to the office."

Crow and I hoisted the woman and her skirt crept up, putting her thong on display.

Another girl at the table piped up. "What are you doing? Pull her skirt down. Everybody can see," she told me.

"Like you gave a shit till now. Get the fuck out of the way. We're trying to save this girl's life," I yelled.

The girl looked pissed but gave way. Crow and I carried her dead weight through the crowd with her boyfriend in tow. We opened the door to the office and laid her on the floor. Her eyes wouldn't come back and her skin was hot to the touch.

"What's she on?" I asked the boyfriend.

"Nothing, we've just been drinking," he told me.

213

"Is that her purse?"

He looked at his hand. "This?" he stammered.

"Yeah, that," I said as I snatched the bag from his hand. I rummaged through and pulled her ID out. "Hey, Crow, her name is Shelly."

Crow began using her name to get her to respond. I started writing down her information while we were waiting for the EMT.

"What does Shelly do?" I asked the boyfriend, who was acting as if this whole episode was an inconvenience.

"She's a dancer," he told me.

Well, if her behavior wasn't enough, the fact that she was a dancer sealed it for me. "What is she on?" I asked again.

"Nothing," he responded.

I'll never get why people care more about getting in trouble than they do about their friends' lives. I shouldn't have had to convince this jackass that he needed to help his girl—it should have been his main priority.

"Look, you're not going to get in trouble. But when the EMT gets here, I need to be able to help them."

The boyfriend looked dumb. He also looked high.

"Don't be an asshole. The girl could die. Any trouble that could come is worth that? Is it?" I asked again just as the EMT came through the door.

They got her hooked up and took her blood pressure. While it was extremely low, her heart was pumping at 152 beats per minute. The paramedics got to work on her and she still didn't respond. It took the EMTs about thirty seconds to make a decision: she was going to the hospital. Her boyfriend didn't make a sound. He didn't tell them what she took. He didn't try to help. He just followed the paramedics as they wheeled his expiring girlfriend onto the elevator.

Finding people passed out is a nightly occurrence in Las Vegas. Transporting people to their hotel rooms or a taxi via wheelchair becomes routine for security. People come to Vegas to pollute themselves for a few days and then head back home. What most of them don't realize is that the desert is a harsh environment. The desert has an effect on people that they seldom recognize. The first few times I exercised after I moved here, I ended up with a crust of salt on my forehead. That's how fast water evaporates.

When you arrive from Anywhere, America, and you're not used to the climate, it can wreak havoc on you. As soon as you disembark the plane, the dryness hits you. Even in the air conditioning of McCarran Airport, the moisture is being sucked right out of you. Most people check into their rooms and head straight for the bar. Time and again, the dehydration is furthered by drinking, and it isn't uncommon for people just to faint where they stand. I've seen it a hundred times. The face goes blanched white and they just drop.

I was on the balcony on a nice fall evening; the weather was mild, and this makes the effect even more deceptive. I watched as a boisterous blond who moments before was regaling her group with an animated story just stiffened and fell straight back, right onto her head. It seemed like a scene from a movie as a trickle of blood seeped from under her blond locks and slowly crept toward the drain in the balcony floor. I immediately called for Crow as I approached the fallen woman. Her friends were standing by dumbstruck. I started with the normal questions: "When did you arrive? How much has she had to drink today? How much water? Has she eaten?"

Crow arrived and looked over the woman. It was taking him a minute to rouse her and her friends were growing frantic. I called for a medic over the radio and began trying to calm her friends when I felt a tap on my shoulder.

"Excuse me," said a tall, dark-haired thirty-something holding two drinks.

I assumed this was one of her friends, maybe her boyfriend, and I stepped aside to make room for him. I stared in disbelief as he attempted to negotiate the bottleneck of people. This fucking asshole actually lifted his foot and stepped over the unconscious, bleeding woman with more care for not spilling his drinks than for stepping on her. I felt like grabbing him and throwing him over the railing to his death. This was the care extended to humankind by tourists in Las Vegas. That's why I never felt bad about fleecing jack-offs.

215

Incidents like these definitely helped warp my perception. They put me in touch with the human condition, or at least the human condition in the environment I'd chosen to take part in. I wanted to care. But when you're faced with so many people who don't, it's a hard thing to not turn that part of yourself off. You may end up not caring, but you still want justice. I've already said that fighting in the club is not the worst transgression one can make. When you add alcohol to an already heightened situation, like men preening for female attention, you can be sure there will be conflict. This adds a special qualifier to a man's behavior: pride.

Pride will get your ass kicked. I've seen it play out a hundred times—an obviously overmatched slouch of a man picking a fight with a cock diesel motherfucker that you know would just tear his head off if three or four security guards weren't preventing this. Slouch runs his mouth and may even take a swing, sometimes connecting. This solidifies in his mind that he has asserted his dominance over Diesel and helps him save face in front of any possibly watching females. Diesel has been dissed and hit in the face. He has no recourse. He can't reach Slouch to render him limb from limb, and when we ask him if he'd like to press charges, he has to say no. To say yes would make him appear weak and only serve to add insult to injury.

This very scenario took place on a busy Friday night. Diesel was a nice guy. He was dressed stylishly and this concealed the fact that he worked out a lot. He was extremely polite, if agitated at the fact that Slouch had shoved him and the woman he was with out of the way to get to the bar. Diesel confronted Slouch about his behavior and Slouch addressed this by causing enough of a scene, it alerted security. Upon our arrival and in a Class A bitch move, Slouch took a swing at Diesel, striking him in the face. We quickly separated the parties before Diesel could retaliate. I pulled Diesel out to the entrance without much effort. He wasn't angry at security and had no reason to fight with me.

"I'm sorry you caught one, man. I hate dudes who pull that shit," I apologized to Diesel.

I truly do hate "men" who throw blows in this fashion. You know who you are, all you guys that clam up when you're face to face with catching a beating. But suddenly you start posturing and talking shit when someone steps between you and your adversary.

"You want to press charges? We all saw him hit you," I said.

A wide grin that identified Diesel as an alpha covered his face. "No way. But you could give me a minute or two in a room alone with him if you wanted," he said.

"Not the first time I've had that request," I told him as we reached the elevator.

He and I climbed in the elevator alone and I hit the button.

"You know, as soon as you cross that rope downstairs, my involvement with you is over. Me or my guys aren't really allowed to involve ourselves with casino security matters," I said.

"Really?" Diesel said with a smile.

I escorted him out and headed back upstairs. Once there, I heard Slouch before the doors even opened. He was giving the guys a ration of shit.

"Just get on the elevator," Johnny told him.

We rode down with Slouch and escorted him out.

As soon as the rope closed, Diesel came out of nowhere and smashed him in the face with a savage shot that sent Slouch sliding across the marble. Blood poured from Slouch's nose.

"That's as nice as it gets," Diesel told him.

Slouch just looked at a glowering Diesel standing over him. He never attempted to stand up. Diesel lingered for a moment and then took off around the corner, beelining for the front of the hotel. It felt good to deliver one of the assholes into the hands of one of the good guys.

The collective patience of the security staff was wearing thin, or maybe it was just mine. The douche bags that one has to deal with on a constant basis all seemed to share the same face, the same bullshit jokes, and the same smug self-satisfaction. We were asking one of these douche bags to leave on a weeknight, a night when it was extremely hard to get kicked out. You really had to work to get thrown out on a night when revenue was hard to come by.

This moron separated himself from the pack by talking shit to one of the cocktail waitresses on each occasion that she returned to the table. I am a man of the people. I know it smacks of socialism, but the workers' party has special rights at work, and the right not to be fucked with is number one. I walked to the sofa on which this moron had his fat ass planted and asked him to get up. The exchange went something like this:

Douche bag: "Why?"

Me: "Because you're leaving the club."

Douche bag: "Why?"

Me: "For mistreating the staff."

Douche bag: "Oh, really? What—she can't take a joke?

Me: "That's neither here nor there, sir. She didn't come to work to be abused."

Douche bag: "That's just great."

He stood up quickly and I saw that, while he was a pretty-good-sized guy, he was soft around the middle. He was noticeably tense in the way douche bags are when they are suddenly usurped by someone who is in their eyes a lesser person. But he couldn't and wouldn't do anything because Johnny and Crow had assembled behind me. The douche bag knew he wouldn't stand a chance of resisting. He gave the waitress a parting shot as we passed the service well.

"Here goes your tip," he told her.

"Just keep moving," I said.

He began running his mouth to his buddy about how he couldn't believe he was being thrown out, about how the club sucked anyway, and blah, blah, blah. All of this was typical douche drivel. We finally reached the elevator and he grabbed hold of the last bastion of the douche bag: economic superiority. He pulled about thirteen thousand in casino chips from his pocket. It was easy for me to count because there were two "chocolate chips," or 5K chips, in his hand.

"I'd give them 3-1 on this that I could kick all their asses. If they could afford it," he said to his friend, who looked noticeably uncomfortable at this comment.

I cocked my head, so as to grab the douche bag's attention, but he didn't look.

"Man, for those odds, we'll let you fight just Johnny. You can even bring your friend," I said loud enough for him to hear.

They both went quiet, neither one making eye contact.

"We don't have to do it here. We can meet at the bar on Sunset, say around 3:30. We'll let him beat the shit out of you and then we'll all go have some drinks on your dime," my tirade continued. I was pissed off at this point and the fact that this asshole had to belittle a girl while she was working, simply for his satisfaction, could not go unpunished.

"What—nothing to say? I thought the action was 3-1."

The elevator door opened and we all got on. The both of them refrained from uttering a word or making eye contact for the duration of the ride. Once we get off the elevator and escort them to the rope, they beat a hasty retreat.

"So don't forget—we'll see you at the bar ... 3:30," I called after them.

I have nothing against people with money. They worked for it, and even if they didn't, good for them. It's the pricks I just can't stand. Their ostentatious displays are tiresome. In Las Vegas, folks with money are everywhere. Mostly nouveau rich, they are constantly asserting themselves in the wrong places. They have to show just how much money they have to those who don't, and somehow that solidifies their superiority in their minds. This superiority leads to behavior devoid of couth or manners.

It was a busy night and the hallway leading to the hip-hop room was crammed with people. An ordered chaos, we had two lines running together in opposite directions. One was for entry to the hip-hop room and the other was for the men's bathroom. I was heading away from the hip-hop room and had reached the head of the restroom line. Having walked the hallway a thousand times, I noticed something glinting off the flat paint in a spot that wasn't normally shiny.

A portly man in his late thirties was standing in front of the shiny spot on the wall. As I approached, I noticed that the glint was a cascade. The man was pissing on the wall and it was running down onto the floor. Never mind that he was in a hallway full of people. Never mind that he was at the front of the bathroom line. Never mind that he was pissing on carpet. This is the sort of ridiculous thing that makes me want to erase people with a single shot to the head.

"What the fuck are you doing?" I asked this dickhead.

"What? The bathroom line was taking too long," he told me.

"So you just up and piss on the wall? What the fuck is wrong with you? Zip it up, Tiny. It's time to go," I said. It was all I could do to keep from running his stupid ass out of there like a battering ram, but I didn't want him to piss on me.

He zipped up his pants just as one of our semifamous VIP hosts rounded the corner. She was made semifamous by her participation in a reality TV show, and while I liked her well enough, that was all about to change.

"He's throwing me out," the dickhead told her.

"No, you can't throw him out. He has a table here," she protested.

"He was pissing on the wall. He's definitely leaving," I told her.

Her protests grew more overt as she pulled me out of earshot of the dickhead. "He's one of my best clients. You can't throw him out. He spends a lot of money," she told me.

It's almost always the same with hosts—they only care about the money.

"Look, the guy was pissing on our wall, basically pissing on the club. But fine, if you want him to stay, I'll let him stay. All you have to do is clean up your client's piss. You're going to make the money, so why would I have a porter do it?" I told her.

I could see the wheels turning as she set her price. *Is it worth it?* she thought for a long time.

The fact that she even took more than two seconds to say no illustrates what goes on in the mind of a VIP host. To her credit, she did decline, and I ushered the dickhead to the elevator. We climbed in with a couple of his friends and he opened his mouth.

"You cheap-suited asshole. What do you make? Thirty thousand a year? I could own you."

Always the same garbage spewing out of their mouths.

"Wow, thank you. You just gave me a raise. Thirty grand would be great," I replied. To tell the gentleman that I made nearly ninety thousand a year working less than thirty hours a week would be futile.

He continued to blow all the way down the elevator. My good humor quickly waned. The idea that this guy was knocking me when he didn't have the potty training of a housecat was impossible for me to swallow. The elevator chimed and the doors opened. His friends exited first and I seized the moment to get right into his ear.

"Yeah, but thirty thousand dollars will fuck you up," I told him so only he could hear.

The fat prick went ballistic. "Fuck you. I'll kick your ass right here."

There was no one between him and me at this point, so for him to attempt to kick my ass wouldn't have been hard.

"What are you going do? You're forty-five and out of shape. You ain't going to do shit," I said, striking the death blow to his ego.

His friends grabbed him and he struggled against them. This was funny to me, because a minute ago, he could have gotten to me without restraint. This was the sure sign of a bitch. But he was content to rant while his friends dragged him off.

Fall was approaching and there was a lot of change happening. The lease on the Ranch was up and Johnny's job change morphed into a life change, so he decided to move in with his girl. This meant I had to move again, my sixth time in four years. The situation was made easy by the fact that one of Greasy's friends from Cali needed a roommate. I moved into an apartment off Smoke Ranch with Greasy's homeboy, Jack.

Jack was as cool as you would think one of Greasy's homeboys would be and we got along swimmingly. Jack had a 9 to 5, and this aided my attempt to minimize the mayhem that normally followed me everywhere. It required me to keep the chaos at arm's length or at least make sure it didn't follow me home. I was just getting to know Jack and I didn't want to disrupt his situation.

The team was changing as well. With Cal heading out to hit the open road to make all his redneck dreams come true, and after Johnny's move to the bar, the team was left two men down. We couldn't afford to let the decrease in manpower affect our ability to run the club. But we also couldn't afford to bring just anyone on. I'd maintained a careful balance of personalities that complimented each other, and few had qualms about executing the tasks necessary to keep the room running smoothly, the tasks that kept us off the radar. That level of comfort couldn't be disrupted, so the decision on whom to bring up had to be made carefully. Luckily, a couple of our Monday fill-in guys distinguished themselves pretty quickly.

Lima had all the tools. While he was short in stature, you could feel the confidence coming off this cat. He was a never-back-down type of dude. But he still had a way with the ladies. He worked hard at the bullshit proving-ground tasks to which all entry-level security guards are relegated, moving furniture and manning garbage posts. It didn't take him long to get noticed. Both hard and soft, I knew he'd fit in perfectly.

Bryant was a good-looking kid with a chiseled physique and he wore a suit well. Bryant kept in shape by lifting regularly, a holdover from his days in the service. He was a little goofy, which we'd come to find out was a lot goofy. He and Lima fell in because they were hired together and worked a lot of the same shifts and positions, much like Stu and I had when I first started. We brought on Bryant as a result of his proximity to Lima. You could say he got in on Lima's back. This was to prove a mistake on my part.

On the first Monday after Lima and Bryant came up, Bryant distinguished himself in another way. I was working my section in the lounge. The club was packed. I stood in my usual spot between my clients and the masses. A tall black gentleman walked up to me and stood in my personal space. This was a common occurrence as real estate was hard to find. If you get claustrophobic, a club job is not for you. He looked at me as though he had a question to ask. I leaned in and turned an ear to him as the house music that was thumping off the walls made it impossible to hear at a distance. He leaned in to ask his question and instead kissed me on the neck. I immediately shot an arm out to create space between us.

"What the fuck are you doing?" I asked him. I looked at him, and he was obviously tweaking, on coke or meth, I couldn't tell. "Beat it, man," I yelled over the music.

There was no way I was throwing him out. Partially because it would take from my time to make money, but mostly because I would have to suffer the endless jokes from the rest of the crew when they found out another guy had kissed me on the neck. Apparently, he was satisfied, and he wandered off into the crowd.

A while later, a call came over the radio from Lima: "FIGHT IN HIP-HOP."

I ran down the back hallway, the quickest way to the hip-hop room. When I arrived, the fight had already been broken up. Lima was leading two portly white guys down the hall towards the hotel's service hallway. Greasy had the black guy who kissed my neck and led him into the old managers' office. But Bryant was nowhere to be found. I hadn't time to look for him, though—I had multiple people bleeding. I checked with Lima first.

"That nigger is a fucking faggot."

This summed up the conversation I had with the two white guys. I could pretty much surmise what had taken place, as it happened to me a short time earlier.

"Get rid of them," I told Lima. "Wait, we want to press charges," one protested.

I could see why, as he had a torn shirt, a bloodied, fat lip, and some nasty swelling around one eye. His friend had fared slightly better, coming away with just a bloody nose.

"Look, two-on-one will never wash with Metro, fellas. And what if a black cop shows up?" I said.

This appealed to their inner racist works and they agreed to leave.

I entered the old managers' office and Greasy leaned comfortably against a desk. But the black tweaker was hyped up. He paced the office like a caged animal. He engaged Greasy in conversation.

"Dog, let me at 'em. I'll fuck their world up," he said.

"Give it two minutes, Greasy, and then get rid of him," I said. I wanted to keep this interaction as brief as possible. I surely didn't want the fact that a black tweaker had kissed me coming out, especially after

223

he had beaten up not one, but two white boys. Besides, I had another problem to deal with.

I tracked down Bryant in his section. "Why didn't you respond to the fight?" I asked.

Bryant looked down at the floor and therefore played his hand before he even ventured an answer. "I didn't hear the call," he said.

Even if it weren't for his body language, I'd have known this was a lie. A nightclub fight is easy to spot. People spread out quickly when a fight pops off, giving the combatants plenty of space. This has the effect of putting a spotlight on the conflict—that's the reason why Greasy and Lima spotted the situation and were able to respond.

"That's not acceptable, man. Your number one priority is situations like the one that just happened. You need your head in the game," I said. This admonishment was necessary. Since it was his first flub, I could give him the benefit of the doubt. Maybe I was reading him wrong and he really didn't hear the call or see the brawl. "It can't happen again. Understand?" I asked.

Bryant shook his head in the affirmative but his shame was evident. I walked away with the sinking feeling that we had a weak link.

Still, Bryant was part of the team, and we were going to do our best to make sure we'd either expose the punk in him or eradicate it entirely. That meant, even though he didn't really drink all that much, we'd include him in the postshift drinking sessions.

One night, we were in the midst of a solid session at the hotel's center bar. As we were on our way to a nice buzz, Lima suggested that he'd set up some girls while he was on shift. They were staying at the hotel and Lima told us they were down to party. Normally, I would be skeptical that girls would want to "hang out"—a convenient euphemism for *fuck*—a half-dozen or so drunk security guards and their boss. But my experiences in Las Vegas told me different. So up we went.

Lima led the way, followed by Kalil, Greasy, Bryant, Crow, and myself. We walked to the end of the long hallway and stopped in front of their door. Lima knocked—no answer. He knocked again.

"Man, these broads are asleep—this isn't live. Let's go get a drink," I said.

I was interrupted by the chain being pulled from the door and the deadbolt turning.

Maybe we'll have a party after all, I thought.

Our hopes were dashed to pieces when a fat Mexican in a stained wife-beater answered the door.

"Yo, is Mina here?" Lima asked.

"She's asleep," the Mexican answered as he closed the door in Lima's face.

Lima braced himself for the onslaught. We howled in laughter as Lima headed back down the hall with quickness. We jumped on him.

"Man, Lima, that broad was hot. I bet her friends are the shit."

"This dude is always talking about dimes, and I've never seen him with anything above a solid five."

The group hammered Lima all the way down the hall.

We piled onto the elevator and hit the button. Content that we'd sufficiently shamed Lima, we all quieted down. The elevator stopped on a lower floor and two khaki-and-collared white guys climbed on, looking rested and wearing their convention name badges.

Greasy turned to one of the men and looked him in the eye. "Sir, have you ever seen a gorilla knuckle?" he asked the man.

"No, I haven't," he answered.

Greasy looked at the end of his nose and cast his eyes downward. Everyone in the elevator looked down simultaneously. In Greasy's hand were his balls, squeezed to the bursting point. The entire elevator erupted in laughter. The two conference attendees were red-faced and laughing, too. There was no way, when they woke up that morning, they thought they'd see another man's balls on the way to the convention.

The elevator stopped on another floor and everyone quieted down, the conference-goers now complicit in pranking the next folks who got on the elevator. Greasy stood there, balls in hand, waiting for the next unsuspecting victims. A black guy with the same convention badge climbed on. All of us waited for Greasy to ask the question.

"Sir, have YOU ever seen a gorilla knuckle?"

He looked again and the man just stared back at him. He was wise to what's going on. He had probably heard the laughter echoing down the elevator shaft, or maybe it was because he saw a gorilla knuckle every time he looked down.

I was working toward fixing the problems I'd created through a complete lack of caring coupled with a penchant for recklessness, and for once, I was actually making progress. Since making money was easy, it didn't take long to right the financial problems. Through this small improvement, I'd convinced myself I was ready to give it another go with Dana. She was game to move back to Las Vegas and give it another go as well. She and I had been seeing each other every time I'd gone to or passed through California. She accompanied me to Tijuana on a couple of trips, even going so far as sweeping all the drugs off the counter and into her purse, putting herself at risk. She was unafraid and willing to go as far as I wanted to go. She was still Bonnie to my Clyde. But I was still tragically flawed. The incremental improvement in my economic situation only served to set me up for a fall. I needed a lot more work than just a superficial fix of my finances. It didn't get to the root of the problem, the chaos in my head, the continuing willingness to invite ruin into my life.

Dana was set to move back in with me. Instead of preparing for her arrival, I fell into old behaviors, a sure sign that I was still ruled by chaos and that my selfishness wouldn't spare her. My perspective of a fresh start gave way to the feeling that, after her arrival, I couldn't just do what I wanted anymore. I formulated the idea that I needed one last hurrah and then I'd be ready.

Monday night was over and my weekend started. I went out with the crew after work for our usual drinking session. Colette had made her way up to the club and was more than happy to come along. One by one, the guys fell off, leaving Colette and I alone.

I took Colette to our apartment out on Smoke Ranch. Once there, I excused myself to the bathroom so I could snort ecstasy. I'd procured a number of pills and a giant bag of coke to fuel my last weekend. I was drunk, so I barely crushed the pill and hurriedly snorted big, thick lines of the stuff. The tingle hit, followed by an intense burn that made me feel like scraping the flesh from the inside of my nostrils. This sensation gave way to an immediate feeling that everything would be okay. That Colette was the woman for me and I had her all to myself. I returned to bed and she was waiting. I didn't have a thought or a care as to what I could be contracting. I didn't think on that for even a moment. I wanted to pour myself into her. I felt that two wounded hearts would come together into a union that might very well heal the both of us. That she could fix and nurture my heart and I would protect hers, and through that, we would both find our way. We made love for hours.

When Colette left, the hypocrisy of my actions immediately took hold. Dana was coming to live with me in two days' time. She was uprooting her life and moving back to Las Vegas for me. She hadn't even gotten there and I'd already betrayed her. I quickly drowned these feelings in a torrent of coke and ecstasy. The two days passed in a blur. Having been up the entire time, I was wound tight when Dana arrived. I helped her carry her things inside and then she reclaimed our bed. I didn't come clean with her. I just picked up our relationship there and made the fresh start I told myself I needed. I fixed this in my mind by telling myself I was at least fighting. I convinced myself that since I'd lessened the damaging behavior, that meant I was trying. I just stamped out the feelings, like I'd always done.

While the club was a world unto itself, one which required a conversion of morals and ethics, I was willing to make that trade. When you came into the club and did something wrong, you were agreeing to play the game. If we extorted money from you, assaulted you, or otherwise involved you in what we were doing, it was because you'd involved yourself. But I could never justify the high levels of bastard that entered my personal life. I could cover them up and keep going, but I could never make them right. I wore an impenetrable mask that covered the pain of those decisions. It didn't help that, after all the bullshit I pulled in the club, they wanted to promote me. After all the shakedowns, all the drinking, all the drugs, the assaults, all the exploitation, they wanted to put me in charge. They wanted to make me a manager.

It only made sense. I was responsible for keeping the floor running smoothly. I'd been a governing force on the floor through four general managers and a host of supporting managers. I knew nearly all the regulars. I had the place laced up tight and had a governing philosophy that managers could appreciate. My philosophy lessened their headaches on the floor, largely kept the bullshit out of their sight, and allowed them to do what they needed. In turn, I was given carte blanche to run the floor the way I wanted, and while the management would never condone all I'd done, they had the benefit of the favorable environment I'd carefully constructed, one that gave them plausible deniability. In turn, my guys knew we were a team and that I'd look out for them as much as I could, covering tracks and managing bad situations. But if you called your own play, shit the bed, and got caught, you'd likely get fired. They had learned this through the incident with Black Hank.

My decision to accept the offer was partially out of complacency, but the club was evolving, too. All of Las Vegas was evolving. We watched as a number of nightclubs sprang up and challenged for the crown. We were no longer the newest, the hottest, the most exclusive club in town. We didn't have a partnership with the hotel/casino with the backing of their huge marketing budget. I sensed our spot was peaking and was now on the inevitable downward spiral that all clubs go through. We were forced to watch an ever-degrading class of people enter the club and with them came problems. Problems like evacuating every orifice in your body—shit, piss, and vomit—like one young man did on the night before he was supposed to get married. I needed to make a move from security because I knew it was a dead end. As a manager, I would at least have the title, and if I could get my personal shit sorted out, I'd be able to parlay that into something down the road. Also, it gave me further run of the club as the only eye on watch. So I took the job.

I regretted my decision to become a manager almost immediately. The move had me straddling the line between leader and subordinate. I was no longer part of the team I had identified with and led for so long. When altercations broke out, I was no longer needed to get involved and doing so meant stepping on the toes of the new leader, Crow. In addition, I was never the management type, save for overseeing a crew of knuckleheads as they indulged whatever drunken, drug-induced flight of fancy that presented itself. I was perfect for that job. Inventories, P&L statements, schedules, etc. left me shaking my head. I knew they were important and kept me in a job, I just didn't care.

I was welcomed into the management team and learned about how they worked the room for their own benefit. They immediately told me about the managers' tip pool, similar in all ways to the security tip pool except for the fact that they had independent hosts working the casino floor to bring people in. Those people paid a discounted admission fee, which was split between the host and the managers. It was brilliant because these hosts weren't poaching guests who were already coming to the club. They were gleaning these guests from the areas around the other nightclubs in the casino. This practice is, of course, frowned upon. But the nightclub biz is cutthroat and every guest represents revenue. Now I knew why the management had given us a wide berth to pull shit. I always felt like they had their own gambit running and it was finally confirmed. Naturally I was going to find the angle to maximize this situation.

Crow took over the security team and would move guys he liked into the spots as he saw fit. Over the course of his tenure, he moved in Collier to take my place on the team. Collier was a big, cornfed white boy with a baby face. He was quiet but rock solid. Alabama was a good old boy and one of the calmest guys to ever put on a suit to work the room. J.J., an ex-soldier with sexual proclivities that made the wildest of us look tame, and finally Mack, a clean-cut, smooth kid, slight of stature but extremely effective at the job.

Now that I was in the ranks of management, my recommendations on hiring held a bit more water. I could help steer hiring and it happened that one of our favorite guys from the after-work spot was looking for a job. Cisco was a jovial guy, an easy-money type that inherently brought a half-assed, angling approach to work. He wanted to work with us after realizing he could make more money as a busser in our room than he could as a security guard in his. He was regarded as a problem nearly as soon as he started. I respected this and I made him my go-to guy when I needed something done. In this role, Cisco always delivered. His readiness to accept any challenge I gave him was born out of the fact that with those challenges came respect. He was a busser, which meant he picked up dirty dishes and trash. But security was no different—the trash was just human. We formed a friendship based on this and mutual respect is a good starting point for any friendship. It didn't hurt that Cisco had an affinity for drugs that rivaled my own.

The first night we hung out, Cisco suggested we stop to blow some of our hard-earned tip money at the blackjack table. Being the high-risk personality I am, I was happy to oblige and we sat down. Cisco taught me basic strategy as we powered through shots of tequila. I pulled a Xanax from my pocket and popped it in my mouth, washing it down with yet another shot. Cisco and I got another, followed by another, then another, then lights out.

I woke up in my truck. The heat of the morning sun had pushed the temperature in the cab to well over one hundred degrees. I was sick to my stomach and disoriented. Somewhere, I'd lost four hours of my life. At best, I'd slept those hours in my truck on the employee parking level. At worst, I'd terrorized people in the casino. At least I hadn't driven anywhere. I opened the door and stepped outside. The air cooled the beaded sweat on my neck and I removed my wrinkled jacket to aid the cooling off. Then it hit me. The sickness in my gut moved to my bowels. Even under the influence of the pills and still partially drunk, panic set in. I was going to shit my pants. I knew I wouldn't make it to the elevator, down to the casino level, and into the bathroom. That trip would take two minutes. My growing nervousness painted a picture of me trailing shit out of my pant leg across the parking lot on my way to the elevator. I did the only thing I could do: I moved to the opposite side of my truck and dropped my pants. Without taking the time to look around, I sat my tailbone against the rear tire and expelled the putrid excrement from my body, being careful not to get any on my shoes. I finished dropping my guts in the parking lot, then jumped into my truck and screeched out of the garage.

As I drove away from work, I dialed Dana. I had to apologize for staying out so late. The phone rang and went to voicemail. By now, she was probably sick of this sort of thing. When I got home, she was waiting. She let me listen to the message, a slurred, sickening string of unintelligible words. The message was a clear signal that I hadn't changed a bit. I had the two following days off and the worry began. Surely if anyone saw me shitting in the employee parking lot, surely they would report it to security. Likewise, if anyone saw a pile of shit sitting in the parking garage, they would report that and security would review the cameras and find out who had done such a heinous thing. I pictured being called into my boss's office after they had reviewed the video and having to explain why I would relieve myself in the parking lot. Not to mention them being privy to the madness that had preceded such an act. I was convinced I would be fired. All the evidence needed to send my career to a humiliating end was sitting in the parking lot.

I lamented this for two days and then I had to go back to work. I got into the elevator to ascend to the top for what I thought could be the last time. I steeled myself for the humbling meeting I was about to take part in. I tried to console myself. This was just another trial in the mess that was my life. If this was to be the polarizing moment, then it would surely straighten me up. It would be remembered by my friends and colleagues as an embarrassment of epic proportions, something that would live on well after I'd been fired. I climbed off the elevator and was greeted by our maître d'.

"Hank," he said, with the same tone and inflection he always did. The rest of my fears were put to rest when my boss approached me with a handshake and immediately started briefing me on the nightly events. This was just another bullet dodged and thus the saga continued, with me doing my best to fuck things up.

I was in the doghouse again for staying out late drinking and carousing. Dana was pissed, and rightly so—it hadn't taken long for me to revert to the behaviors that had sabotaged our relationship the first time. She was dedicated to taking a new path herself, and after my parking garage incident, she did her best to show me my behavior and the damage it was causing. That being said, I decided against taking the right path. Instead, I'd just drink myself into oblivion while continuing to ignore the fact that this was a new level of sickening behavior.

When I arrived at work that afternoon, I was looking to get a buzz on as fast as possible. I needed a drinking partner, and since none of the security team had arrived, I'd chosen the hostess, Molly. Molly was an attractive girl and the security team and I spent a great deal time debating on whether her breasts were real or not. They were the right size for her body type and build, but they were just too perfect. I voted for fake and would later find out I was correct.

At any rate, I asked Molly if she felt like having a drink and she accepted. She ran her own business and worked two jobs. Dealing with the stress of this had left her ready to blow off a bit of steam. I had the bartender pour a round of chilled tequila. She and I ducked into the A/V closet that ran the media room. Not a moment later, we emerged and I headed straight for the bar to round up another couple of shots. This certainly wasn't acceptable boss/subordinate behavior, but it was a story told in clubs all over Las Vegas.

Kate, one of our servers, got wise to what was going on. "What are you guys doing in there?" she asked the obvious.

"What's up, girl? You want to be on deck?" I asked.

Never one to turn down a challenge or a drink, she accepted, and the three of us were back in the closet downing shots. This continued on until Kate bowed out due to the fact that she still had to be straight to serve her guests. Molly, however, continued to match me shot for shot. When the glass total reached fourteen, we knew we'd done some damage. This was solidified when Molly greeted a couple of guests.

"Good evening, this evening," she muttered. Then Molly took a misstep and looked as though she might run into the wall before she righted her path and walked them to their table.

Mikayla, a mutual friend of ours, showed up seemingly out of nowhere. We immediately involved her in the carnage and another round of shots was ordered.

Shaun, one of our other managers, showed up to relieve me and observed the shape I'd put our hostess in. He seemed miffed but reserved judgment, and since she was in no shape to be helping guests, Shaun ordered Molly to retire to the managers' office. I had to do payroll before I could leave and it was the only thing standing between us and the next drinking destination.

I had ordered dinner and it arrived just as I was sitting down to do the payroll update on the computer. I convinced Mikayla that we could expedite the process if she would just feed me while I worked on the computer. She sat behind me and cut my steak, gingerly holding each bite over my shoulder while being careful not to spill on my suit. In the pantheon of good times to be had, being fed by an attractive Asian girl has to be in the top ten. I finished my steak, entered the payroll, and the three of us moved on to the next club.

We headed to the burlesque spot, and since I knew the bouncers, they comped us a table in VIP. It wasn't long before Kate joined us at the club, having been cut from her shift for having some drinks on her as well. I knew Shaun would keep this in confidence and that no one would see any trouble for having gotten too drunk while working. This was part of the game and Shaun was no stranger to getting bent on shift himself.

We whiled the night away watching the burlesque revue offered as entertainment in the club. In between acts, we watched as the tourists would get on stage to dance. The onstage talent varied from hot to heifer as girls from everywhere but Vegas got up there to have a go.

One by one, everyone called it a night until Molly and I were the only two left. We were both completely bombed and talking about God knows what. In the grips of a brownout, I said something to her that I can't remember. She pressed her fingers to my lips, looked at me, and wandered away. I assumed she was going to the bathroom, so I waited. She didn't return. I assumed I'd insulted her and she left. But I knew Molly was wrecked, and since I was responsible, I wanted to make sure she was going to get home safely, even if she was going to hate me in the morning. I dialed Mikayla to get Molly's number. Mikayla didn't answer. She would later tell me this was due to the fact that she was in the bathtub puking. I headed off to my truck genuinely worried about Molly but unable to do anything to help the situation.

The next day, I headed in for my shift and Molly was there, safe and sound, sober and working. She told me that casino security had filled in the blanks for her when she called them to see if they'd found her purse. It seems that Molly had been wandering the fifth floor of the parking garage looking for her car. Even if she could have found the car, it wouldn't have mattered, as she had left her purse behind in the club. Security put her in a taxi and even paid for the ride. She'd lost her phone on the way home. But her neighbors returned it after finding it on the steps in front of her apartment. She used the phone to call casino security and thankfully her purse was there. The bouncers we knew had turned it over to lost and found, proving Las Vegas isn't a totally heartless place.

We laughed a lot in the club. Sometimes at the airs people put on to impress each other. Mostly at the gross ways people abuse themselves and others. It's been said that all humor is at someone's expense, and if that be true, then the only difference is the amount of malice involved in making fun of someone. So while the room harbored plenty of malicious humor, every once in a while, a moment of innocence shed light into the darkest corners.

One busy Friday night, I was walking through the vacant dining room on my way to the patio bar to line up a round of shots for the fellas. Alone in one of our plush chairs was a kid of about twenty-five years old. He was passed out cold. I tried to rouse him, but he wasn't moving. I lifted my mic and made a call: "Crow to the dining room."

As usual, this brought nearly the whole team running. If it sounded like something could happen, you could be sure the whole team would respond. Crow, Greasy, and Lima arrived around the same time. Crow was immediately annoyed and started pushing the kid's shoulder, causing him to stir a little.

"Hold on," Greasy said as he ran out of the dining room.

We were all left to wonder what the hell he was doing when Greasy returned holding a miniature can of shaving cream. The rest of us let out a collective chuckle at the juvenile prank Greasy was about to play in a multimillion-dollar club.

Greasy sprayed a healthy amount of shaving cream on the kid's hand and proceeded to tickle his face. The kid drunkenly smashed his face full of the shaving cream, his eyes and nostrils full of thick white foam. He bolted from the chair, startled and without the ability to see. He reeled around the room for a second as he tried to get his bearings until he finally realized where he had been sleeping.

"Oh, real funny—what the fuck?"

The kid was scarcely equipped to deal with what was happening to him. He was so drunk, he didn't know what to do with the shaving cream that was all over his hands and face. Greasy took mercy and pulled a napkin from one of the side stations to help the kid clean up.

As we escorted him to the elevator, one of his friends recognized him.

"Jesus, Brian we've been looking all over for you," his friend said.

"Look, bro, your friend has to go. He was asleep in the dining room," Crow told him.

"His punk ass can't drink anyway. I'll take him to the room. But can I come back?" his friend asked.

"Absolutely ... just let Pauly know you'll be returning," Crow told him.

Meanwhile, Brian had fallen asleep again on the banquettes that sit in the elevator lobby. His friend just smiled and watched as Greasy put more shaving cream on Brian's hand. But this time, Brian wasn't all the way out. He sprang up and recognized his friend, who was laughing with us.

"Man, what the fuck? You're letting them do this to me?" Brian yelled as he scraped his hand on a trash can.

"Shut up. You're passed out and that shit is funny," his friend said as he grabbed Brian around the neck and corraled him onto the elevator.

Seldom does the line between celebrity and an escort out of the club intersect. Celebrities almost never mix with the average patrons of a club, and if they do, it's purely by chance or their own choice. One particular evening, I was waved over by Reagan; she was pointing frantically toward the end of the bar. I called for security over the radio and headed to where she'd been pointing. I spotted the trouble immediately. A gigantic 'roided-out beast of a man was screaming at another guest, who was holding the patio door open with one hand. Roid Beast was raging out and the other guy looked petrified.

"Just go outside," I said to the petrified man.

He looked relieved and took his out. As I turned my attention to Roid Beast, I was joined by Crow and Alabama.

I didn't know what the problem was between Roid Beast and the other guy. All I knew was that I couldn't have a highly aggressive, weight-lifting, psycho problem in the club. Johnny and I were enough.

"Hey, brother, it's time to call it a night," I said to Roid Beast.

He was still pissed and he didn't look very happy with the instruction I'd just given him. His girlfriend was a petite blond who was standing on the banquette and leaning on his shoulder. She had gotten the gist of the conversation through body language and the fact that I had two guys flanking me.

"Hey, honey, show them how strong you are," she said.

I smiled at this. "Yeah, honey, show us how strong you are," I said.

I was taunting the guy, but it was necessary. You want to show someone who's contemplating physical action that you welcome his attempt. It's literally peace though superior firepower. Roid Beast got this and he started walking towards the entrance. But it didn't keep him from talking shit about how he could kick our asses all the way to the elevator. We reached the elevator just as the doors closed, and I stuck my arm in to keep the doors from closing.

When the doors opened, we saw the former heavyweight champ of the world standing there in shorts and tennis shoes. As far as I know, he's the only one we let out of the dress code to that extent. The champ was flanked by two pretty females. At this point, we probably should have just let Champ ride down, but Roid Beast was getting more and more agitated. He was beginning to yell and we just wanted to get him out before he got too worked up, so we climbed on the elevator and pressed the button.

In the elevator, Roid Beast kept up his tirade about kicking our asses. We all just stared at the elevator walls or doors and ignored his bullshit. The ride will would be over soon. But Champ started to get agitated by the anger that had suddenly come into his otherwise serene presence.

Champ spoke ever so softly: "We got a problem here?"

I raised an eyebrow as both Crow and Alabama did. We looked at Roid Beast in an attempt to calm him. But Roid Beast didn't see us or hear Champ because he was caught up in his own world.

"We got a problem here?" Champ asked again, this time a little louder. "I don't want to get a problem. We got a problem on here?" Champ's voice was beginning to climb, and you could hear a slight but distinct climb in tone.

Roid Beast looked at us. He could hear Champ now. I raised another brow. A smile crept across Alabama's face. Crow shook his head at Roid Beast. Before we got on the elevator, it was debatable if Roid Beast was the toughest guy present. Crow, Alabama, and myself would all provide a formidable opponent if things were to be one-on-one. But now that we were on an elevator with Champ, all debate had ceased. He was in charge if he wanted to be.

"We got a problem here? I don't want to get a problem. If I get a problem, I get a third strike, and I go back to prison," Champ said.

He had begun to shake his head and look down at the floor of the elevator. We were all wondering what the hell we were going to do if Champ started trying to knock people out on the elevator. I personally hoped that he would direct his energies to the Roid Beast, as he was "the problem" anyway. We were all very quiet now, as Champ owns the floor. "I don't want to get a problem," he whispered.

DING. The elevator bell went off and mercifully, Champ didn't start swinging. We all disembarked quietly and led a very chilled out Roid Beast to the rope, where he exited and said, "Thank you."

Champ smiled and thanked us, too, as he led the ladies into the casino.

But not all encounters with sports figures went so smoothly.

Take the case of an American football player who came into the club one night. He was a cornerback who played for a team with a Southern exposure. I didn't know who he was, but I noticed the ICE, designer jeans, and the swagger. Crow knew who he was and comped him into the club. The only stipulation was that he had to remove his hat to comply with the dress code.

Later that night, I passed Mr. CB on my way to the office. I noticed he'd put his hat back on. This was typical, for people to put their hats back on after being told to remove them. Crow was right behind as I passed Mr. CB. I pointed to my head and looked at Mr. CB. Crow nodded, as he was thinking the same thing. When Crow stopped Mr. CB, my instinct told me there was going to be a problem—just something in his body language.

Crow politely asked him to remove his hat as I took up a position behind Mr. CB. Just like I thought, Mr. CB refused to remove his hat. "Well, then, I'm going to have to ask you to leave," Crow said.

Mr. CB was obviously incensed by this refusal to recognize his celebrity and he gave Crow a half-hearted shove to show he meant business.

Mr. CB was an athlete whose profession required him to be in great shape. As such, his body was made up of pure muscle. It was this false belief in his own athleticism that led his hands to write a check that his ass couldn't cash. The average corner weighs 194 pounds and stands five feet, eleven inches. Crow and I were both over six-four and two hundred forty pounds.

I immediately grabbed Mr. CB under his left arm and mashed his head into the wall. "You don't put your hands on security. It's time for your ass to go," I said.

Crow pushed the button and the elevator door opened. Crow grabbed Mr. CB's right arm and we pushed him into the corner of the elevator. He cursed us the entire time.

We'd gotten Mr. CB onto the elevator, but he was still struggling.

"You motherfuckers ain't strong. I can get out of this anytime I want," he told us.

I quickly regripped and got underneath him. "Go ahead, motherfucker," I replied.

I had designs on slamming his ass to the marble if he went crazy trying to get loose. Mr. CB sensed that this confrontation was about to get a lot worse and I could feel his body go slack, but I still didn't loosen my grip. He had already proven himself a cheap-shot artist, and if he was going to take another shot at me or Crow, we'd have to return in kind.

We hit the bottom floor and the elevator door opened. We led him to the rope, still careful to keep him locked up. The rope opened and we gave him the customary shove into the lobby. Crow and I got back into the elevator to head back upstairs. Crow opened his hands and they were covered in tiny cuts that were just starting to bleed.

"What happened? You all right?" I asked.

"Yeah, I'm fine. I was trying to get his bracelet off. Did you see the size of those rocks?" Crow asked me.

Yes, we'd even try to roll a football player if he showed his ass in the club. Celebrities—they're just people.

The eve of another new year was here. We were preparing for another night's festivities and the night was going to prove to be the busiest NYE of all time. We prepared for the crowd and set the room up for the massive influx of people that would be coming through the doors.

The night was running smoothly and we were in the middle of the second dinner shift. The lounge was full of people from the first dinner and the booze had been flowing freely all night. I was standing on the perch when I got the call: "The champ is here."

Our first idiots of the night had made themselves evident. I made my way to the bathroom as Crow was leading two men out of the restroom. One was visibly pale and being partially held up by his friend. I hit them with the setup, but they weren't going for it. The healthy-looking man was a little pissed that I had accused them of doing drugs or having gay sex.

"My friend is sick and I'm helping him. Is that so outrageous?" he asked.

Actually, yes, it is, I thought.

"You are in a nightclub in Las Vegas. Two men in a stall. The last thing that springs to mind is that one man might be looking after the other because he is sick," I said.

The man's agitation grew as I continued to probe for the opportunity to milk them for a payoff.

"Don't you find it weird that your first inclination was to believe we were doing something wrong?" he asked.

"Sir, I work in security. It's my job to find people doing something wrong and I've been doing it for a long time, so I'm very good at it," I told him.

"Well, in this case you're wrong, and I think it's a sad commentary on this club if that truly is the case," he told me.

I began to think I might have very well been wrong on this one. Wrong for the first time. This guy's behavior ran contrary to every dumbass we'd ever pulled out of a stall. This guy really was just helping his friend out because he was sick. That had never happened before. I quickly recognized that this could be trouble.

"I'm sorry. I have a lot of experience in this sort of thing and this is the first time I've been wrong. So again, I'm sorry. Please go back and enjoy your dinner if you can. I hope you feel better," I said in an attempt to mitigate the damage.

The man seemed satisfied with my apology and they returned to their table. After they took off, I was left to ponder the encounter. This situation was a good one—a situation where one person was helping another in a time of need. It illustrated to me just how far I'd fallen in my views on people-at-large. My knee-jerk reaction to humanity was to first assume the worst, then try to manipulate the situation to benefit me and my band of fellow miscreants. When the situation was something other than what I was used to, I still tried to turn it to our benefit. I felt bad, but only for minute.

It was New Year's Eve in Las Vegas, and for that shit, you better have your boots laced and your helmet pulled tight. I went back to work. A few weeks later, we received a scathing letter from the gentleman. He was still outraged about the whole incident. He was stunned at how a high-class establishment could tolerate such behavior from its guests. He did not discredit the fact that I was simply using the tools I had at my disposal given my experiences in the room. He did, however, hint at the fact that he had felt like he had to pay us off, which meant the message was loud and clear, even if I was losing my touch a bit. But another message was loud and clear as well: club life in Las Vegas is a far cry from real life anywhere else.

The new year began and it felt like the walls of the valley were closing in. The Las Vegas valley is wide and approaching urban sprawl, but since a huge number of its inhabitants come and go, it can still feel like a smallish town. Spend too much time in the land of neon without breaking the outer rim and it might very well consume you. A few of us were on the verge when Johnny asked Greasy and I if we'd go to Arizona to help his parents move. We jumped at the chance to get out of town for a few days. So we packed up and headed out.

Johnny's parents lived in mountains. Its high elevation and vast pine forests were a world away from Las Vegas. The plan was to stay downtown and hit some bars where Johnny knew a few people; the next morning, we'd get up and help his parents.

We got there in the early evening and, after saying hello to Johnny's parents, we headed for the downtown area. We stopped at one of the more popular bars in town, a spot where Johnny's boy was the GM, so naturally the booze flowed. Arizona being a pretty white state and Johnny's hometown being a pretty white city made the fact that Greasy was with us a novelty to the locals. It wasn't long before we had company.

Four local girls approached Greasy and me after Johnny headed across the street to book a hotel room. They were pretty, college-age chicks, and to them, Greasy may as well have been a celebrity. Johnny soon returned and announced that he'd straightened out our room at some historic hotel across the street. Since we were always trying to get a freak party started, we ordered shots—Jaeger bombs for everyone. We all drank and bullshitted for a while. Round after round of shots came to the table. Seven came and seven went down. One of the girls bowed out of the festivities but the shots still came in sevens. When the seventh shot showed up, Johnny and I alternated who drank. It was close to midnight when Johnny told us we had to go. Our hotel, it seemed, closed the doors at night, locking all the patrons inside.

Johnny had given the manager a hundred to keep the hotel open, thereby giving us an extra hour at the bar. We bid the ladies a final farewell after they declined an invitation to take the party to our room across the street. We hustled into the hotel and ambled up to the bar; apparently, Johnny had paid the bartender to stay open as well. A skinny kid dressed in chef's attire sat on a stool on our side of the bar. The bartender, a woman made pretty only by her Amazonian size and the fact that I was innumerable shots deep, was waiting for us. We all sat down and ordered drinks. Small talk ensued.

"We're from Vegas ..."

"On vacation ..."

"Like to drink ..."

"Can we buy you guys a round?"

All was going swimmingly, and I started in on the bartender. "You know, girl ... being tall like you are, you and I could have, like, ten genetically superior babies."

She warmed to this and I suddenly found myself with an opportunity to still have a freak party. We were talking and getting along spectacularly until I heard voices pitch up two seats down. I turned just in time to see Johnny punch the chef in the face. As he did, the force spun his barstool, and on the return trip, he punched him in the face again.

Greasy grabbed Johnny as I stood up to assist. The force of the punches was diminished by the fact that Johnny was seated and the barstool had moved, so Chef was little more than stunned.

Chef was rubbing his jaw. "What was that for?" he asked Johnny.

"You're talking shit. He was talking shit," Johnny said, simultaneously talking to Chef and trying to convince Greasy and I that he was justified.

"Johnny, man, just chill out," Greasy said in an attempt to get him to relax.

Luckily, Johnny saw the reason in this and extended his hand, which Chef refused to shake.

"Yo, man, do you want to defuse this? You see the man has his hand out. Just shake it," I told Chef.

He still refused to shake. This was bad for several reasons.

Johnny was one of the most unreasonable people I have ever met when he's drunk. *Hothead* didn't begin to describe how he could be. He had the shortest of fuses, and since he was on about six types of steroids, he was currently the human equivalent of an A-bomb. Johnny had already punched Chef in the face twice, and it was just pure blind luck that we didn't have to pull raging-bull Johnny off the guy after the initial two-piece.

I leaned on Greasy and Johnny to get my point across. "Look, bro, in life, there are two roads a man can take. One is the road to respect, which is shaking this man's hand. The other is the road to getting your ass kicked. Now, which do you want it to be?" I asked him.

Apparently, this flourish of poetry helped Chef see his lousy position more clearly. Or perhaps it was the fact that the hotel security guard was giving him the thumbs down sign from behind us. Regardless, Chef extended his hand and shook with Johnny.

We attempted to order more drinks but the bartender thought it was a good time to close and the security guard, who had finally found his balls, agreed with her. The staff closed up shop and we retired to our room. Since it was a historical building, our room was built like a cavernous boxcar, with high ceilings and wooden floors. There were three single beds with metal frames that looked like they had been taken from an insane asylum. There, on one of the beds, sat two cases of beer, compliments of Johnny's boy across the street. We drank a couple beers and sat in the room pondering what to do next when it became evident—Johnny attacked me.

It was a full-on scrap, but not in the I'm-trying-to-destroy-you-or-hurt-you-permanently sort of way. I picked Johnny up and attempted to slam him, when I toppled over and he landed on top of me. My hip slammed into the metal bed frame. The result was the worst bruise I have ever seen. Johnny sat up and punched me a couple of times. I pushed him off with my feet and, as he came back, I moved. His momentum carried him over the bed and onto the floor. I jumped on him and proceeded to choke him. I had it sunk and could have choked him unconscious but refrained. That was my mistake.

Johnny reached up and grabbed a handful of my flesh and partially squeezed/partially attempted to rip it off my neck. I let go of the choke and kicked him away from me. I held my hands up to indicate I was game if he wanted to continue the battle. I also winked to let him know I was going to have to escalate the violence due to him nearly ripping my neck off. But Johnny had gotten it out of his system and the battle was put on hold. It was all in good fun, so we sat down and cracked another beer. We talked a while and were just about to crack another cold one when Greasy suggested we head downstairs to poke around. He was hungry and his logic was, "They have a chef, they have a kitchen."

The hotel was deserted and we found the kitchen quickly. None of the refrigerators or pantries were locked, so I helped myself to a few handfuls of cheese and some nuts. Greasy found the walk-in and he ducked in, only to emerge with a huge tube of ground beef.

"Dude, we got to take this. You know how much this costs?" he asked me.

"It's fucking hamburger. What the fuck are we going to do with, like, twenty-five pounds of ground beef? We don't have a cooler. Just put it back," I said.

He wasn't happy about this, but Greasy dove back into the walk-in and returned with a sack of something.

"What are you doing now?" I asked.

"They got these little cordon bleus. We're eating this shit. Get the oil right there," he said.

I handed Greasy the handle of oil while he retrieved a pot. He potted the oil and stuck in a thermometer. While were waiting for the oil to heat up, Greasy found the kitchen torch and proceeded to char the wooden handles of all the utensils in the whole kitchen. The oil was still not hot enough, so we stepped out into the bar. I jumped behind the bar, and since the taps were operational, I began sampling all the beers. Greasy stayed put to make a phone call and I moved to the front of the hotel.

As I finished my beer, I decided to try and arc a stream of piss over the handrails that flanked the entrance. Though I tried my hardest, I couldn't make the second handrail. I finished and headed back to find Greasy. I found him still on the phone, standing at the bottom of the stairs.

"Hang up the phone—we're hanging out," I told him.

Greasy looked me off and continued his conversation. So I punched him one good time in the face.

"Dude, what the fuck?" he said a split second before he shot a right hand into my stomach and doubled me over.

Since Greasy's a trained cage fighter, I considered this single gut shot a reprieve. He hung up and we returned to the kitchen to eat cordon bleu and drink our beers.

When we get back to the room, Johnny was already asleep. We killed the lights and went to sleep.

A sound roused both Greasy and I at the same time. It was coming from Johnny's side of the room.

"Yo, Hank, I think something's up with Johnny," Greasy whispered.

"Johnny, you all right over there?" I called out.

Johnny sat upright in bed and Greasy turned on the light. We saw black Jaeger vomit covering Johnny's face, his shirt, and the bed. Johnny then finished puking black all over the bed. When he was finally convinced that he was finished, Johnny got up and headed down the hall to clean up in the communal hotel bathroom.

"Man, I'm glad we woke up, Greasy. He could have choked on that shit," I said.

"Yeah, no doubt. But what are we going to do with this mattress? It's ruined," Greasy told me.

I was still shitty drunk and the idea of cleaning up vomit with no towels and water from the bathroom down the hall was unappealing. "Fuck that. Let's just flip the mattress and let that bitch go back to bed."

Greasy agreed and we flipped the mattress over, trapping all the puke underneath. Johnny returned and then did one of the most animalistic things I have ever seen: he cracked a beer to wash the puke out of his mouth.

Greasy and I watched incredulously as Johnny sat on his puke-filled mattress and finished his beer.

"It fucking smells in here. Open a window," Johnny slurred to us as he got up and proceeded to a low-slung window. He threw open the sash and nearly fell head first out of the second-story window. I grabbed his waistband and arm to steady him.

"You know your girl would kill us if we let your ass fall out a window. Go to bed," I told him.

We all went back to bed, only to wake a few hours later because the frigid, thirty-degree wind was blowing like hell through the window. But that was bearable compared to the smell of the room.

The odor of booze-soaked, half-digested Italian food mixed with sour dairy product permeated the room. The rankness of the vomit quickly overwhelmed the need to sleep off our approaching hangovers. We policed up our luggage, including the unfinished beers, and headed for the lobby. The only other guests, a married couple who looked spry and ready to take on the day, greeted us when we got there.

The man smiled and had a hearty chuckle at the sight of us. "Oh, it was you guys in here with us last night. We didn't know if it was a herd of elephants, an earthquake, or World War III," he said.

We didn't say a word as we pushed the front door's emergency bar and headed out into the frigid dawn.

I understand that fighting people, pissing on floors, and generally acting like an animal is gross, foolish, and shows a staggering lack of respect for oneself and others. But once we started getting away with things, the recklessness became a sort of contest. The more outrageous the behavior, the further we were apt to push things. For myself, I needed to see how far the rabbit hole went. How far down could one go? To use an addict's terminology, was there a true rock bottom? I was in good company for sure. I'd surrounded myself with people as crazy, maybe even crazier, than myself. While the majority of this book covers what I went through by myself, I wonder what the fuck my guys were up to when they were on their own. It couldn't have been good.

One night, we were enjoying a few post-work cocktails. Since I was in charge and the low man on the totem pole, I drew closing duty. I was the governing force in the nightclub at the end of the night. That meant the bar was open for me and the guys and anyone else who could be trusted and wanted to drink, which was pretty much everyone.

We had been drinking steadily throughout the night and had a pretty good buzz going. Greasy, Crow, Lima, and I were sitting around one of the lounge tables with Iris, one of the cocktail waitresses. Iris had been working that night and had decided to stay after for a couple drinks. The boys welcomed her company, as she was a hot-ass Mexican dime piece and a self-professed freak. The low point was that her boyfriend had come over from one of the other clubs in the casino to meet her. But we didn't really care that he was there—it was casual and as usual, it was, the more the merrier. He was in the business and as such we extended him the hospitality he would show us if we were at his club.

We were all drinking, rolling C-Lo, and getting along swimmingly. The shit-talking was reaching epic proportions, which usually involved calling one another's manhood into question, claiming we could beat the shit out of each other, and disputing who would win. For reasons unbeknownst to me, Iris' boyfriend had decided to join in the shit-talk. He was amongst people that he had just met and started running his mouth. Not the smartest move given the company, but I liked the fact that he was sure enough to assert himself. But it wasn't long before Lima took offense to a couple jibes from the kid.

Both of them being of Latin descent, I sensed that there was some blood-in/blood-out shit going on. At any rate, we cooled the C-Lo game and decided to head downstairs for a couple drinks. We gathered up and a few went to the restroom. The verbal sparring grew heated when Lima questioned the kid's ability to hold a woman like Iris in check. Lima fired a barb and the kid shot back, "Why don't you show me how?"

Lima's blood was already up and this was a direct challenge. We all knew what the kid was saying without him actually saying it, and this was a bad move on his part.

"Fuck it—let's go downstairs, then," Lima told him, readily accepting the challenge.

The kid hit the button to call the elevator. "Let's go, Lima," he fires off again, not a hint of fear in his voice. That's the beauty of liquor, I suppose.

Lima walked right up and got in his face, but the kid didn't flinch. I admired the kid's moxie, but I knew Lima would fucking destroy this fool. Discretion is the better part of valor, and since Iris' man refused to exercise any, I decided to step in.

"Look, nobody is going anywhere. Nobody's fighting. After the rest of these jackasses get back from taking a piss, we're all leaving together," I told them. This lightened the mood of the Mexican standoff.

"Yeah, fuck it—I'm going to piss right here," Lima said as he unzipped.

I knew he was drunk enough to piss on the carpet and I grabbed him by the back of his jacket and slung him towards the bathroom hallway. He went flying and Iris' boyfriend laughed. He opened his mouth to continue ragging on Lima.

"Don't," I said, cutting him off. I had just managed to defuse the situation before it got out of hand, and I didn't want him to agitate Lima any further. "Look, he's alrea—"

I was cut short as Lima came off my right shoulder. He one-shot the kid right to the jaw and the kid just dropped like a ton of bricks as

Lima stumbled over his falling body. "Wake that nigga up," Lima said before the kid evens hit the floor.

Lima stumbled and nearly fell before catching himself on the wall. The kid was out cold on the floor. He was stiff as a board and I'll be goddamned if he wasn't SNORING. Iris' boyfriend had taken a one-hitter quitter and dropped straight into the land of nod.

Just then, Collier entered from an adjacent room. "Holy shit. Is that dude knocked out?" he said with a smile.

"Yeah, he's fucking out. Get him," I said, handing Lima off.

I knelt beside the kid and I couldn't believe how loud he was snoring. I shook him and clapped my hands. He didn't wake. I slapped him a couple of times and still he didn't stir. I was laughing because this kid was knocked the fuck out. I was also shitting because we could all lose our jobs if we had to call the ambulance for this.

Iris returned from the bathroom and went hysterical. She screamed his name and tried to wake him up. I explained what had happened and she lost her shit, taking hysterical to a new plateau.

Crow rounded the corner and we finally had a trained professional on scene. The once-auxiliary fireman gave the kid a chest rub and he finally stirred.

"What happened?" he asked.

"I don't know, man—I think you fell," I told him.

"Really? That's weird," he said.

"You're telling me. I turned around and you were out. You're lucky you didn't hit your head on the way down," I said.

We helped him up and got him a bottle of water. Iris pushed between Crow and I and she started to tell him what had happened, but I quickly waved her off. We didn't need him getting his blood up after we had just woken him up from getting KO'ed.

"How you feeling?" I asked.

"A little spaced out."

"I guess it's time to call it a night," I suggested.

He agreed and Iris took her boyfriend down.

We gave them time to clear the area and then we corralled Lima and took him downstairs. It was decided that, since he had entered psycho-kill mode, he shouldn't drive anywhere. I told him he was staying at my house and we all decided to meet at a 24-hour Mexican-food joint not far from my apartment.

We headed across the casino on our way to the parking garage. Directly in our path was an area cordoned off on the casino floor where a number of workers were laying new carpet. I watched as Lima cut between a row of slot machines and we became separated. Lima stepped over the ropes and into the workers' area. I called out to him but he just turned around, flipping me the double bird as he hurled expletives about me and my mother. I was cut off by a bank of slot machines and had to go around so I could get to him.

I came around just in time to see Lima trip backwards over a guy laying carpet. The guy was pissed for obvious reasons, as a shitty, drunk Mexican had just fallen on him. Lima was cursing him out as he continued walking. He finally reached the end, crossed the rope, and was confronted by casino security. I hustled around the last bank of slot machines and arrived for the tail end of the conversation.

"Well, if you were a real man, you would," Lima slurred into the security guard's face.

I could only imagine how the first part of the exchange had gone. This was a bad situation. Fucking with casino security while drunk was the surest way of losing your job. You got eighty-sixed from the property for drunken antics and you lost your job by default. It's hard to work if you're not allowed on the property.

"Look, I'm sorry. I'm driving him home. As you can see, he's a little out of hand," I told the security guard, hoping he won't press the issue.

Luckily, he was satisfied with my apology. We finally reached my truck and headed for the Mexican joint.

"Let's bump Wu Tang," Lima said. "Wu Tang, bitch. Your fucking mother likes that shit," he continued the drunken onslaught.

Since he was in a delicate frame of mind, we bumped fucking Wu Tang and Lima slurred the words. On our way to the Mexican joint, Lima threatened me with bodily harm more times than I cared to count. We met Collier at the Mexican spot and Lima ordered twenty dollars' worth of burritos that I paid for.

"You want anything else, asshole? How about a fucking churro?" I asked.

He wasn't there to answer because Lima had moved on to fucking with the fake plants and mad-dogging the few customers the restaurant had. I decided to get the food to go, as it wouldn't be long before he had picked a fight with some poor patron.

After stopping to pick up some beer, we headed to my apartment. I told Dana I was home and then I returned to the living area to lay out the food and two fresh beers on the poker table that served as our dining-room table.

Lima refused to eat any of the three burritos he had ordered. I returned to the bedroom and retrieved a number of muscle relaxers. I took a couple and gave Lima a couple as well. I hoped this would put him to bed. I ate as Lima waxed poetic about knocking people out, fucking Iris, and fighting me. I returned to the bedroom and retrieved some Lortab, another dose for Lima and myself.

Now Lima wanted to play poker. He was telling me how he was going to destroy me and take all my tip money. We got the money and chips out. He wanted to play Heads-Up for a hundred a hand. When I counted his money and informed him that he only had three hundred, he changed his story.

"Bitch, you can't even see the cards. We aren't playing poker for money," I told him.

"You scared?" he asked as he reached for his beer. He knocked his beer over and thus committed the cardinal sin of spilling shit all over my poker table.

"Fuck that. It's time to go to sleep," I said as I cleaned up the spill. I returned to the bedroom for the coup de grâce and came back with a handful of Xanax. "Take these, lay the fuck down, and go to sleep," I told him.

Lima downed the pills with his beer. "Take me to my car," he demanded.

"You're out of your mind. You're in no condition to drive, and you don't even have your keys. You lost them in the casino. We already went over that in the truck," I told him. I got a blanket and laid it on the couch. Since the pills had gone to work on me, I headed for the bedroom.

The haze was just beginning to settle over my eyes when Lima called into my bedroom, "Yo, Hank, take me to my car."

"Lima, you don't have your keys, and you shouldn't be driving anyway," I said.

"I got my keys right here, motherfucker," he said.

I walked into the living room. "Where are they? Show them to me."

I normally didn't shatter people's illusion when they were this fucked up, but I couldn't stand it anymore. Lima searched his pockets to no avail.

"Just lay down, bro. I'll take you in the morning." I returned to bed and lay down.

I heard the front door opening and closing a number of times as Lima wandered in and out. He returned to the door of the bedroom. "Yo, Hank, where's my car?"

I contemplated for a moment feeding him some more pills. I'd already given him enough to tranquilize a rhino. I feared giving him more while he was this drunk could possibly kill him, and the ones I'd already given him had done nothing but made him more unreasonable.

I stormed into the living room. "Your keys aren't here. Your car is at the casino. I'll take you in the morning," I explained once again.

"Bitch, I'll just walk, then. Since now I know where my car is," he told me.

"Well, go, then," I told him.

I felt terrible for telling him this when he was in such a state, a state that I was partially responsible for. But I was at the end of my rope—I was tired and drunk, too, and I'd spent the last few hours keeping this fool out of trouble. I opened the door for him and he walked out. I knew in my heart of hearts that he'd be back, so I left it unlocked.

I returned to the bedroom and lay down. A short while later, I hear the front door open and Lima walked in.

"Yo, Hank, where's my car again?"

Dana, having listened to the proceedings for the last two hours, had had enough. "I'll drive him home," she said.

I walked into the living room, where Lima paced the floor.

"Give me a minute to get dressed. We'll take you home," I told him.

251

I returned to the bedroom to get dressed. But when Dana and I emerged from the bedroom, Lima was gone. Dana and I climbed into her car and drove up Jones heading toward the 215. We saw Lima walking across a vacant lot strewn with rocks and brush.

"LIMA!" I yelled his name.

He flipped me the bird and took off running. The sight of a drunk, pilled-out Mexican dressed in a light-gray suit running across a desert lot in the early morning sun stopped a number of nearby construction workers. They watched with us as Lima tore off in the general direction of the Strip. He didn't get far before he took a tumble and went end over end down a small gully. He got up and, even from distance, it was obvious that the fall had taken the wind out of his sails. He stood up and brushed himself off. The fall had scrambled his brain a bit, as well, and he walked slowly in the opposite direction of where he was heading.

Dana and I pulled into a housing development and we met him at the edge of the vacant lot.

"Lima, get in the car. We're taking you home," I told him.

"Fuck you!" he screamed.

Those were his last words until we got him home. I wasn't sure if he was thankful for the ride, if the tumble he took in the desert had adjusted his attitude, or if the pills had finally kicked in. But he sat quietly in the back for the whole ride.

"Thanks for the ride. Thanks, Dana," Lima said as he climbed from the car.

"How you getting in?" I asked.

"Through the window. It's unlocked. See you tomorrow, dickhead," he wished me well.

As Dana and I pulled away, we heard breaking glass.

"Just go," I told her.

While there was some damage control necessary after the incident between Lima and Iris' boyfriend, it didn't take much to remedy the situation. No one wanted to lose their jobs over an incident like this, and making too much of it would have required asking some serious questions about how the night had unfolded. Questions nobody wanted to answer. Not me. Not Lima. Not Iris. Not even Iris' boyfriend, and he was the one who got knocked out. Iris didn't press very hard to defend her man, and we soon found out why.

It was a post-work drinking session and the order of the night was Dragon's Breath and C-Lo for tips. The work night had been lucrative and we were rolling off for pots that would reach a few hundred dollars. Iris had gotten so drunk on shift that she couldn't complete her paperwork, so one of the other cocktail waitresses took care of it for her. She was passed out on the couch next to us while we shot dice and drank ourselves into oblivion.

The crew had finally grown comfortable with their winnings or uncomfortable with their losses and we decided to get a drink up the road, away from the casino. Tyrell was one of our bussers. He was also an uncompromising opportunist, and since Iris could barely walk, much less drive, he volunteered to take her home. I told you before that Iris was a self-professed freak, and I think this was the sole reason for Tyrell playing Captain Save-a-Ho. She was wasted and Tyrell no doubt saw an opportunity. But we needed to get her home safely, or at least in the realm of safely. We were all walking to the parking lot when I got a bright idea.

"Yo, Tyrell, give me Iris' keys. I'll drive her car," I told him.

Iris owned a BMW M3 and I could think of nothing better than borrowing her car and driving it as fast as possible. Tyrell flipped me the keys and took Iris to his car.

Greasy and I retrieved the car. I screamed through the parking garage learning to drive the autoshift. I dropped Greasy off at his car and we agreed to meet at our regular spot on Sunset. I screamed out of the parking lot and made a right on the Strip. I slammed the car through its gears and sped past the police station. I slowed only to stop at the light and make the left on Sunset. That's when Greasy pulled up beside me in his Mustang and revved his engine.

That meant the race was on. As soon as the light turned, we took off. I screamed off the turn. We wove in and out of early morning traffic. The speedometer in the BMW climbed quickly and I left Greasy behind. I slowed around 90 mph to let Greasy catch me. I saw he was newly dedicated to winning this race and I depressed the accelerator. I pushed car into fifth and once again left Greasy behind. I was screaming past people on their way to work. I reached 120 mph and then I realized I had another gear. I pushed it into gear and the car had another life. Safety was secondary to seeing how fast this thing would go. The speedometer pushed past 130 mph. The only thing passing me was a plane that was taking off of a McCarran airport runway.

It finally occurred to me that if I continued at these speeds, someone could get killed. I was so tied up in seeing how fast Iris' car could go that I passed the bar. I turned around and Greasy was waiting for me in the lot. I hopped out completely psyched by the speed.

"Man, that shit is fast. Where is everybody else?" I asked Greasy.

"I guess they all called it a night. Bryant has Iris and they're going to the Dayside Inn," he told me.

Greasy and I decided to go in and have the required shot and a beer before we hit the road. After our round, Greasy told me he was heading home. It was now nine-thirty in the morning and I wanted to drop Iris' car off and get home myself.

Greasy took off and I called Bryant. He told me they were at the Dayside Inn, but when I arrived, they were nowhere to be found. I called Bryant again and he was mysteriously unreachable. I contemplated abandoning Iris' car with the keys inside and walking home, as my apartment was just up the street from the bar. I called Iris in a last-ditch attempt to do the right thing. I wasn't expecting her to pick up the phone, as she was pretty much wrecked when we left work. But to my surprise, she answered.

"Hey, Iris, I have your car. Where are you?" I asked.

"We're heading to my house. Meet us there."

She gave me directions and I headed off. As I got close, I got lost. I pulled off to the side and tried to call her again.

A car screeched to a stop in the middle of the road and some guy I didn't recognize screamed at me out the window, "It's two streets down. Third house on the right." He looked thoroughly pissed and he screeched his tires as he pulled off.

I followed his directions and saw Iris and Bryant standing in driveway. "Who the fuck was that guy?" I asked.

"That's my boyfriend. He's just pissed," Iris told me. "He woke up on the couch while Bryant was sitting there. He got pissed and left."

I'd be pissed, too, if my girlfriend was inviting guys from the crew that had seen me knocked out over to my house. Still, Iris invited us in.

"You guys want a drink? I only have vodka," she said.

"I appreciate the hospitality. You got any painkillers?" I asked her. My buzz was waning, and that just couldn't happen.

"I don't know. I think I have some Soma. Let me get them." Iris retrieved the pills and handed me four, when Bryant piped up.

"Can I get a couple?"

I knew Bryant didn't take pills. I recognized that he was trying to prove to Iris that he was down. I also knew this was a weak play for pussy. He was willing to go down a road he knew nothing about just to impress her.

Lesson time, I thought to myself.

"Sure, Bryant. But let's take 'em with those shots of vodka. It hits you harder," I told him.

A short while later, Bryant was asleep on the couch when Iris and I decided to go for a drink up the street.

Iris was an attractive girl, but she also had an almost constant stream of cold sores around her mouth. "It's how I know my immune system is low," she told us once. It wasn't so much the fact that she had the cold sores—she didn't have any then, and so it wasn't that big of a deal—but I also knew that she was reckless as hell and found herself quite frequently in the company of strange men. Now, I knew that I'd slept with a prostitute multiple times without using protection, and that flew in the face of my decision-making when it came to Iris. But to me, there was an ocean of difference in risk between a woman who approached sex as a business, who therefore took the necessary precautions, and one who got wrecked on the regular and was willing to go with anybody.

I was very familiar with the level of caution someone with that life approach showed, and this was enough to dissuade me from venturing into her pants, even though I knew she'd be game. She had a boyfriend, I had a girlfriend, and both of us knew this. The loyalty piece for her was flexible, just as it was for me. My only real loyalty was to the crew, my core unit. The brotherhood I felt with the guys was something I hadn't known since I was growing up. My friends were my family, and these guys were blood to me. Everything else was negotiable.

Iris and I drank for quite a while, long enough for me to ensure that Dana had left for work and I wouldn't suffer any immediate trouble when I came home. We returned to Iris' house and I woke Bryant up as he slumbered on the couch. He had to drive me home. Awhile later, I learned some information that made me happy with my decision not to sleep with Iris. It was the day Bryant came up to me and asked me if I ever had a pimple on my dick.

I had been faithful to Dana since she'd returned to Las Vegas, even if I was giving myself a pass for sleeping with Colette two days before she arrived. I was passing up all the females who throw themselves at you on a nightly basis and I was giving my best effort to turn over a new leaf, to make the best of things between Dana and me. I hadn't seen Colette for a couple of months when, out of the blue, she showed up at the club on a Monday night. She lingered at a distance until I called her over. We held a short conversation that was not at all genuine on my part. I was trying to distance myself, and being no stranger to body language herself, she read it loud and clear. She went upstairs and I told her I would join her later for a drink. I waited long enough for the door to slow down and for David to come back with our cut from the door.

I went upstairs and found Colette hanging out in the hip-hop room. The lights were up and Lima was shooing some of the stragglers out of the room. Since Colette was family, she was bellied up to the bar and was in the care of Gordon, one of our bartenders. Gordon was a black kid from Africa and he was enamored with Colette. I couldn't blame him—Colette was an extremely attractive woman. She knew just how to push buttons in men and always had their attention. Gordon was pouring her a fresh shot of tequila when I sidled up next to her.

"Make it one more," I said and Gordon obliged.

Colette and I clinked our glasses and tossed one back. I noticed she was on edge and drinking with a purpose. I felt like this was because I had slighted her at the door. My heart was filled with love for her and I had to deny that feeling to preserve the relationship I had started over with Dana. I couldn't show Colette that I had an interest other than friendship. This denial would never wash internally or externally. The love I felt for Colette was oozing out of my eyes every time I looked at her. I was down for her no matter what, and my inner denial just muddled the situation.

Colette was onto me. Her intuition made me transparent. But for me, the denial was enough. I was sure this cut Colette deep and she sought to bury it under an avalanche of drink. I slid down to the end of the bar as Gordon poured her another huge shot.

She better not drink that, I thought to myself. I was concerned for her safety, as though prostitution was a safe endeavor. I was mad at Gordon for pouring her the drink. I couldn't know whether he did it to set me up an easy mark or he just did it to foster more insanity in someone he didn't know. We all know that's part of the fun.

"You're one away," I said to her.

She looked at me. I read betrayal in her eyes and then she killed the entire glass of tequila. She slammed the empty on the bar and walked out. I wondered if it was for good. My answer came quickly. Not twenty minutes later, I got a call from Colette. She was hysterical.

"Hank, I'm in the bathroom. I'm in the bathroom. I need you to come get me right now," she cried.

I was alarmed because I'd never heard her like this.

"Please, you have to come and get me. Security was outside and they were waiting for me. Please come." She was begging. Colette didn't beg.

"Where are you? Which bathroom?" I asked while I headed for the elevator.

"The bathroom, by the poker room, by the mall," she whimpered through the phone.

"All right, stay there. I'll be right there," I told her.

I rushed across the casino. I assumed security had followed her because she was a known prostitute. I was amazed that they would be onto her, because when it came to her business, Colette was always on top of her game.

As I reached the bathroom, I recognized the security guards who were standing outside. "Hey, fellas. How's it going? There's a young lady inside. I came to get her," I told them.

"Yeah, she said her boyfriend is coming to get her. You her boyfriend?" he asked.

"No. She's just a good friend. I'd like to take her out of here if I could," I said, deferring to their sense of justice and hoping they wouldn't hassle me too much. I knew if I were working security and someone was willing to take a potential problem off my hands, I'd let them. Plus I knew Colette had a rap sheet as long as my arm, and she'd been trespassed in more than a couple Strip casinos.

"Sure, man. We just followed her over here because the pimps were getting at her. She was giving them hell. But if you got her, it's cool," one of the guards told me.

Colette emerged from the bathroom as if on cue. She hugged up next to me and curled under my arm. She was wasted.

"Thanks, fellas. I'll get her home safe," I said.

I was relieved that they weren't pushing the issue. I walked Colette to my truck and she was only partially under her own power. I was supporting her, guiding her. I opened the truck door and helped her into the cab.

We drove her up the street to the 24-hour diner that she and I frequented from time to time. I needed to get her something to eat and give her time to sober up. I pulled in and parked the truck. Just as I pulled the keys from the ignition, Colette wrenched the door handle and the door swung open. She had one hand on the handle and the other hand on the seat. She leaned out of the door without swinging her legs and her drunken, uneasy momentum carried her out of the truck and onto the pavement face first.

I jumped out of the truck and hurried around. People in the front of the restaurant saw her fall and their faces said it all. I helped her up and I got to see the full extent of the damage. Colette had landed on her face. She was bleeding from her mouth. She had a fat lip, multiple scrapes, and a huge egg on her forehead. "Oh, God," escaped from my lips as I picked her up from the pavement.

I sat her back in the truck and retrieved a water bottle and a towel from behind the seat. I tried my best to clean her up. I wiped the tear-streaked blood from her face. I didn't know where to start. I needed ice for her head and her lip but I couldn't leave her unattended to retrieve it from the restaurant. She'd already mangled herself in a split second. I knew I needed to get her home.

But I didn't know where she lived anymore. We'd been out of touch since Dana returned, and last I knew, Colette had left her apartment. I asked her where she lived.

"Green fairy," was all she could muster.

She was drunk and fading in and out of consciousness. I was worried she had a concussion. But I wasn't going to take her to the hospital. I just needed to get her home so I could clean her up.

"What side of town do you live on now, Colette?" I asked.

"North. Craig. Green Fairy," she yelled at me before she faded out again.

At least I had a direction now.

I headed out of the parking lot and drove onto the ramp leading to I-15. I was hoping she'd come out of it by the time I got to Craig Road, at least enough to give me a better sense of where, exactly, she might live. When we split off I-15 and onto the highway leading to North town, Colette rolled down the window and began puking down the side of my truck. This was not a good situation. I was driving around with a bloody, battered prostitute who was puking. I knew I had a warrant out for my arrest for failure to pay the ticket I'd gotten on the way back from Laughlin. We spent the next three hours driving around North Las Vegas.

Colette would come to and give me partial directions, then check out again. She would mutter something about green fairy. I tried everything from being nice to being angry to pleading. Colette moved between belligerent and inconsolable. She would wake up trying to fight me and then move into periods of extreme despair. The most wounding exchanges were when she would show me her heart.

"You're the only one who ever showed me any respect. The only one," she cried. "Why can't you just love me?" she asked again and again.

259

I hadn't beaten her up but I might as well have. I'd hurt a woman who had undoubtedly experienced unknown horror. Through my weakness, I'd managed to get inside her walls and wound her. She'd let me in and I'd hurt her, just by being me.

Colette was a dynamic woman. She was thoughtful and kind. She had a pure heart and I truly believed that she only wanted to be loved. The single thing that kept me from committing to her was the fact that all my friends knew she was a prostitute. For that, I am ashamed. The way she looked at me with those pleading eyes. When she would smile at me, it would electrify her face, a physical happiness that would cause her body to shiver and threaten to burst. I never wondered if that's how she looked at them. Colette had the simplest of dreams—all she wanted to do was open an ice cream shop. She just wanted to have a normal life scooping ice cream and taking care of people, making them smile. A dream we could have accomplished together very easily.

Colette finally sobered enough to tell me where to go. It turned out that the street she lived on was called Green Fairy. I carried her into the house and cleaned her up. I laid her in bed and crept out of the house. As I climbed into my truck, I worried that she might have suffered a concussion. I wondered if she would wake up. I called her the next day to check on her, but she didn't answer. I wondered if she remembered what had happened. I wondered if she thought I had beat her up. It sickened me to think she might. I only ever laid eyes on Colette once more.

The next day, I was on my way home from a poker session. I'd had a losing session and was pissed off. As I waited to make a left turn onto the 15 on-ramp, I handed the last of my cash out the window to a bum that was posted up on the median. When you're losing, it's as if the cash doesn't matter. That gut-sickening feeling that you should at least do something good with some of it overwhelms you. I have no doubt that many gamblers feel this way. Sometimes it's so overwhelming that they can't handle the swing and end up doing something drastic. Not me, though—I just handed the bum a wad of cash and immediately felt better about the whole situation. After all, there was more cash to be had that night—all I had to do was hustle.

The light changed and I pulled a left, gunned the engine, and slipped into traffic. As soon as I made the move onto I-15, a Nevada Highway Patrol car slipped in behind me at an accelerated speed. I knew I was sunk. I still hadn't paid the ticket I'd received during the trip to Laughlin. Failure to pay the ticket meant the court would issue a bench warrant for my arrest and suspend my license. Since my license was suspended, I couldn't renew my registration. With those two pieces of the puzzle firmly in place, the third fell right in—I was also driving without insurance. This was all by foolish design, as I'd wanted to see how long I could roll with a warrant without getting picked up.

When the blue lights fired up, I pulled over immediately. A portly kid stepped to the passenger-side window. I was wondering how he'd met the minimum physical requirements for the job.

"Do you know why I'm pulling you over?" he asked.

"Yeah, my registration isn't up to date." I handed him the necessary documents and he returned to his car. I contemplated calling Greasy to let him know I was going to jail. But I knew it would take awhile to get processed, so I figured I'd just call from inside after I found out where they were taking me. He returned and the prelude to jail began.

Doughy cop: "Hank, do you know there is a warrant out for your arrest."

I gave him my best denial look.

Me: "No. What's it for?"

Doughy cop: "I can't tell you that. But I need you to step out of the car."

Me: "Sure, no problem."

I climbed out on the passenger side and spied his partner—a matronly woman who was also made of dough stood about fifteen feet behind him. It occurred to me that they could both appear lumpy because of the body armor, but their cheeks carried the bloat of too many meals eaten in their car.

Me: "Do you want me to roll up the window?"

Matronly/doughy cop: "SIR, STEP TO THE REAR OF THE VEHICLE."

The woman yelled as she slid her hand down to her weapon. I smiled and shook my head. So many cops had only one speed. I stepped to the rear and assumed the position. His search was fumbling and not very thorough. I was mentally breaking down their relationship, looking for a way to drive a wedge into it and hopefully make it out of there with just a warning. But that was going to be a tall order. The portly kid was new on the job and the broad was his T.O.—Training Officer. This explained the overzealousness with her mouth and her gun. It wasn't long before I was in handcuffs and being whisked off to jail.

"Why didn't you take care of your ticket?"

Why did they always ask questions they couldn't care less about? For a moment, I faltered and forgot that I don't talk to cops. "I didn't have the mo … You know what? It doesn't even matter."

I stared out the window of the cop car and watched the lights of the Strip pass by. It wasn't lost on me that, just the day before, I was drunk and driving 130 mph down a busy street and I could have been picked up then, making the arrest only about a million times worse in the eyes of the court. I'd always been lucky that way. That is, if lucky meant still going to jail.

I wondered if this was where I belonged. I wondered if this was where I might someday end up. For most of my life, I'd thought I was but one bad day away from serious prison time. I messed with the cuffs a little to see how he had put them on. Was the keyhole up or down? Did he double-lock them? If I had a comb, could I ratchet-click them while sitting on my hands? This passed the time and gave me something to think about, other than the fact that I was headed to a cage.

We arrived and they passed me through to the CO, where my information was copied and my shoes were taken and replaced by a shitty pair of plastic flip-flops. They did allow me to get a few phone numbers out of my cell phone so I could make some calls and get someone to bail me out. Then they threw me in the concrete holding cell and told me someone would be coming to fingerprint in awhile.

I called Greasy while he was on his way to work. He offered to come bail me out after work and I told him I'd just wait until morning court and get out on OR, my own recognizance. Greasy then proceeded to tell me that he got sentenced to two weeks over Christmas for a traffic infraction. He had received this sentence in morning court.

This whole experience had just changed complexion. "You've got to get me the fuck out of here," I told Greasy.

This response elicited a few turns of the head from the denizens of the holding tank.

"I will, but I have to go to work, and it might be close. We don't get out of work until 4:00."

"Just get here ASAP."

I called my roommate Jack and we got to talk for thirty seconds before the phone cut off. Apparently, you can't make collect calls to out-of-state phones while in jail. I looked around at my cellmates, a slew of Mexicans, a black kid around twenty-five or so, and a twitching meth freak who was using the only roll of toilet paper as a pillow. I found this amusing, as there was no way he was going to fall asleep. He just rolled over again and again on the metal bench. No rest for the stupid.

I wait for the CO to come get me for fingerprints. When it was just the two of us, I popped the question: "Miss, I'm in here for a traffic infraction, and I would really appreciate it if you might let me use a phone for just a minute or two. I can't reach my roommate—his number is an out-of-state."

She finished fingerprinting me and told me she'd come get me when the duty sergeant took a break. I was stunned by her humanity.

It was a while later when I was sitting in the cell and I heard, "Man, fuck the motherfuckin' po … lice. Fuck, bitch po … lice, too."

I saw an OG black dude with a Jheri curl still cuffed and being processed. He was giving the COs a ration of shit and therefore making life difficult for everyone who was there. Once in the jaws, one should not make trouble. It only made life more difficult. I saw my chances to use a phone evaporating.

"Man, fuck you. Fuck you, nigga, workin for tha po … lice. Ol' Uncle-Tom-ass nigga."

Please don't put him in here, I thought. I picked up the phone and dialed Greasy. He picked up and gave me the information efficiently, as he was no doubt working the line.

"I already talked to Jack. He's going to bail you out once you hit the system. Call me when you're out and I'll come get you."

I hung up the phone and let the relief just wash over me for a second. This relief didn't last—sure enough, Mr. OG got put in the tank. The tank was already near capacity and there was no room to sit. A couple of drunks had even taken up residency under the benches.

"Man, move, lazy-ass nigga." He kicked the toilet paper out from under the meth addict's head, then pushed his feet off the bench and took a seat. "What, nigga?" he screamed at the meth addict, who glared at him.

I sat silently and waited for my name to be called. A headache of epic proportions had set in and I couldn't wait for them to call my name. Finally, it came: "Carver, Hank O."

I hustled to the door and the woman led me to a lineup. "Did you get a chance to talk to someone yet?" she asked.

"Yes, thank you very much."

I was amazed at her humanity and caring, especially after she'd just been verbally abused by the OG. This feeling, too, was short-lived as I realized she had led me to a line for further processing. I was going into population. I waited in line for a time and I finally reached the front. I was ushered into an infirmary-type place and took a seat in front of a nurse.

"I need your right hand for a shot," she told me.

"I really don't feel comfortable taking a shot from you. I'm not going to be in here that long," I told her.

"That's fine—we'll put you back in the tank and you can wait there."

The idea of going back into the tank, where a potentially volatile situation could erupt with the drunken OG and the host of other freaks, did not appeal to me. I extended my hand for the shot and then I was led into another holding cell where ten other men were lined up.

"Strip down and put your belongings in the plastic bag in front of you."

"All the way down to your bare asses," the CO told us. Now I was standing butt naked with ten dudes in a cold-ass concrete cell. The CO called out a bunch of sizes to another CO who was standing outside and one by one, orange jumpers were distributed. He handed a box containing disposable underwear to the man on the end. Each of us took a pair and put them on.

Don't know what disposable underwear is? Think hairnet, with two holes for your legs. I put on my jumper, which was around three sizes too big. I had to cuff the legs and arms four times to have it even remotely begin to fit.

We were led to pick up our mattress and then led into population, which was locked down for the night. Everyone was in their cells, and I was put into a cell that already contained three people. Luckily, there was a bunk, and I put my mattress on top and climbed up.

My head was killing me because my blood pressure was through the roof. I knew I was getting out in a short time, but I was totally distressed. I sat up in bed and looked around the room, all concrete and steel. The neatly arranged belongings of the prisoners sat on the floor—some letters, envelopes, a box of saltines, a few Styrofoam cups. I could never do this. I didn't and never will do incarceration well. If I ever found myself in a situation where all the chips were down, I would most likely be a suicide-by-cop type. I lay back on the too-small mattress and tried to sleep, but no rest for the stupid.

I lay awake until I heard, "Carver, Hank O." echo off the steel. I jumped off the bunk and grabbed my mattress. I processed out, grabbed my paperwork, and got out of my jumper the same way I got into it, in the company of ten other dudes. Not wanting to take a second longer, I just pulled on my boxers over the mesh jail drawers and exited the private bathroom. I took a seat next to twelve other crooks. A short time later, they ushered us onto a caged van and dropped us off in downtown Las Vegas. I called Greasy on my cell.

"He's out, cuz," Greasy screamed to our coworkers. "Where are you going to be?" he asked.

"I'm going to the Golden Nugget to get a beer," I told him.

"Cool, I'm on the way."

I headed into the GN and took a seat at the bar. "Shot of tequila chilled, beer back. Thanks, man."

I killed my drink and Greasy rung me. "I'm pulling up."

I hustled out onto Fremont Street and Greasy saw me first. "Right here ... left."

I saw the Mustang and ran up the street to the car. I climbed in.

"What the fuck are you running for?" he asked.

"Man, I don't know—let's just get the fuck out of here."

We took it back to the club, where I was given a hero's welcome and everyone wanted to buy me a drink. We tossed back a bunch of rounds and then took it to our late-night spot. Greasy, Crow, Johnny, and Lima—the whole crew was up for some serious drinking. It was like I had just been released from an actual prison sentence.

We'd been drinking steadily when nature called. I stepped into the stall and unzipped. It was then that I realized I still had my mesh jail drawers on. I already had my pants off and I was removing the mesh panties when Johnny walked into the restroom.

"What are you doing?" he asked.

"Nothing, man, just taking a leak," I answered.

"What the fuck are your pants off for?" he asked.

I had to come clean—he had seen my pants. "All right—I have my jail drawers on and I'm going to put them on Greasy like a hairnet."

"That's fucking awesome. You got to do it." Johnny cosigned the idea with almost too much zeal.

"It's not that awesome. It would have been you if you hadn't walked in on me," I told him.

I walked out and showed him the hair net. We were both exiting the restroom when Greasy walked in. One look told it all.

"What are you guys doing?" Greasy asked.

"Nothing," we said in stereo.

But Greasy wasn't buying. "Nah, fuck that—you two are up to some shit."

I showed Greasy the jail drawers and told him he was going to wear them like a hairnet. "I guess it'll have to be Lima."

We all headed back to the bar and Johnny did his best to get Lima looking the other way. I fully stretched the mesh drawers/hairnet and laid it atop his head like a crown. Lima just stood there with the mesh panties on his head, making no attempt to remove them. The crew was crying with laughter. Lima took a long draw off his beer.

"You know that's fucked up, right?" he asked.

"Yeah, I know," I told him. "But it's been a fucked up night."

I headed in to begin my work week with the court date looming over my head. Things had gradually begun to get better in most aspects of my life, or at the very least, the recklessness had slowed to something approaching responsibility—as close as I was going to get, anyway. I viewed this as just another opportunity to fix something that needed repair, and since I was being forced, I might as well go with the flow. I didn't want real trouble, and defying the court when you're in the clutches of the system is about as real of trouble as you'll find. I welcomed the discipline I sadly couldn't provide for myself. I suppose I needed some guidance on the path to improvement. At any rate, I had plenty of time to think about this as the club had slowed as we entered summer. This gave us plenty of down time that we had to fill.

In our business, the lack of clientele left us with nothing to do, and so the level of boredom was high. That night, the topic of interest was caning, as in getting-your-ass-beat-in-Singapore-for-spray-painting-cars caning. Someone found a small piece of bamboo in one of the flower arrangements and it had made its way back to the old managers' office. We were discussing caning versus jail time and which we would choose if faced with such a decision. We looked up pictures on the Internet so as to be more informed when making our choice. The decision was unanimous: give us the cane. This led us to while away the time by testing the cane on each other in a sort of small-scale experiment. It wasn't long before some of the guys raised issues of trust on the severity of the strike.

Being the cane-wielder first opened you up to the possibility that your partner might decide to thrash you soundly, and then you would find yourself without recourse. It was decided that this would be the main interest of the experiment. It was an experiment in team building, building trust through shared experience and pain. The lot of us ended up with welts on our forearms. This brand of fun was short-lived and took place after the last of the guests left. Crow and I took over the maître d's computer to play a scrambled word game. We had been playing for awhile when two females on their way out of the club stopped to say hello.

One was a tall, good-looking blond with a soft figure. Her friend was a petite, pretty brunette. The blond was enamored with Crow, as many women were. Crow was annoyed that she was disturbing our game, and he attempted at least a couple of times to bid the ladies good night. Each time, he became a bit more forceful. The ladies wouldn't be put off, despite Crow's best attempts. Rudeness seemed the quickest way to a club floozy's heart. Other members of the team would stop by the podium for short-burst play on the word game. All of them took notice of the young ladies who wouldn't leave.

So our gears shifted from trying to get rid of them to trying to get one or more of the team members laid. The time came to close and the nightly drinking commenced. We broke out two of our best parlor tricks to entertain the ladies—Dragon's Breath and Sleaze Cinema. Dragon's Breath was a mixture of liquor that you set on fire and then drank. Sleaze Cinema was a DVD our promoter put together of clips from old pulp films. The clips ran together in a weird mix of sex and violence. The alcohol flowed freely, and when it took effect, someone once again raised the topic of caning, aka team building.

The drunken revelry brought the cane out and the team was really ready to bond. With the hearts of both the caner and the canee emboldened by booze, the blows became more vicious. I don't know what it was about watching a testosterone-and-booze-fueled contest of pseudo-manhood trials that aroused the ladies. But of course they wanted to be part of the team. I imagine they just wanted to have a crazy time in Las Vegas, something they could always remember, that they could take home with them, an authentic experience. The ladies wanted to do something that they could pretty much count on no other women doing while they were in Vegas. Well, they had found the right guys.

The team quickly decided that we weren't going to cane the ladies arms on the grounds that they were more delicate and we didn't want to mar their body in an area people could see. The guys fell in step with leading the women down the path we wanted them to go, which was to bare their asses so we could see what they were working with. This was a gamble, and while we're a smooth unit, getting two chicks to unclothe in front of a half-dozen drunk, obviously forward men was anything but a sure thing. So when the blond dropped her pants and leaned over the leather chair, it was almost unreal.

I gripped the cane and cracked off a nice one, just enough for her to feel it and raise a welt across both cheeks. She enjoyed the first one so much, she asked for another one. "Harder," she said.

I obliged, winding up, and the next one raised a welt about seven inches long across both cheeks. The brunette was to go next, even though she was a little more apprehensive. But no one wanted to be left out of that crazy Vegas story, even if it meant suspending your good sense for awhile. Giving in to my inner sadist, I cracked her across both cheeks a little harder than the blond. We took them back to the old managers' office and they signed the wall right above the celebrity pictures that doubled as the staff's look-alike/yearbook pictures. I suppose the ladies had a good time and no doubt went back home with the story they came to Vegas in search of.

That Friday, we were all talking about the caning and how we should keep it under wraps. The fact that it had even transpired blew our minds. What and how in the hell did those girls think and do to get themselves into that situation? That night, the club was jumping when we got a call from Greasy to report to the old managers' office. When we got there, he was with a good-looking Spanish girl and an older man. "They want to see what's up with the cane," Greasy said.

We were all taken aback by the fact that someone had come upstairs and asked for the cane. But we didn't do much detective work to find out how she had gotten there. We chalked it up to the fact that there's no shortage of freaks in Las Vegas and this girl and her old man were no exception.

She invited everyone to take a turn caning her, and the harder she got hit, the more she liked it. Everyone lined up to take their turn, never minding the fact that we were leaving the club essentially unsupervised to cane this girl's ass. She signed the wall with a bold stroke and returned to the club for some drinks. Long after we'd caned the Spanish chick, I received an email from Greasy with a link to a porn site, and there she was on celluloid getting pounded by a grotesquely muscled dude.

In addition, we learned that Alabama hooked up with her later. After the deed was done and she was sitting there on top of him, she said the CIA was looking for her and she proceeded to pull a dagger from under her pillow. "A damn dagger, son," Alabama would say in that long drawl. He told us he thought she was going to ritual kill him right there, black widow style.

By Saturday, the sheer ludicrousness of caning women made sure that everyone was on the prowl for willing participants. The club would yield two more that night, a couple of Jersey girls with a truckload of attitude. They were in their thirties and not as open to suggestion as so many twenty-somethings. When we first approached them, the girls were outraged, a little insulted that we would think they would take their pants down and let us smack them with a cane. But they kept hanging around different members of security throughout the night. Eventually, they'd had enough drinks to convince them that letting five or so strange men spank their bare ass hard enough to leave welts was a good idea.

By Monday, we all agreed that it was getting out of hand. All it was going to take was one of these girls feeling the morning-after regret and we were all sunk. On Monday, when a ghetto-talking white girl from San Francisco took a shine to Crow, we all agreed again that we had to put the exclamation point on a wild week at work. This chick was definitely from the hood. She had a bunch of shitty, jailhouse-looking tattoos—names, dates, initials. Her loose talk and forward demeanor gave her away as a prostitute, most likely a track ho. But out of all of the women we caned, she had the best ass. It was almost a shame to raise the big red welts across those lovely cheeks. I wondered if it would affect her work.

When it came time to sign the wall, she didn't so much sign as tag it up, graffiti style. She added a cityscape and a crown to her signature. Once she signed, she became really forward with Crow. Apparently aroused after the caning, she cornered Crow and made her play. The idea that a 5'6,"110-lb. girl can corner a 6'6," 250-lb. man is outrageous, but somehow she managed. The rest of us vacated the old managers' office and left Crow in there with her. We held the door from the outside so he couldn't escape. When he finally got out of the room, he cursed us for leaving him. Crow would tell us that he had to push her away after she pulled her underwear aside and exposed her labia, which he said resembled taco meat. Since the week was over and we were beginning to run the potential risk of a serious problem, we decided to retire the cane for real this time. But team building would live on as one of the most unreal experiences of the time.

That was one thing we definitely excelled at—leading the fairer sex down the wrong path. I knew they wanted to go that way anyway; we just made it easy for them and didn't call them hoes after the fact. One night, Greasy, Cisco, and I were having the requisite post-work cocktails and prowling the casino floor. We were joined by Carla, our new hostess. Carla quickly realized she wasn't going to be able to hang with the accelerated drinking pace we'd set and she bowed out after just a few rounds. Even though she was fairly intoxicated, she still wanted to drive home. While it wasn't a terribly responsible thing to do, who among us was going to tell her anything to the contrary?

We walked her to her car and she drove away. We wouldn't see Carla for the rest of the weekend, as she called in sick for the next two days. She cursed us for plying her with that much alcohol. The three of us thought it weird that she couldn't hang as we were just getting started. With no female company and the gamble in us well oiled, we headed for a roulette table. We picked the only one that had room for the three of us.

Already on the table were two girls, a blond with a heavy New York-Italian accent and a slight Asian girl with long, dark hair. We bought in and began placing random bets, playing for longevity. We introduced ourselves to the girls. As always, we were in it for a good time and the women could have done worse for company. As soon as the waitress arrived at the table, shots and beers were ordered. The women, not wanting to be left out, ordered shots as well. They came back in a hot minute and another round was ordered immediately. Two rounds later, the women were thoroughly enjoying their first night in Vegas.

They didn't seem at all upset that we had made them violate their agreement with their friends, who were asleep in the room. They had agreed to take it easy on their first night, as they had plans of going to breakfast and the pool in the morning.

271

"This is Vegas. This is what you came here for, isn't it?" I asked.

They agreed and yet another round was ordered. The party always went well when you were winning, and the croupier was doing a nice job of making sure we were. All of us were stacked up a fair amount. The women became more agreeable and the night was progressing nicely.

We had invited them to come to the club the next night and told them we would show them a good time. The blond asked for directions to the nearest restroom and I pointed. She didn't return for a long while. I soon found out why when the Asian girl suddenly went pale. She covered her mouth and a thin jet stream of vomit escaped from her fingers. It made a perfect line across the roulette table. We all looked at her a bit stunned. The croupier, an older Asian woman, began to raise a stink, as the girl had puked on her table.

"It's fine. She's fine," I said, sliding a stack of chips across the table. Everything is negotiable in Vegas.

Placated by the tip, the croupier retrieved a towel and discreetly wiped the razor-thin line of vomit from the green felt of the table. What was disturbing was the fact that the Asian girl did not move from her spot at the table. She had choked back down the vomit that had entered her mouth and was ready to place the next round of bets. She even ordered with us when we had another round. Thoroughly grossed out by her unapologetic vomit episode, the three of us excused ourselves and left her to rack up for her friend. The girls never made it to the club to see us. We found it only mildly disturbing that a normal night of drinking for us served to retire a bevy of females.

Of course, all of this staying out late with female accompaniment put my relationship with Dana back in the same box it was in the first time. But this time around, Dana wasn't comfortable just sitting around and taking it. She rummaged through my stuff and discovered one of the journals this book is based on. It contained things I feared admitting even to myself, all the nasty bits, the trophies I'd kept from my conquests, all the basest pieces of my being. She went on a further discovery mission, and I'm not even sure how far she went or what she found. I do know it was the end of our relationship, though.

I finally had to face the things I'd done to her without her knowing. Out of all of the people I'd wronged, I wronged Dana the most. She loved me like you should love someone, with all your heart. But I didn't love myself. I suppose it was the next logical step in making things right in my life. Dana was willing to accept and forgive me for those things, but I wasn't ready to forgive myself, and so I left her, this time for good. Even though I'd finally done the right thing in closing the door, Dana wasn't ready to accept the finality of it either. Jack told me that after I'd moved my stuff out of our shared apartment, she stood there in our nearly vacant space and asked him, "Do you think he's coming back?"

I feel worst about this. I just imagine her standing there and saying that. That even though she knew it was over, the last piece of her was still not willing to let go of me. I know that I broke her heart. That, because of me, it lay shattered into a thousand pieces, and there amongst the true and crystalline pieces will forever lay a piece of my own heart, black and shrunken.

DIAMONDS

Any bouncer with skin in the game will build a clientele of folks who come to the club to see them. The handshakes you receive from your people throughout the year will supplement your salary, so the more, the better. Greasy was exceptional at this. There was always a steady stream of people coming to see him, and it didn't hurt that his face had been a fixture on the door for nearly his entire career. It also sometimes seemed like the entire nation of Brazil would come to see him. The statement "I am with Greasy" was like some sort of universally accepted password to get through the rope without paying cover. But Brazilians like to party, and you could count on the women being easy on the eyes, so it was never a problem. Almost never a problem.

We were handling the line on a Monday night when one of Greasy's teammates was brought down by security. Flavio was one of the co-instructors of the combat school Greasy trained at and probably the second baddest dude in the club that night. The first baddest was the guy Flavio was with, Tico. Tico was the owner and head instructor. Flavio was worked up and the reason was easy to see—he was bleeding from a gash on his neck. The gash was deep enough that you could lay your pinkie finger inside. He was pissed off and only wanted to go back up to finish the fight.

"Greasy, they cut my neck," he protested in English.

"Tell us what happened," Greasy said, trying to calm him down.

What had happened was a dispute in front of the men's room. Flavio was trying to pass the men's room lineup in the tight confines of the hallway, when apparently a gentleman didn't want to give way. Blows were exchanged between Flavio and the gentleman, when the gentleman's friend pulled a roadhouse, breaking his beer bottle on the wall, then attempted to slash/stab Flavio's throat.

Now, you might think that's an overreaction to such a slight as not respecting one's space in a crowded nightclub. But that's how quickly a confrontation can escalate to a life-or-death situation. When security arrived, the original man was trying to pull Flavio off the bottle-breaker. Greasy and I calmed Flavio down when Tico arrived to help further our cause. The reverence Flavio held for Tico as his instructor pretty much ensured he would listen to him. Word came over the radio that Crow was bringing down the other two men. I suggested to Greasy and Tico that it might be better to take Flavio around the corner.

They took him around the corner to a lounge area in the casino. I waited for Crow about halfway between the front door and where they'd taken Flavio. I saw Crow lead the two men through the rope, where casino security was waiting. The bottle-breaker looked woozy on his feet, and the original man's face was already turning black and blue. It was two-on-one, and even though they managed to cut Flavio, they'd definitely lost the fight. Crow told me it took four security guards to remove Flavio from the bottle-breaker's nearly unconscious carcass.

Flavio suddenly came streaking across the marble floor to get at the two men. Greasy and Tico restrained him and Crow and I aided them. Flavio desperately wanted to get back into the fight. I couldn't say I blamed him, as one of them had tried to end his life. If that bottle had entered his neck a couple inches forward, it would have opened Flavio's jugular and covered a whole bunch of club-goers with arterial spray. Security would then get to hold a murderer for Metro as we tried to keep Flavio from dying in the club.

The men saw Flavio, who was struggling to get at them, and they hid behind the casino security guards. Thankfully, Flavio calmed down when casino security turned their attention towards us.

The casino security asked Flavio if he wanted to press charges, but Flavio refused. Casino security gave the pair of guards holding the men a nod and the two men were led from the casino, presumably to be eighty-sixed and to lick their wounds. Their night was over. Flavio's night was obviously over as well. The fact that his neck had been been flayed open and would require stitches guaranteed that.

Casino security finished taking down Flavio's information and then handed him back his ID with a piece of paper. They told us all to take it easy and stay safe and we gave them the same courtesy. A huge smile crossed Flavio's face as he held up the piece of paper that contained the names and addresses of his two attackers. If you work in the security field long enough, you will grow a very different idea of what justice means.

The fact that someone would try to end another person's life over a slight at the club was just par for the course. People treated Las Vegas like it wasn't the real world. Fueled by alcohol and drugs, people made some very unreasonable and reckless choices, but for us, reckless was routine.

Toward the end of the night, Greasy and I moved into our relaxed mode at the door. The money had been made and we were waiting on Devin, the cashier, to bring back our cuts from the door proceeds. The usual late-night suspects were filing through the door and the night was slowly winding down. Patrons loved to buy us drinks and they would continually bring them down to us. We had a good buzz going and Greasy and I were sitting on the bench bidding guests farewell, catcalling drunken women, and talking shit to each other. Sally was one of our regulars. She was a thick Puerto Rican transvestite with long brown hair, big fake tits, and a giant round ass.

Sally responded to Greasy's call.

"Ms. Parker. When you going to let me fuck, Ms. Parker?" Greasy was channeling his drunken energy into cinematic references.

Sally came over, sat her ass on my lap, and started a conversation with Greasy that centered on her tits. Her voice was soft, but her face was rough. Men, for the most part, do not make good women, though I once saw a bevy of Asian beauties who were once men and sheepishly admitted I would venture to see what it would take to hit bottom.

At any rate, Ms. Boricua was sitting on my lap and Greasy was fondling her tits. "Squeeze 'em. You're not going to hurt me," she said.

Greasy began squeezing harder.

"Harder. Come on, you're stronger than that."

Greasy obliged by sitting up in the seat and leveraging himself down onto her tit. His fingers were turning white and she was just smiling, egging him on. Greasy finally gave up and just stared at her tits, smiling and shaking his head. With both her nipples fully erect, she kissed Greasy on the cheek and stood up.

"See you next week," she said.

Greasy was amazed that she didn't cry out in pain. He told me he really was trying to pop her implant.

"What the fuck would you do that for?" I asked.

Another time, Greasy, Crow, and I were departing from work one evening when we spied one of our regulars passed out on a slot machine. It was Big Turk. Turk was a large black man. When I say large, he was pushing four bills, easy. He was well-liked by all of us, and we knew he'd been celebrating his birthday that night. Apparently, he'd gotten separated from his group and couldn't continue, so he'd just decided to take a nap.

We couldn't let him sit there for casino security to roust. As we approached, we saw that there was an empty champagne bottle near him. He had probably consumed the entire bottle himself. Big Turk was a drinker.

We roused Turk from his slumber and he was genuinely happy to see us. He was sure to let us know it was his birthday. He'd seen us all earlier and was now definitely on autopilot. We'd talked to Turk earlier in the evening and we knew he was staying in the hotel. We picked the big fella up and the three of us struggled under his enormous dead weight. We walked him slowly, step by step, to the front desk of the casino. Along the way, we got enough information out of him to at least narrow it down to a name—Doug Clark.

We parlayed this information to the front desk clerk as Big Turk let him know it was his birthday. The clerk gave us the room number associated with the name and we set off to find the room. Hauling the drunken dead weight of a four-hundred-pound man is about as fun as it sounds. Though we were all good size and certainly strong enough, walking the man all over the casino and hotel was no easy task. We traded off—two walked Big Turk and one rested while clearing the way of unsuspecting casino patrons. We really should have gotten a wheelchair.

We walked Turk to the room number that the clerk had given us and all of us were glad when we finally arrived. Crow knocked on the door. We heard a stirring and so he knocked again. After what seemed like an eternity, the door opened. A short white kid in a wife-beater stood in front of us rubbing his eyes. No doubt he was in disbelief at the sight of three men in suits holding up a four-hundred-pound black man.

"Is Doug Clark here?" I asked.

"I'm Doug Clark," he said. Just the answer we didn't want to hear.

"This isn't your brother, is it?" I asked, even though I knew the answer.

Doug just closed the door in our faces. No doubt he thought this was some ridiculous late-night prank and he wasn't in the mood.

We dragged Turk back down to the lobby, this time interrogating him the entire way. By the time we reached the desk, we hoped we would have enough reliable information to give the clerk. We narrowed the search down to two adjoining hotels and we have the clerk ring both for the listings of Doug Clark. We found the exact room but its occupant answered and immediately hung up the phone. Not a good sign, and we all decided that dragging Turk the mile or so to the hotel room just to have someone not answer the door was not going to happen.

We pulled a credit card from Turk's wallet and got him a room. We dragged him back upstairs and deposited him on the bed. We cracked the imported water and made Turk drink it all before he passed out. That was the good thing about the brotherhood—we shared—if you were in, you were taken care of.

This sort of brotherhood extended even after you worked for the nightclub. We took care of each other. When you're in the business, you're in it together, and that was really the point. When you're all dirty, you're all clean—close ranks and help each other stay out of trouble. I benefitted from this phenomenon quite a bit during my tenure.

We were six drinks deep and just getting started on a Monday night. The handshakes were plentiful and the coffers were full. A celebratory mood was in the air. I walked onto the patio and found Kalil and Murphy well into their evening of drinking. I sidled up to the bar and in no time we were congratulating each other on doing a fine job. The fact that the club was in decline wasn't an issue. At this point, we were merely plugging holes on a sinking ship. Another club had opened up and taken Monday nights. With their casino marketing budget and track record of proven nightlife winners, we became old news. The fact that the management above us was inept and had no idea what the club business in Las Vegas was like ensured that we would never make a comeback. So we whiled the time away drinking in plain sight, living it up, and riding the train to the end of the line.

A cocktail waitress came by as we tipped another round of shots back. "What are you guys doing?" she asked.

"We're running this shit," Kalil answered, obviously feeling his buzz.

"Right into the ground," Murphy added.

Murph was completely right. We were in full-on trouble mode, exploiting every opportunity to make money while fully taking advantage of our position in the club in every way possible. We shut down the patio and I made my way into the lounge. I stood in the well and ordered a round for the cocktail waitresses and myself.

Groupdrink was a sport in the club and everyone had to have a good time, even if they didn't really want to. The times someone didn't want to were few and far between. I was standing in the well when two black men in suits stepped in and demanded to be served.

"I'll need you guys to step out of the well," I said.

They stood their ground and I stepped forward. I squared up with the man in front. "I'll need you to step out of the well," I said again.

"We want a drink," he said again.

"And that's fine—I'd like to get you one. But when you step into an area that we keep off limits to guests and start demanding things, you make me think you don't respect the staff or the club. That can't happen," I said.

My blood was up and their disrespectful attitude concerning the boundaries of the club was agitating me. I was ready for a physical confrontation, itching for one. I really just didn't care anymore. The men could see this and decided it wasn't worth it. They stepped from the well.

"Now, if we're being respectful, I'm buying the drinks," I said.

I ordered a round of shots for myself and the men. Another round followed, and the men turned out to be all right. They were in from St. Louis on business. Murphy sidled up and I introduced the men. He shook hands all around and ordered another round of shots.

Murph leaned into my ear and told me he'd had a problem with them earlier and sent them into the well to get a drink because he knew I'd start shit with them.

"Thanks, bitch," I said.

"Ah, it worked out fine, didn't it?" he said.

We took the shots and then set about closing the club. The club cleared, except for the staff, and I sipped from a beer while standing alone at the bar. A guy in his mid-twenties emerged from the media room and stepped up to the bar. He whistled at Reagan, Johnny's girlfriend, to get her attention.

"Let me get a goose and cran," he said.

"Hey, man, you have to go. The club is closed for the night," I informed him.

"Man, I do what I want. I'm a Vegas native. I've lived here all my life. You're just visiting," he told me.

I was in no mood for shit-talking from some clown, so I closed the distance and stood right next to him. He didn't turn to face me. "That may be. But I run this, and your ass has to go, now," I said.

He looked at me and dismissed me with a wave of his hand. "Get my drink, bitch," he said.

I weigh what to do for a split second.

I snatched the kid under the arms and started running him towards the elevator. Johnny came from behind the bar and Collier hurried behind him. I got to the elevator and threw the kid against the door.

"Get the fuck out of here, clown-ass motherfucker. You're barking up the wrong tree. You don't come in here and talk that shit!" I screamed.

Johnny stepped between him and me. "Hank, we got this—calm down."

Johnny was right—I shouldn't have been involving myself on this level. It was my job to defend them and twist the story when they banged this kid's head in.

Johnny and Collier put the kid on the elevator and took him down. The crew assembled at the bar and the booze flowed freely. By the time I left with Greasy, I had a full head of steam going. We were headed downstairs to meet for Molly at the center bar of the casino. I stepped off the elevator and there sat the kid. He immediately stepped into my face.

"That's messed up—you threw me out of the club," he told me.

By this time, I'd calmed down and changed my focus. I was going to visit Molly along with the rest of our friends and I just wanted to be on my way.

"Just get out of my face," I said as I walked past.

He didn't follow and Greasy and I rounded the bend heading into the casino, when suddenly Greasy stopped in his tracks.

"Shit, I forgot my bag," he said. "I have to go back and get it. My gun is in there."

I told you earlier it was always good to have a gun on the premises, just in case, even if it was next to a big bag of coke and a plethora of pills. Greasy and I turned around and the kid was there to greet us.

The kid started up again. "I can't believe you threw me out. You're an asshole."

Just as fast as my anger had turned to good cheer, it turned back once more. Now I'd had it. "Fuck you, punk. I will beat the shit out of you right here," I seethed in his face.

"I'm not scared of you," he mustered.

I slid my hands into my pockets for what came next and stepped right into his face. "I can see the fear in your eyes," I said.

Greasy would later tell me that he saw the kid's lip quiver at this. I didn't see that, however, as I threw the kid a vicious head-butt to the temple.

"Whoa, whoa, whoa. Hank, what the fuck, man? Shit. Take a walk," Greasy said as he pushed me out of the lobby and into the casino walkway. "What the fuck are you doing, you crazy bitch?" he asked.

The kid was reeling from the head–butt and Greasy hustled me into the casino.

"'I can see the fear in your eyes.' What kind of shit is that to say?" he asked me. "You about to get us all fucked up, starting shit downstairs."

I knew he was right, so Greasy and I hustled for the parking garage to avoid a security response to the incident. Someone watching via the casino cameras may have seen what happened.

The next day, I got a call from my old boss, Danny. Danny was the manager on scene when we choked out the kid and made him piss his pants, so he knew the drill. Danny asked me if I head–butted a kid the night before in the casino. I told him the story and he told me that the kid was the sommelier from a restaurant that was also in the casino. Well, now—I was probably pretty well fucked, and I might even be taking Greasy with me since he covered for me. But as luck would have it, Danny was his boss. The sommelier was pissed and wanted to pull videotape from the casino so he could press charges and have me fired. I explained my side to Danny. He knew me as an even-keel sort of character, and if I was pissed enough to smash my head into the head of their sommelier, then he must have deserved this. Danny was a good dude and he buried it for me. So nothing ever came of me giving his sommelier the Glasgow Kiss, and I was able to avoid getting fired once again.

Even though I was supposed to be in charge, I was by no means the only crazy member of the management staff. The big boss played it clean, and while he would have his shift drink, vodka-cran, he made sure he was out the door before the mayhem started. Kalil would get his drink on for sure. Murphy was a different breed altogether. Murph was a beloved member of the crew. He was a tough guy, a hard drinker, and definitely had a long, sick love affair with substance well before he became a manager in the room. I worked with him a long time before it came out that he was gay. I never suspected and it certainly didn't matter to me once I found out.

He didn't take offense to the locker room maleness of the team when we called each other gay. Or told one another that we would pound each other out and therefore take the manhood of said poundee. He took this in stride and never bothered addressing this non-politically correct treatment of his sexual orientation. He knew we respected him.

One evening after work, we had retired to the center bar to get drunk and find our way into whatever might happen. At one point, the conversation became heated between Murph and one of our barbacks, a tough kid from back East. Back East started calling him a fag, faggot this and faggot that. "You big faggot!" he screamed.

Back East knew Murph was gay and was using it as a direct insult. Murph just smiled a wry smile, took it like a champ, and the conversation moved on. No one noticed that when Back East went to the bathroom, Murph excused himself shortly after. When drinking at the center bar, we always used the high-limit-slot bathroom. The attendants knew us. It was secluded and there was seldom anyone in there. This made it a perfect place to treat our nose or execute whatever other clandestine behavior that might be necessary.

Back East went into the restroom and Murphy followed. Back East was taking a piss when Murphy kicked him in the ass and slammed him against the wall. He threatened him with bodily harm should he ever call him that again. Murph turned him loose and basically dared him to retaliate. Back East knew better. It could have been because Murphy was his boss, but I believe it's because Murph is one tough guy and Back East knew he couldn't beat him in a fight. Soon afterwards, Back East asked for a transfer back to the restaurant from the nightclub. He switched positions but never snitched—he never violated the code, even when he could have easily gotten Murph in serious trouble and likely fired. Thus another human resources nightmare was avoided. I think that Back East knew he'd disrespected Murph. Also, before this incident, Back East was a stand-up guy, so he owned it and righted his wrong.

Disrespect is rampant in the service industry. You'll get guests from all walks of life, and while most are just out for a good time, some just can't help but try to take shits on the staff and treat them as inferior. One evening, I was following Lima on an escort out. They were a middle-aged couple, and while the man was quiet, the woman was ripping into Lima for throwing her out. She was insistent that she was not drunk. By the time I joined the group, they were nearly at the elevator.

"What the fuck is wrong with you? Don't you know who I am? Do you know how much money I have?" She was asking all the usual questions, so they failed to get a rise out of Lima.

Work long enough and you've heard them all. So this lady came up with a new one.

"Huh, Chief? Why don't you go back to the reservation?" she asked Lima. She was playing the race card, which was nothing new, except this time, she had the race entirely wrong. "Where is your feather?"

Lima smiled and looked at me. I just shook my head. This woman showing her racist side against someone who wasn't even of that race was supremely stupid. The fact that she even began the tirade proved that she was in fact drunk, and that was solidified by her inability to identify that Lima was a Mexican.

It became apparent that she would continue to say anything to get a rise out of him, so Lima quelled the onslaught.

"Look, why don't you take some of that money and get your roots dyed," he told her.

A look of horror struck her face and she was robbed of the power of speech. No doubt she was given pause by the fact that a man of lesser position in her eyes could reach into her and pluck out all the pride she had with but a single sentence. Personally, I hadn't even noticed that she'd let her dye job go.

But Lima picked up on it and let her have it where it hurt the most. Any woman takes pride in her beauty, but in one of advancing age and diminishing sex appeal, it was the Achilles heel. She looked as though she were going to cry. Her man choose now to come to her rescue.

"Now, hold on," he piped.

The elevator opened and Lima opened his arm to guide them on.

"You're out of line," the man told Lima.

This, I cannot endure—a man who lets his woman disrespect someone who is just doing their job and then chimes in to play Captain Save-a-Ho when she gets disrespected back.

"Nah, man—you hold on. You stood by and let your woman call a member of my staff everything under the sun. Just because he's doing the job I asked him to do. She insults him and talks a bunch of racist shit. He says one thing and now you want to save her? Sorry, you missed your chance. You should have asked her to leave and told her to be quiet if you wanted to defend her honor. Now be quiet and leave our club," I said without giving him space to utter a word.

The man remained quiet, no doubt used to being thoroughly redressed. He'd been shamed into silence and his woman had been embarrassed into the same state. The couple ambled off into the casino and we never saw them in the room again. It made me reflect on how small some people's lives were. Sure, I was living in unreality. I was a drunk and a drug user. I had certainly mistreated some people close to me along the way. But I still struggled. Struggled not to let the bad parts of my character overtake the good ones. People like that had just quit fighting.

Even though I wasn't technically security any longer, I never lost my penchant for the action involved, especially handling a fight. I was accompanying Greasy on an escort out of the club. Two gentlemen had been arguing with another pair, and after a warning they failed to heed, it escalated into a physical confrontation. Once in the elevator, the shorter of the two began berating us. All the usual fare—low rent ... underpaid ... meathead ... skinhead ... black boy ... blah, blah, blah. He even began to wag his finger at me to get his point across. He left it in my face, trying to stir me up. I was calm with the fact that I could rend this man limb from limb without much effort if the need arose, and I was sure I could take his best shot without much problem. If being in the business this long had taught me anything, it's that fighters fight and pussies talk.

The elevator bell rang and he flicked me in the forehead. He might have thought that such a small gesture wasn't going to get him touched.

He was wrong. I immediately grabbed him by the lapels and slammed him into the wall. I crossed my hands and began choking him with his own shirt. He struggled, but he was weak and out of shape. His face went red with the effort.

Greasy reached in and grabbed my forearms. "Let me do that," he said.

Realizing what my position was again, I released the idiot's shirt and Greasy snatched him up. For a moment, he could breathe, until Greasy spun him around and coiled his arms around the idiot's neck from behind. He locked on a chokehold and began squeezing. Greasy sat down on the bench as the idiot writhed to get free. Not satisfied that the choke was deep enough, Greasy dropped to the floor as the idiot's face went purple.

The idiot's friend, who earlier was ready to argue and fight, just stood by and watched as his boy suffocated. By now, people had heard the ruckus and were looking in the elevator lobby. When I turned around from straightening my suit, there were twenty people watching Greasy choke this moron out on the floor. I watched as his eyes started to roll back into his head. I wanted to let Greasy finish the job and choke him completely unconscious. Hopefully the kid would evacuate and piss himself. His face was a deep purple and I watched his eyes fight to come back.

"Greasy, let him up, man," I said.

Greasy looked at me in disbelief because I was actually asking him to back off.

"It's not worth it. I don't want the fucking paperwork. Just let him go."

Greasy released his choke and pushed the moron off him. His friend helped him up.

"You were lucky this time. Maybe next time you'll do the smart thing and just leave," I told him.

The kid helped his shaky friend out past the ropes and into the casino. I wondered if I was finally going soft. The guy had assaulted me, even if it was a flick in the head, and I knew he deserved what he'd been getting. I just didn't know if it was worth it anymore.

The club rang in the new year in subdued fashion. We had our drinks and made our rounds, but the room seemed quieter. It wasn't just the decrease in business or the change in clientele—it felt different. It was as though it was a prelude to the economic fallout that was on the horizon, the one none of us could quite see yet. Molly and I met on the roof of the hotel. We shared a glass of champagne and watched the fireworks as they went off over the neon of the Strip. After midnight, the guests cleared the club for the most part and we celebrated with a few shots and a few laughs. As usual, a few people took it too far. But for once, I found myself not in that crowd. Molly and I left together and the night ended rather calmly.

Upon my return to work, I would become privy to a dark turn the night took after my departure. We had a kid named Billy who worked for us as a busser. He was a super nice kid and a hard worker, the kind of guy you'd want as your little brother. I'd dubbed him Nice Guy Billy and the name stuck. Just about everyone called him Nice Guy when referring to him. On New Year's Eve, Nice Guy was having drinks, and when the rest of the group left, he went, too. What follows is a piecemeal recollection of what happened with Nice Guy after he left the center bar.

Though no one would claim it, someone gave the kid cocaine. Nice Guy wasn't the drug type, and he was a pretty naïve kid. But in the end, everyone is in charge of their own buzz and what they do with themselves as a result. Apparently, he wandered the casino for the next few hours until he turned back up in the club. The morning girl was there, and that meant it was around nine in the morning. She was completely sober and recanted the story of what Nice Guy did when he arrived back in the club.

Nice Guy sat down in a chair in the office across from her. He went on and on about how he couldn't find his keys and therefore couldn't leave the casino. He had been searching for them all this time, and when he couldn't locate them, he returned to the club to have a look. She offered to help him when the conversation took a bad turn. Nice Guy started talking about how he wasn't worth anything. He couldn't even keep track of his keys. He couldn't even do that right. How all women did was walk all over him and they didn't respect him. She said

287

he was growing visibly angry and he was shaking. Then he suggested he should just kill himself.

"Yeah, that's what I'll do—kill myself," he said.

Then Nice Guy picked up a pair of scissors from the desk and began trying to slash his own wrists. The office girl freaked at this and bolted straight out of the office. She didn't return to the office until she was sure he was gone. The HR manager contacted us about the incident and we closed ranks. Nice Guy might have been a troubled kid, but we didn't want him fired. In our minds, that wasn't going to solve anything. He was allowed to stay, but after that, he was Nice Guy Billy aka the Suicide Kid.

A year later, on January 3, 2008, Greasy and I, as well as a host of people who had worked with Nice Guy, went to attend his funeral. As his parents told the story, he fell off a parking garage in downtown Las Vegas. Those who knew Billy know better. Maybe we should have let him be fired to get him out of the environment. He was a good kid and just wasn't built for the life. I know I feel bad for adding the Suicide Kid to his moniker. I don't know where his head was when he made the decision to jump. But I do know that sometimes, the burden gets too heavy. I was the guy with a pistol in his mouth once.

We were summoned by the ladies' bathroom attendant. One of the stall doors was locked and the woman inside was not responding. Alabama went in while I waited outside. He came out with a disgusted look packed inside of a huge grin. "She threw up and her pants are down," he said.

"What do you mean? She passed out kneeling on the floor?" I asked, trying to get clarification on just what the fuck we were dealing with.

"No. She's sitting on the toilet. Her pants are down. She threw up in her pants ... panties and all of it."

Now this was new. How were we going to get her out of there? We couldn't very well have her pull up her soiled pants and walk out of the club trailing vomit out of her pant legs. Plus, just the idea of vomit being close to her nether regions added a most unsavory element to the predicament, not to mention it being unsanitary.

By now, the rest of the team had assembled to find out what was going on. We filled them in and the jokes began. After a round of laughs and some serious discussion on how to get her out of there, we decided on finding her friends. It didn't take long to identify her friends. One thing you could always count on was the fact that at least one of the security team had noticed a particular woman and her friends and could identify the group if for no other reason than to hit on them later.

Her friend, a pretty blond, went in to survey the scene and came out a short time later with a sick look. We offered to call a wheelchair for her to help get the woman back to their room, which she accepted.

"What am I going to put her in? I can't pull up her pants. Do you guys have any extra clothes here?" she asked.

"This is a nightclub—we don't have any extra clothes," I told her.

We certainly don't have any extra clothes to give to a girl who threw up in her pants, I thought. *Who does that?* When puking, you should turn away from yourself to ensure you don't get any on you. How the fuck would you manage to vomit in your pants? I was running this through my head while the girl told me she couldn't believe we didn't have anything to give her. Did she believe we had people puking all over themselves on a regular basis? Well, we did, but we didn't keep extra clothing on hand for people who couldn't handle their booze. We just threw them out.

"There's a gift shop downstairs where you might be able to purchase something to take her out in," I told her.

The girl went downstairs and returned a short time later. She entered the ladies' room to dress out her friend and we sent in the wheelchair when it arrived. The girl definitely had a sense of humor in choosing an outfit for her friend to wear while being wheeled out of a Vegas nightclub. The sight of this woman slumped in a wheelchair wearing a huge white T-shirt with large red letters that read *I GOT TANKED* was a moment of poetry. Her friend thanked us on the way out.

The decline of the club was all too real. The management had tried what it could to reignite the business and keep the club relevant, but there was just too much competition now. Maybe our club couldn't reinvent itself fast enough, maybe we didn't have the space, or maybe we just didn't have the funds to keep up. One thing was certain: it was now the age of the megaclub.

People started to jump ship or look for new opportunities. Crow was set to make the jump to management, much like I had. Alabama had secured a sweet gig as security director for a premium retail outlet. It will always be a smart move to parlay your security gig into another position as quickly as possible. Bouncing is a dead end.

I was riding out what the club had left. Since I had the place wired, the income-to-output ratio was still working for me. I was burnt out for sure and I needed to make a move. I just wasn't sure what move to make or where to go. The environment was malleable and it was easy. I know a bunch of people were still in love with what the club had been, and that kept them there. Even though the inevitability of not being able to sustain our lifestyles was right in front of us, we failed to act.

It was a Saturday night and we had broken up a fight. We'd just gotten the parties separated. It had taken a moment, as both of the men were quite intent on killing each other. They had to be pulled apart by pretty much everyone in security and management. Me, Alabama, Crow, Mack, Murphy, J.J., Kalil, and Greasy were all involved. One of the men was immediately whisked downstairs and out of the club. The other man was brought into the lobby to await ejection from the club once we'd gotten word that the other man was clear. The man we held was a good size, six-foot and probably two hundred pounds. He'd gotten the worst of the fight, as blood poured from his nose over his lips and down onto his shirt. He was still obviously upset and struggling with security.

Kalil stepped in, attempting to calm the man down. "Look, just relax. We don't want to hurt you, and we'll turn you loose if you'd just calm down," he said.

The man was having none of this. That's when he did the unthinkable—he spit phlegm and blood all over Kalil's face.

"Oh, you motherfucker." Kalil's voice cracked in anger as he attacked the man.

All of us attempted to get a piece. Murphy immediately grabbed him by his bottom jaw and attempted to tear it from his face. Kalil was swinging wildly, trying to get a piece of the guy who was already being slammed, pulled, dragged, and punched in every way by everyone imaginable.

That this guy would spit on someone, which is about the lowest thing you could do, was outrageous. Add to this the fact that he had blood filled with God knows what pouring down his face, and he'd put himself in harm's way.

He was dragged into the hall with people handling and hitting him all the way. It was as though all the late nights, all the insults, all the fights, the confrontations, the petty slights, all the stress wrought on us by the job were being taken out on this guy.

I closed the doors to hide us from the camera that covered the hallway. The spitter was pinned to the floor with everyone on top of him. His face was smashed into the carpet to prevent him from spitting on anyone else. Kalil had his foot on the back of his head and was looking like he was deciding whether or not to break the guy's neck. Part of me wanted him to just give the kid what he deserved and step down hard, thereby snuffing a piece of human garbage from existence. Spitting blood in another person's face is low. The AIDS or hepatitis this guy might be carrying could affect Kalil's life and his therefore family. But the guy with the busted nose doesn't care. All he knows is he's been punched in the nose, he's bleeding all over the place, and someone has to pay.

I walked up and put my hand on Kalil's shoulder. He turned and looked at me with the specks of blood and spit all over his face. Kalil was wild-eyed, and I believe he was truly contemplating killing this kid.

"Don't do it," I said. "This asshole ain't worth it."

Kalil thought long and hard. He just stared at me for what seemed like forever.

I shook my head negative. "Let's go clean that shit off your face and let the guys get rid of him," I said.

Kalil finally relented and took his foot off the back of his head. He looked relieved, and I was, too. I don't think anyone's life would have been the same if we would have been involved in killing that kid.

On one nondescript Monday night at the club when the crowd was sparse and we were drinking to kill time, a stuffed-shirt moron wearing a button-down started the requisite half-hearted confrontation with another guest. His skills were limited to shooting his mouth off and knowing just how far to go with it to avoid getting his ass kicked. We escorted him onto the elevator and he continued the verbal assault. What he failed to realize was that all of us had come to the end of our proverbial ropes. Thoroughly fed up with self-inflicted long nights and dealing with bullshit on a nightly basis, the releases we had used to cope with this had long since been rendered useless.

Even the formerly grand monk robes of Crow had grown tattered and worn. I realized this when Crow was escorting out a loudmouth and closed the rope behind him, at which point the kid kept mouthing off. Crow turned to address the kid and I noticed he was heated. I attempted to step in and Crow, with hands clasped in front of him, simply said, "I got this."

So when Crow slammed Mr. Stuffed Shirt to the floor in the elevator, I wasn't surprised. When you go into work every night asking yourself the question, "What human garbage am I going to have to deal with tonight?" it takes a toll. Further, when you add the physical, mental, emotional, and moral costs of working in such a toxic environment, you come to realize just what a heavy price you've paid.

The club, just like all of us in our own way, had fallen into ruin. Mr. Stuffed Shirt was just the final straw. Lima was berating Mr. Stuffed Shirt, who was face down on the floor, when a roach crawled out from the corner of the elevator.

"You think you're tough, huh? Lima asked the question he already knew the answer to.

The man stammered and tried to answer.

"Man, shut up. Kiss the roach," he told him.

The vermin crawled ever closer to the man's face. I questioned whether we were really going to degrade him further by allowing it to crawl on him. Why assert dominance over another man? Was this where we were now deriving our worth? Why take out our frustrations on him? Were we punishing him and those like him for our own self-defeating ways and unrealized dreams? I didn't have the answers to those questions. All I knew was that it was enough. At some point, you have to forgive yourself for all the wrong. You have to stand up, start making the right decisions, and reclaim your humanity.

CRAPS

I attempted to reclaim my humanity, or at least reestablish my sense of right and wrong, by attempting to right a wrong. LA Ricky, one of security supervisors from downstairs, had killed himself. Ricky's first attempt had been by shooting himself with a handgun that was too small in caliber. Ricky recovered in the hospital and returned to work. He seemed like he was getting along all right, when one night, he made the rounds collecting a few pills from various people in the club under the story that he was suffering from insomnia. Ricky went home, took all the pills at once, and achieved his goal. Everyone who knew Ricky loved the guy. Sometimes the burden just got too heavy.

Ricky's memorial service had taken place at the club, and after the shift ended, everyone stayed to have our usual shift drink. We drank to Ricky's memory and shared a few stories about how Rick did his thing. I left to go home with Molly. I wanted to be around something positive. The rest of the crew stayed and sent Ricky off proper. Murphy, being a true Irishman, kept the party going until the morning crew showed up, including the office staff. The same office girl who had handled Nice Guy that fateful morning and tried to snitch on him to HR, ended up snitching on Murphy for his late-night/early morning antics.

Once the big boss, Chet, heard about the party, he started reviewing video cameras. Everyone involved was preserved on digital, and digital doesn't lie. Murphy was fired since none of the drinks were paid for. The security team dodged the bullet, though, as the drinking had been authorized by a manager. Still, Chet put them all on a last and final warning—any further infraction would result in termination. He even pulled Crow's offer of moving into management.

All of this might seem fine to the average person. Everybody except Murphy got to keep their jobs after a clear violation of company policy, and so it would seem a slap on the wrist. The problem comes in when you understand who Chet was. Chet was a jackass of epic proportion. Security had saved him from numerous acts of creepiness towards females. Acts that could have resulted in possible sexual assault charges or, at the very least, aggravated groping, if that's even a charge. The dude was constantly in the club getting drunk, grabbing chicks, and showing his ass. Like the time he was cursing out a senior hotel VIP host while he was sliding down the wall drunk. Each time, security was there to bail him out and cover his tracks.

My conscience couldn't bear the idea that this asshole was now going to try to hold someone responsible for drinking, even if it was on the company's dime. He'd forgotten the code. If we're all dirty, we're all clean. So I submitted an anonymous letter to HR and the corporate offices. The letter filled them in on the misdeeds of the venue GM and his second in command. I added his second in command by virtue of the guy being a fucking clown crony. His favorite shit to do was sexually harassing the cocktail waitresses. I just couldn't bear the hypocrisy of it anymore. I sent the letter and it was covered up by all involved. It did, however, result in an increased presence by Chet and his dickhead crony. In hindsight, this growing of a conscience is what cost me my employment.

One day, I walked in with a huge hangover and Glen, my boss was waiting for me as soon as I got off the elevator. His face was long.

"What's up, Glen?" I asked.

"We've got to go downstairs, big guy."

I knew what this meant—the end of line had come. I knew I was being fired and I went quietly. The fact that they knew they had a rat in their midst left them no other play. Apparently, it was me who had violated the code.

I sat down across from the HR manager, who just a few years prior had championed the cause of a naïve security guard who'd been doing the right thing. I was in front of her again trying to do the right thing or at least expose the wrongs. I didn't know anymore. But it was a step in the right direction. The discussion was brief. She said she had video of me taking beer from behind the bar. I denied this. I told her the only thing she had tape of was me retrieving bottled water from behind the bar, and as far as I knew, we were allowed to drink all the water we wanted.

I'd had a thousand drinks under that roof, and they couldn't get me on camera. She knew it wouldn't wash, so she changed it to misappropriation of company property. I knew this was bullshit, too. But I was tired of fighting to get back to a place I knew would keep me in perpetual decline. I needed a clean slate. So I took what came down.

The next day, I came in to pick up my last check. I handed the HR manager a copy of the letter I wrote. She told me "they" knew, because of the language, it was either me or Crow who had written the letter. In retrospect, I'm sure that to them, it read like one of a thousand security reports we'd written over the years. Then she called Chet in so he could send me off. Chet entered and took a seat. He waited for a moment and sat there just smiling. He was gloating. He wanted me to know he'd won. I wanted to smash the smug look off his face. But he saved me by opening his mouth. He gave me a line about his willingness to provide me a reference and how it was a bad deal I was getting.

I looked him right in the eye. "It is what it is, Chet."

Then I picked up my check and walked.

Afterwards, I had the same reaction anyone does to losing a job. I got drunk and went gambling. I took three months off before I needed to get back in the game. I decided that I was going back to what I knew best—security. A friend of mine suggested that I go to work for a one of the megaclubs, so I did. I went through one interview, and even though the security manager raised an eyebrow at the fact that I wanted to head back into security from a management position, he still said he was going to give me an opportunity.

I showed up in my new black suit and went through the orientation. First off, they made me purchase my earpiece. I guess they figured I'd take better care of it if I had to pay for one. Still, it left a bad taste in my mouth as they repeatedly told us how much money they made last year.

Great, assholes—you made millions, and you make guys who get twelve bucks an hour buy their earpieces. But whatever. I figured this was the new era in nightclubs in Las Vegas. I also thought it was bullshit that they made us pool our tips and they were to be issued on a check.

The only reason that you'd require a tip pool is so the management could skim off the top. Now, I know the IRS was beginning to realize how much cash was being made off the books in Vegas, and they were asserting their power in making sure that money got taxed. But still, the management would have no problem squeezing that money. When you have a whole bunch of guys dropping cash with no real idea of how much is going into a huge pot, I have to imagine that not all of it made it onto those checks. It's what I would have done. It didn't matter to me anyway. I fully planned on skimming and not dropping all my tips anyway.

After orientation, they assigned us our spots. They started me in a four-table section. I thought this odd, as new guys usually started out in the garbage positions. For a moment, I thought it was because I had experience and they knew I could handle the spot. I was off to a running start on making dough.

But having the new guy in a four-table section wasn't happening. A security vet told me that was his section, and he moved me into a section with just two tables. *No big deal,* I thought. I still had two tables and I was learning where I was in the pecking order. This was fine by me. But my time in the two-table section was short lived also when another vet pushed me to working a line inside the club, the line to the upstairs roof deck.

Now I was going to get paid. Handling a line, any line, is the number one way to make your money in Las Vegas. People would be handing me cash all night to get past the line to go upstairs. I was in charge of a golden goose. The other security guard who ran the line came by and introduced himself to me. He told me he was going to work the front and I'd work the body of the line, making sure people didn't stray out too far and weren't making it hard to get by to other areas of the club. That was fine with me.

"So how do you want to work the payoff? You want me to take the hit and signal you or vice versa?" I asked him.

"What do you mean?" he said. The kid, who was all of about twenty-three or twenty-four, looked genuinely puzzled.

"When someone wants to pay to pass the line, you want to take the cash or do you want me taking it?" I spelled it out for him.

"We don't take cash here. They pay out front," he told me.

"Seriously?" I asked.

"Yeah, we don't take cash here. They don't have to pay to get upstairs," he said it again.

Here we were, literally sitting on top of a mountain of potential cash, and this green-assed kid didn't even know. He didn't even realize he could make thousands of dollars just for letting people pay to pass. I got it. He was new in the game and believed he could get in trouble, just like I did when I started. I played my position, though, and wondered how I could make the angle work.

I watched the kid closely, looking for a way in, a way to turn him. I noticed he wasn't even really doing his job—he was just talking to every girl in line and basking in the attention. I respected that he was taking advantage of the power his position provided, but he was missing the big picture. He was so new to the game that he didn't even know that women were just one of the perks of the job.

But I knew I could work the angle—it was what I did. It was what I always did—find the angle. I watched the club start filling up, and as I saw people filing in to get drunk, get high, get laid, it finally dawned on me: I didn't want to find the angle. I didn't want to turn this kid out and get him to do what I wanted him to. I didn't want to spend time in the same environment with a different address. I didn't want to spend time talking to the same people, only with different faces. I didn't want to watch as they mistreated themselves and those around them. I was done. I headed for the exit and didn't tell a single soul I was leaving. I even took their radio.

EPILOGUE

It was a perfect measure of time and place. The stories you read could never happen now in the super-corporate, ultra-homogenized world of Las Vegas nightclubs. The business has been white-washed and sanitized. There's just too much money at stake and too much competition. You can't even be the top dog, date an heiress, and drive around high without paying the price. But you can still find your way into dark corners if you like—they're still out there. You just have to be willing to pay the price. I was, and it almost led to my ruin.

When I think about the confluence of events that brought me to the place, those things that allowed me to have the experiences I did, I realize it was equal parts light and dark. If I'm being honest, it was probably more darkness. I loved the club and all its toxic beauty. There were days I relished walking through those doors. Sometimes I walked onto the perch and surveyed the floor and thought that I must have the best job on earth.

Those days were tempered by the moments I found myself in a dark hole, and instead of climbing out, I went down. I went as deep as I could go. I would love to say that it was Shannon's fault I went down that path, but no one person can have that much influence on someone's life. Her indiscretion only forced me to face down what I was inside.

I looked at every taboo and tried to punch a hole through all of them. I wanted to be in it up to my elbows and found myself in it up to my neck, but the moral erosion I experienced was gradual. Las Vegas takes you in pieces so small, you still think they're all yours.

At the height of it all, a very influential man in town told me that I was made for this business. At the time, I remember thinking he was paying me a compliment, but I don't want to be made for this business. Who wants to be good at manipulating people? Who wants to be good at hurting people? Who wants to be good at creating a web of lies woven so thick, even they start to believe? I played the role so well, I wore it like a second skin.

There were many times that I was within a hair's breadth of ruining my life. I put myself at risk so often that my daily life was maintained in precarious balance. In an instant, it all could have come tumbling down like a house of cards. But it didn't. It was as if I was being protected, so that I could do something better, that real and true and good thing that everybody wants to do in their life. A lot of people I knew over those years will never get their chance.

Even when I thought I was finished with the lifestyle, it didn't go easy. You can't taste forbidden fruit and expect to come out unscathed. Living a nihilistic existence for so many years exacted its price. While I came through the experience physically whole—no STDs, no DUIs, no lasting financial problems, and I hadn't killed myself—my mentality wasn't the same. Maybe it never will be. The want to destroy myself has lessened over the years, but still, there were episodes where the darkness reared its ugly head. It seems that kind of freedom dies hard.

If there's a takeaway for me from my days in the nightclub, it's that I lived, in every sense of the word. I had a whole bunch of experiences I wanted and some I didn't. But I also didn't live one of those lives of quiet desperation that your boy Thoreau wrote about. I'll never be a guy that wishes he'd taken it to the limit at least once in his life. The difference between daring and reckless is almost nonexistent; it just depends whether you get it right or not. I still have that recklessness inside me. It's down there with the darkness, always lurking. The only difference is, now I care about keeping it tamped down.

I care about my wife, Molly. Yes, I married the cocktail waitress who was wandering the parking garage. I care about our beautiful son and his upbringing. I care about building a strong family and working hard. I went back to the fundamentals I learned while I was growing up, the fundamentals that I thought were a sham just years prior. Hard work gets you somewhere—that was foundation I started working on when I came to Las Vegas, and that's the path I'll continue on. I went far enough down the path less taken to know that there's always time to turn back. Oh, and I finally made it to Hollywood when I sold my first screenplay. It's set to be produced in late 2015, and it's got nothing to do with the club business. So that's a dream come true for me.

As far as the nightclub business is concerned, I couldn't care less. It's all a farce, smoke and mirrors for young people. It's the ultimate disposable environment. People working in the game now will find that out soon enough. It can be fun for sure, and if you're in the midst of what you think are the best years of your life, please enjoy it, but save your money. There's very little room at the top, and your stay will most likely be short. There will be a whole new crew of the young, hungry, and beautiful right behind you. . I thought I had it all, because so many seemed to covet that which I found at arm's length. In the end those things proved empty, at least for me and my guys. Still it doesn't keep people from seeking them out and the story continues to unfold nightly under the never-ending neon. But I promise you, no team, now or in the future, will ever be as slick or wild as we were. You can bet on that. And that team and the brotherhood we shared is the only thing I miss.

My name is Hank. I drank and drugged. I played till it hurt. I broke some hearts and had mine broken. I risked it all, in every way, and in the end, I still came out on top. Las Vegas will seduce you. Not me, though—I went willingly.

301

Printed in the United States
By Bookmasters